Pit Yourself Against Challenges from FUN to GENIUS Level

THE NATIONAL GALLERY

GREAT PAINTINGS SPOT-THE-DIFFERENCE

40 FINE-ART PUZZLES

ilex

An Hachette UK Company
www.hachette.co.uk

First published in the UK in 2017 by ILEX,
a division of Octopus Publishing Group Ltd
Carmelite House
50 Victoria Embankment
London, EC4Y 0DZ
www.octopusbooks.co.uk
www.octopusbooksusa.com

Distributed in the US by
Hachette Book Group
1290 Avenue of the Americas
4th and 5th Floors
New York, NY 10104

Distributed in Canada by
Canadian Manda Group
664 Annette St.
Toronto, Ontario, Canada M6S 2C8

Publisher: Roly Allen
Editorial Director: Zara Larcombe
Commissioning Editor: Zara Anvari
Managing Editor: Frank Gallaugher
Art Director: Julie Weir
Designers: Ginny Zeal and Kate Haynes
Senior Production Manager: Peter Hunt

ISBN 978-1-78157-423-2

A CIP catalogue record for this book is available from the British Library

Printed in China

10 9 8 7 6 5 4 3 2 1

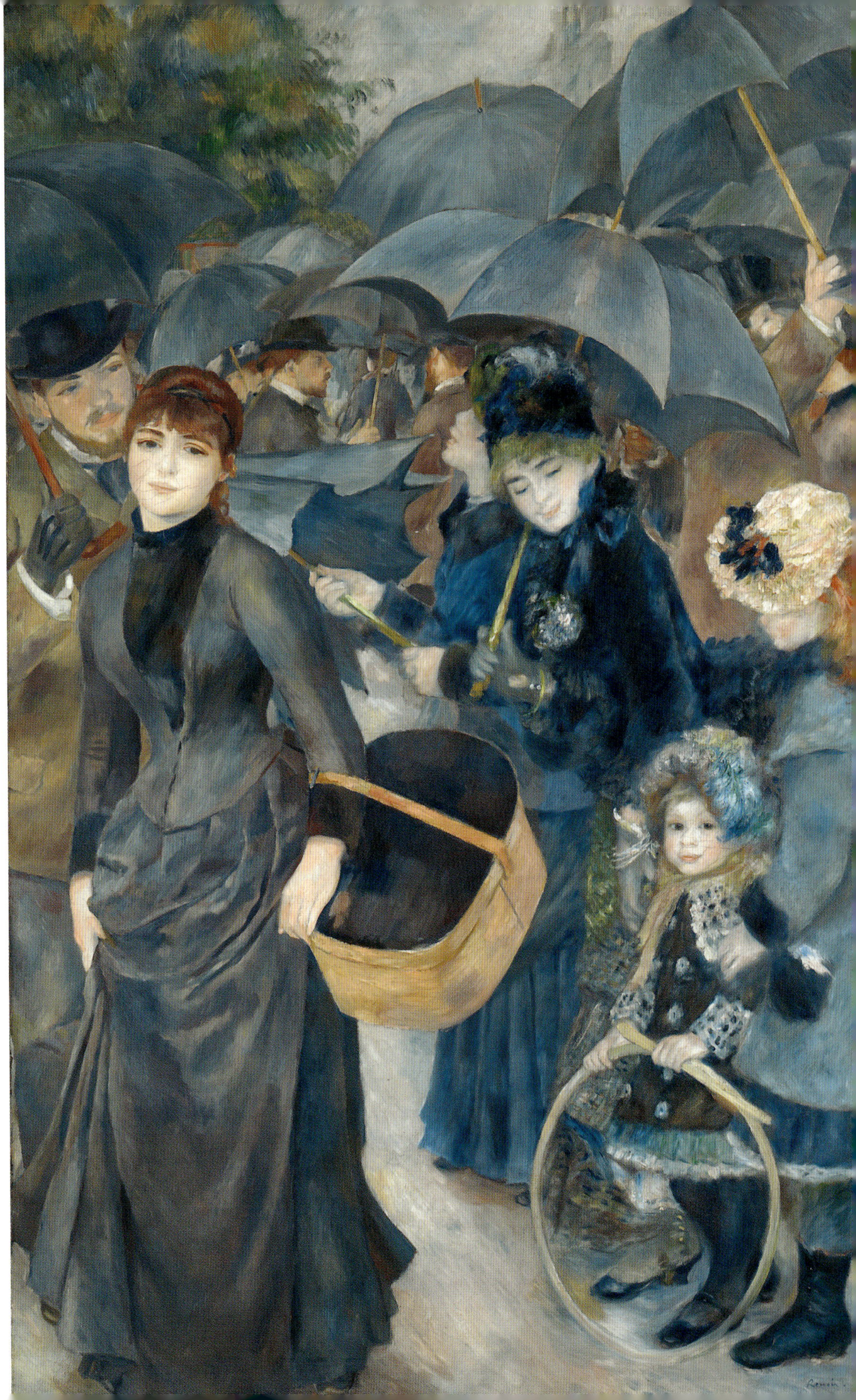

CONTENTS

INTRODUCTION

Great works of art deserve a closer look. This carefully curated selection of great paintings provides a fun opportunity to appreciate pivotal works in the National Gallery's world-class collection.

Here, 40 visual puzzles take you on a journey through art history, from Early Renaissance paintings by Italian masters to pieces that paved the way to the birth of Modern Art.

Each puzzle contains a total of 20 differences to spot – and the devil is in the detail. As you search for incongruities, taking in each individual artist's brushwork, technique, use of colour and a range of other creative decisions, you will be rewarded with a deeper understanding of what makes these artworks so masterful.

Paintings include depictions of Parisian leisure time rendered in expressive brushstrokes by the Impressionists, stunningly detailed Venetian vistas from Canaletto, picturesque landscapes (Constable), dramatic seascapes (Turner, Claude), and sensual mythical scenes (Rubens, Titian).

The answers are included at the back, and captions provide hints and insight into each painting, be it on the meaning, subject or technique behind the piece.

Spot your Bronzino from your Botticelli, your Monet from your Manet, with this grown-up activity book that combines the pleasure of puzzle-solving with the contemplative study of fine art.

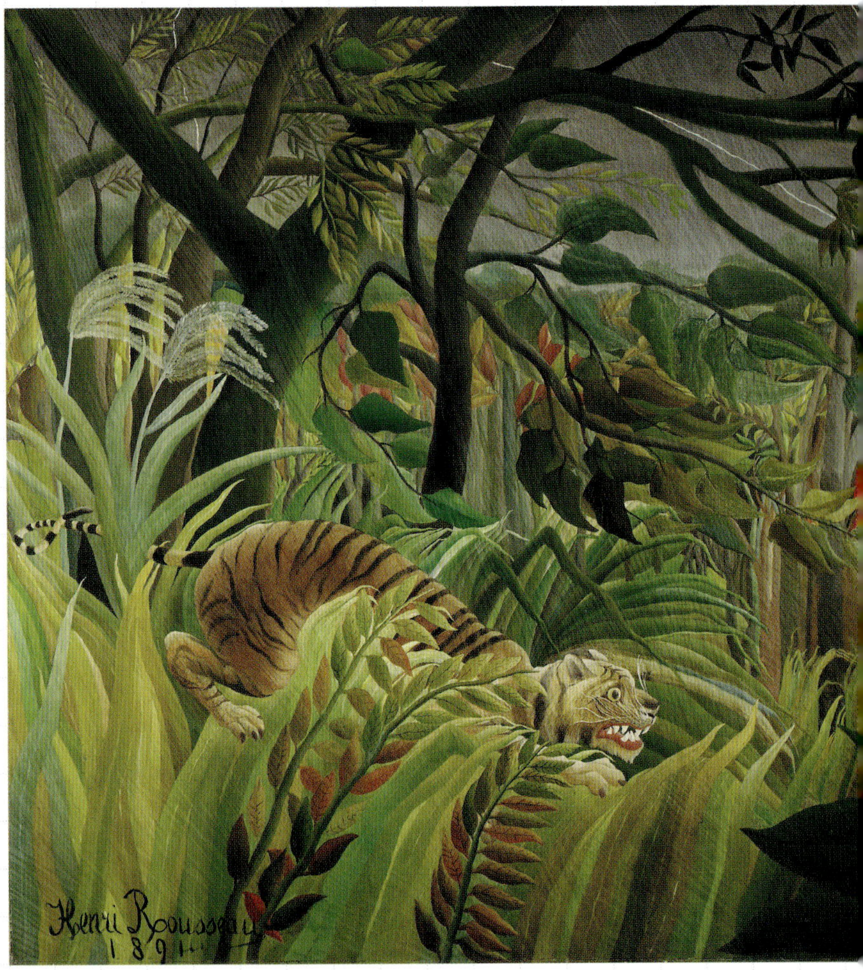

SURPRISED!
Henri Rousseau (1844–1910)
1891
Oil on canvas

In the first of Rousseau's famous jungle scenes, a storm breaks out while a tiger, deep in foliage, is on the hunt. There is a great sense of atmosphere, the forks of lightning cracking in the moody gray sky, and of movement – the sprawling foreground vegetation, the bending branches and diagonal streaks of rain.

60

Answers to the puzzles
are in the back of the book:
follow the grid references
to discover the changes

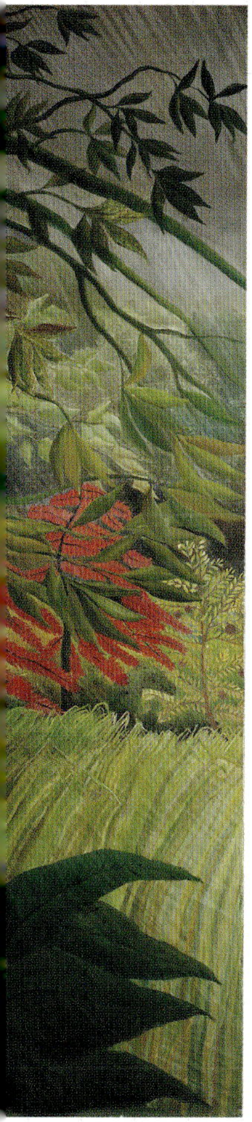

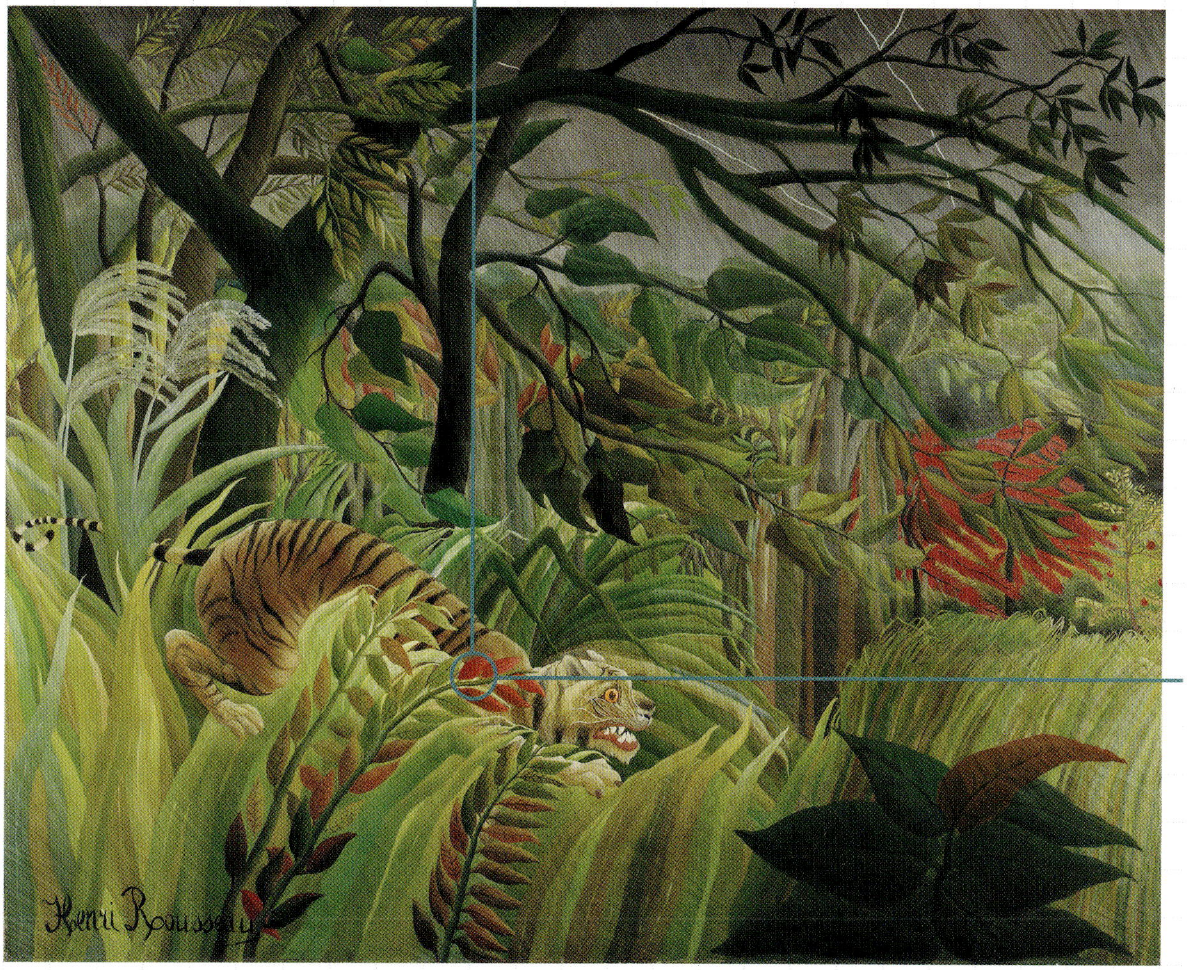

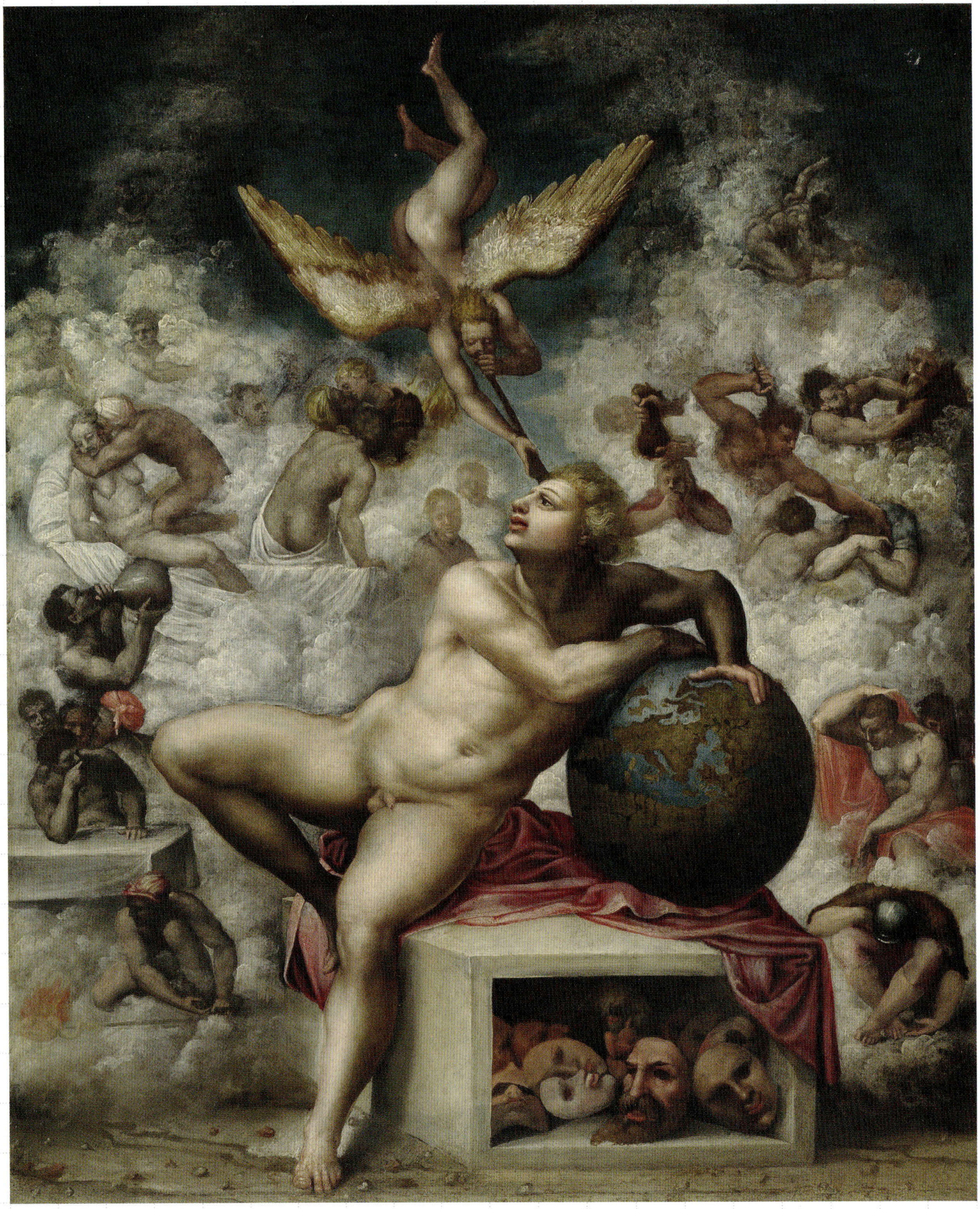

THE DREAM OF HUMAN LIFE

After Michelangelo (1475–1564)
after 1533
Oil on slate

Hidden in the background of this allegorical image are scenes representing six of the Deadly Sins. Among the clouds figures embrace, wrestle and drink. Can you tell which of the seven sins has been excluded? The central figure rests on a globe of the Earth, while an angel above plays a trumpet.

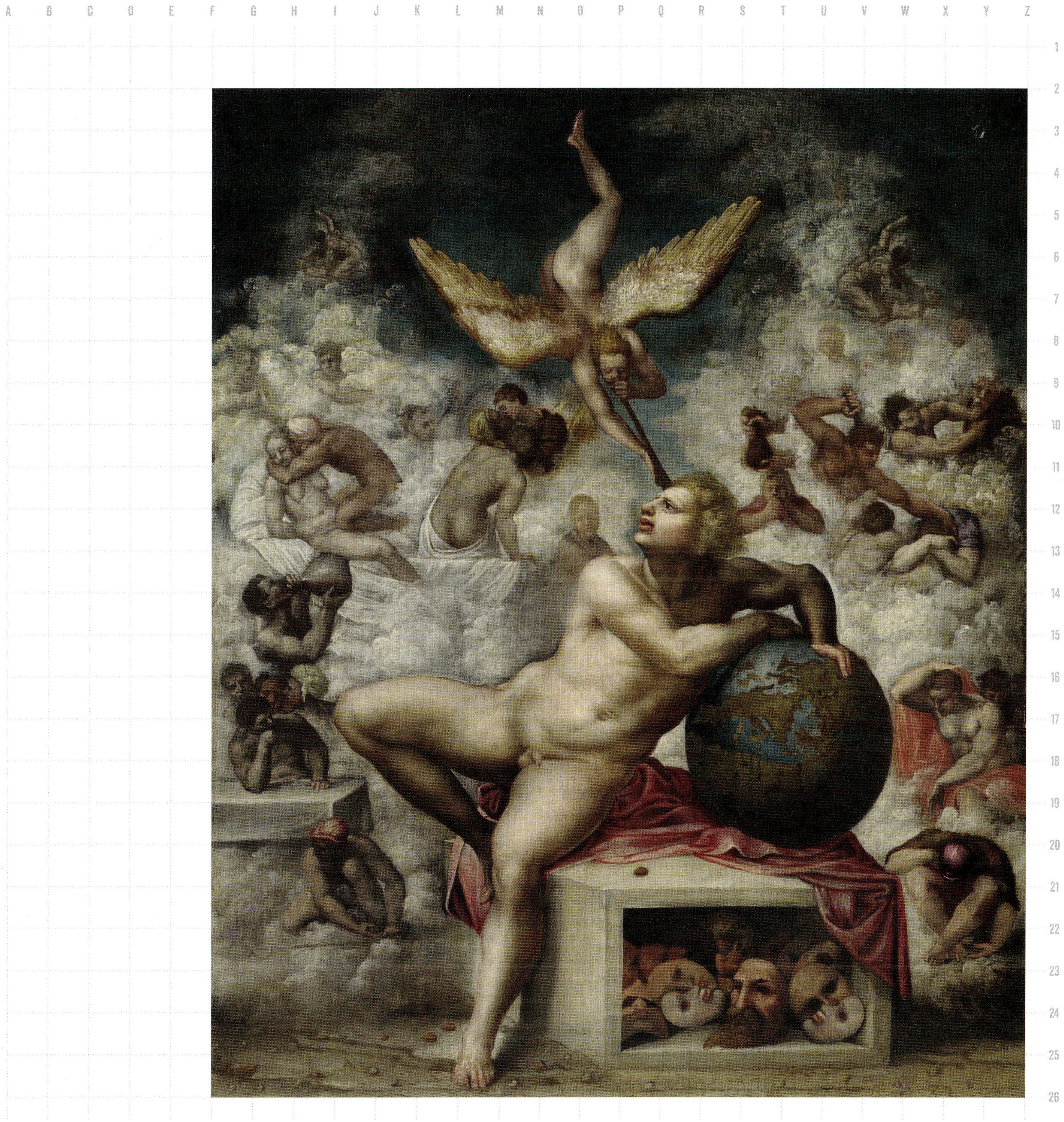
A B C D E F G H I J K L M N O P Q R S T U V W X Y Z
1 2 3 4 5 6 7 8 9 10 11 12 13 14 15 16 17 18 19 20 21 22 23 24 25 26
A B C D E F G H I J K L M N O P Q R S T U V W X Y Z

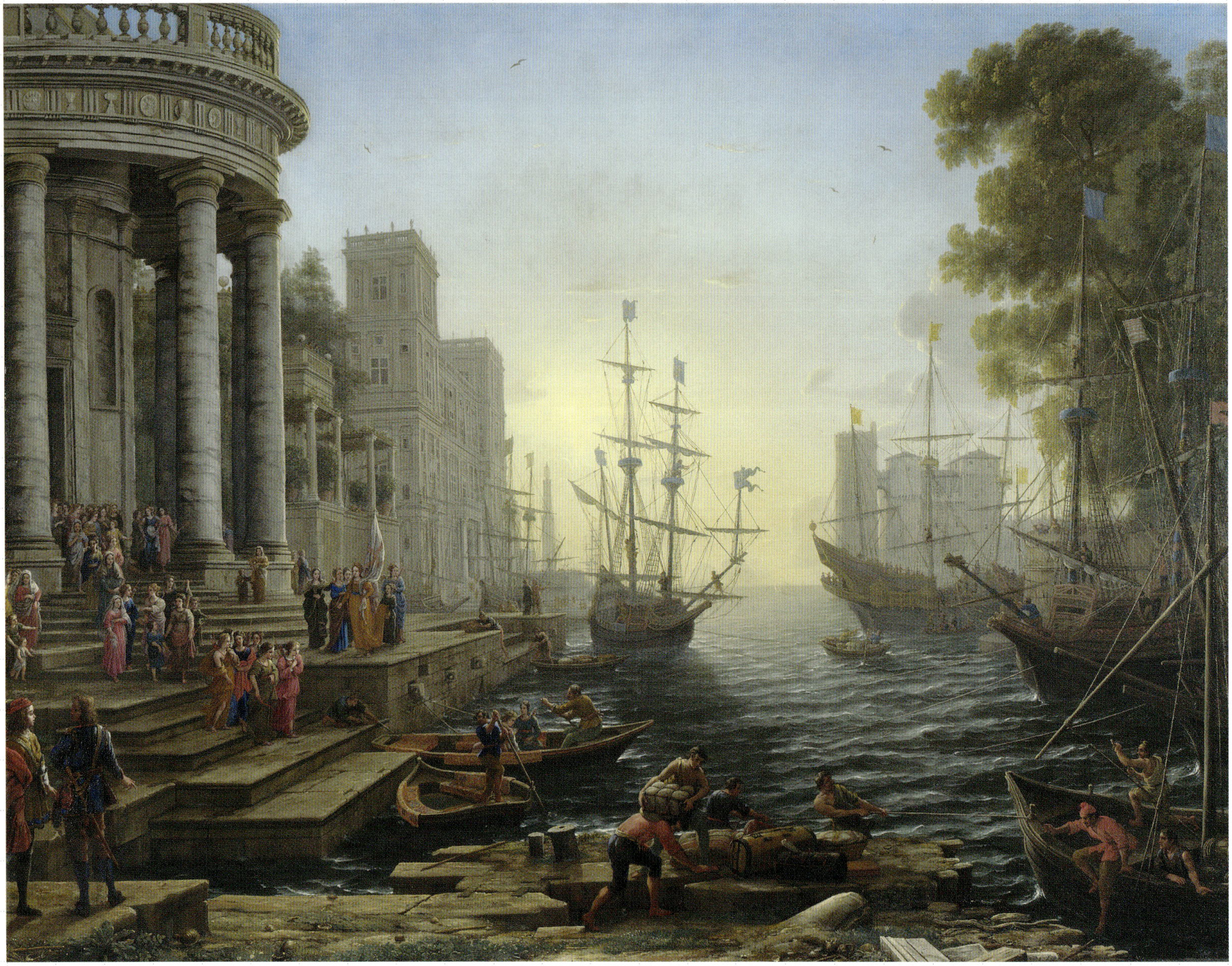

SEAPORT WITH THE EMBARKATION OF SAINT URSULA

Claude Lorrain (about 1604–1682)
1641
Oil on canvas

Claude's finely detailed seaport scene depicts Saint Ursula embarking on a fateful journey to Cologne, where, according to legend, she was martyred along with her 11,000 virgin handmaidens. In a yellow dress and carrying a flag, can you find Ursula? The bows and arrows in the hands of the maidens reveal how they died.

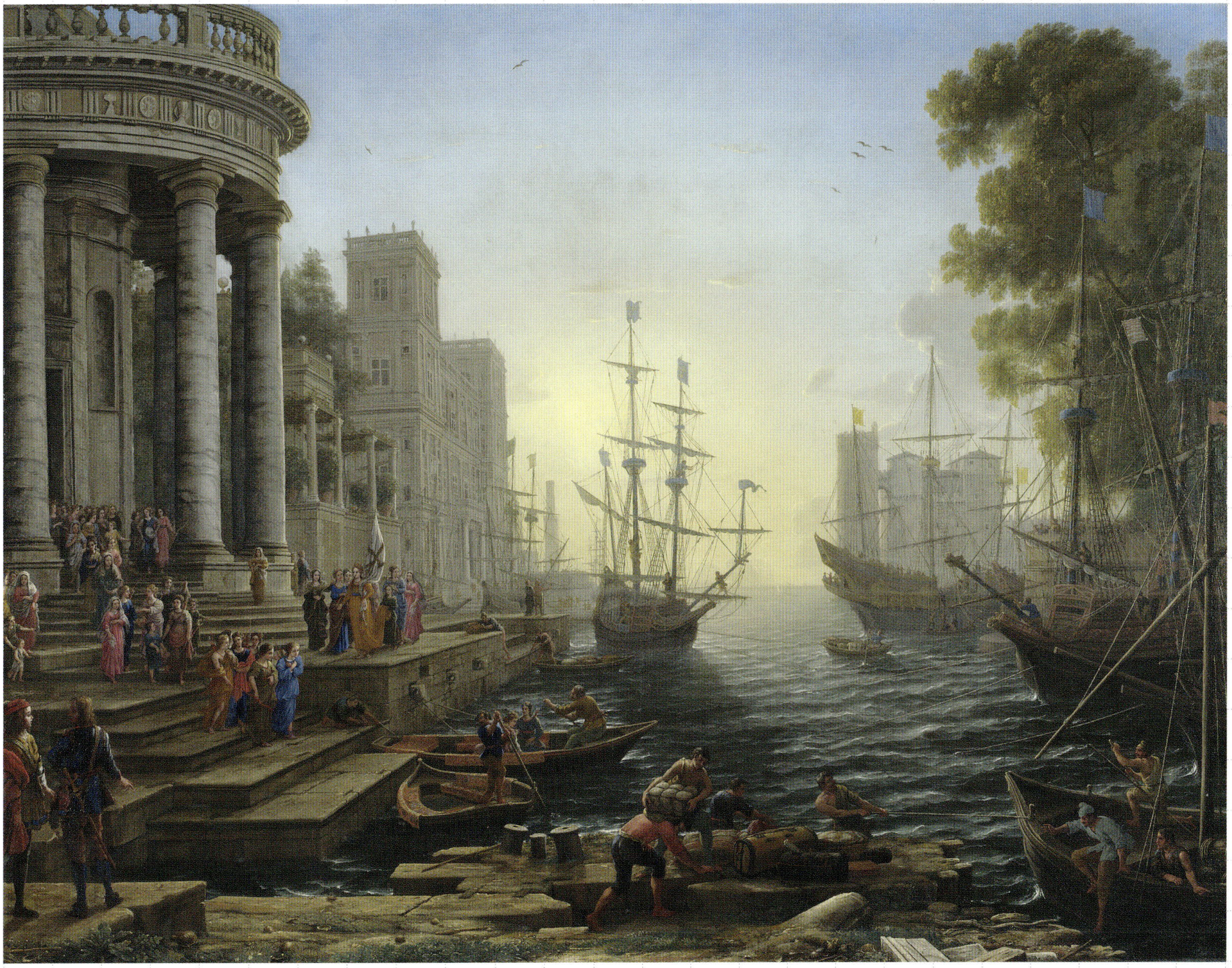

A B C D E F G H I J K L M N O P Q R S T U V W X Y Z

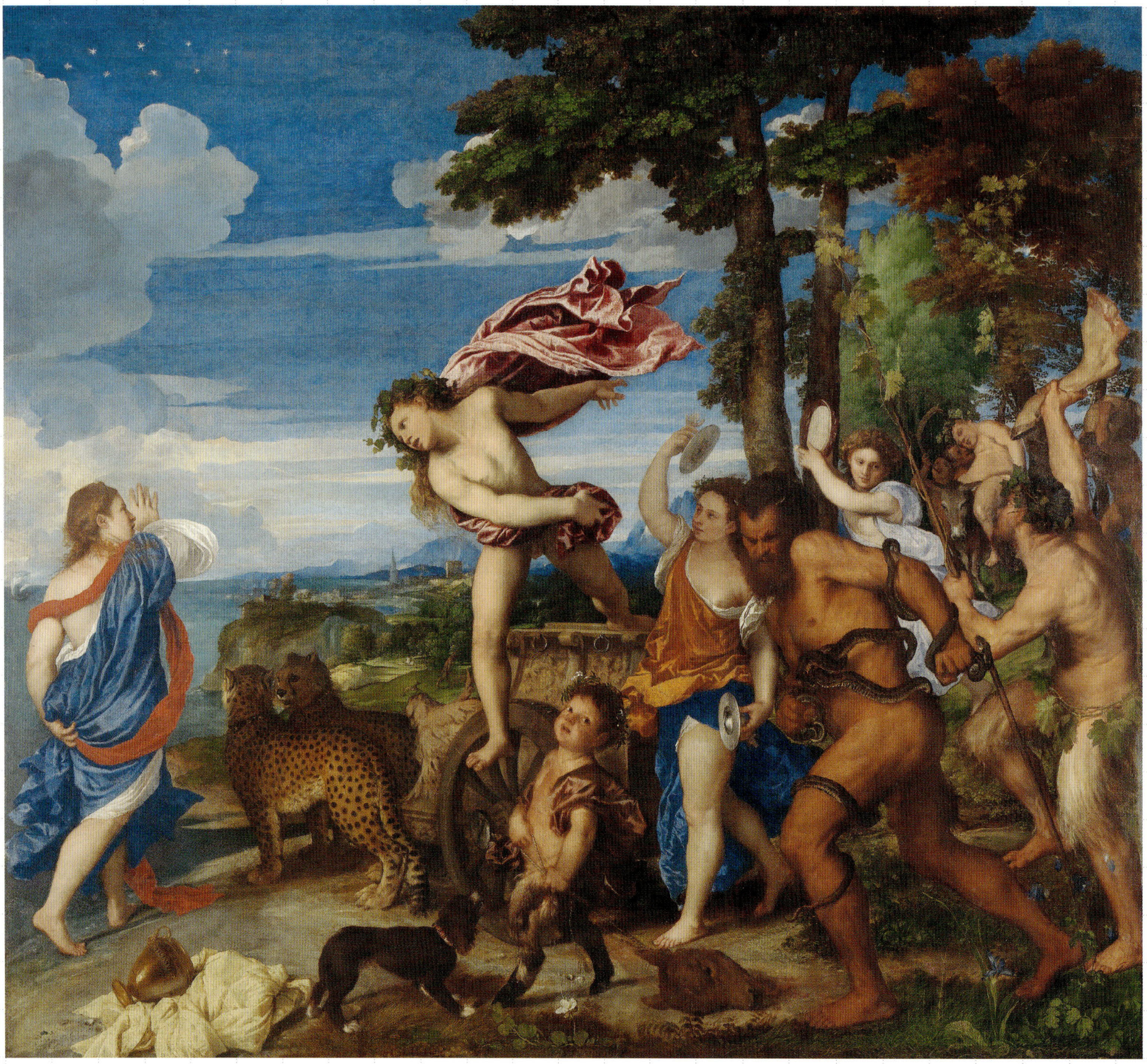

BACCHUS AND ARIADNE

Tiziano Vecellio, known as Titian (active about 1506–died 1576)
1520–1523
Oil on canvas

For Bacchus it is love at first sight as he springs from his cheetah-driven chariot to greet Ariadne. Abandoned on the island by the distant ship to her left, she will soon join the stars above her as a constellation. Can you spot the single white caper flower, a symbol of love?

A B C D E F G H I J K L M N O P Q R S T U V W X Y Z

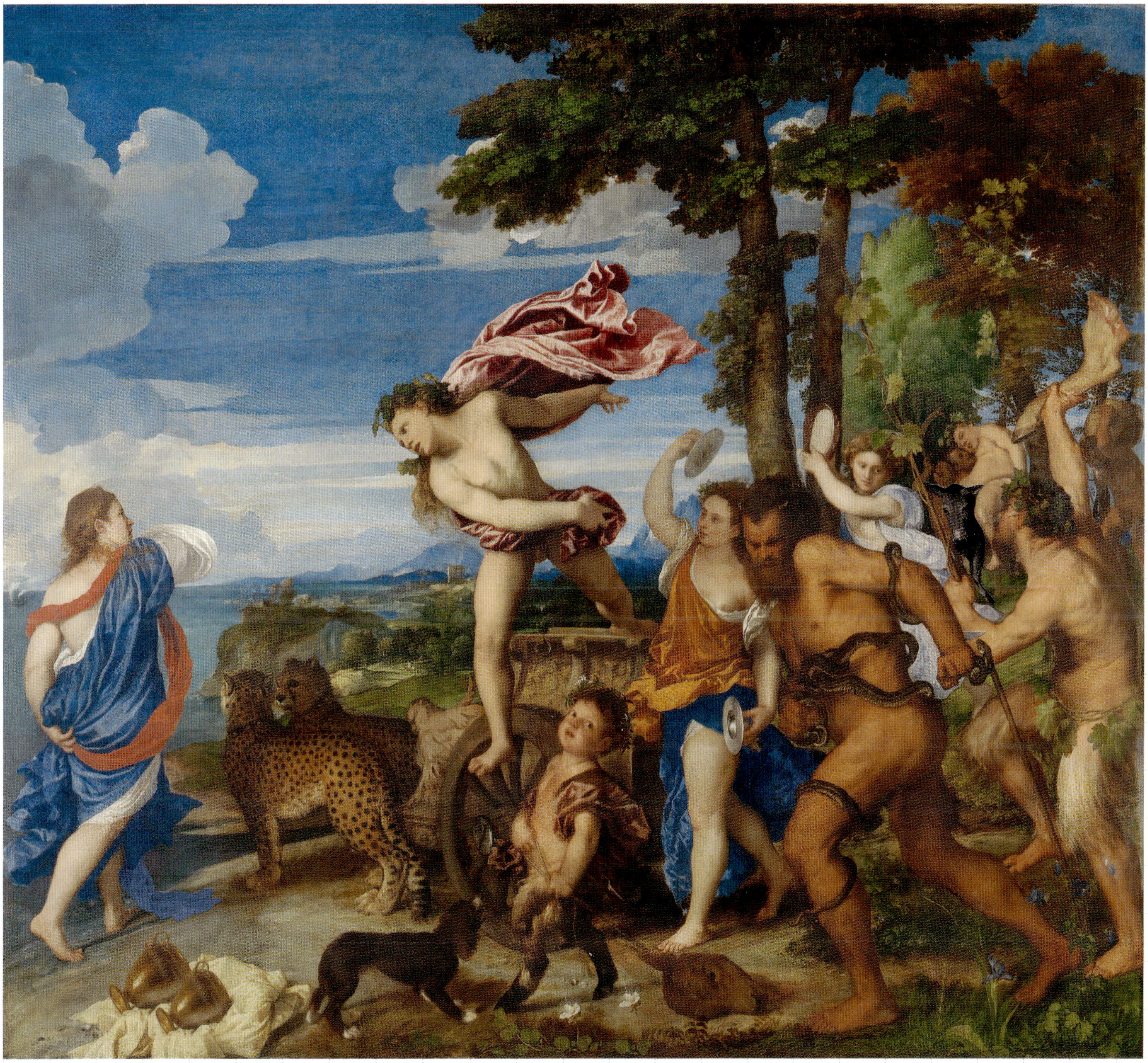

1 2 3 4 5 6 7 8 9 10 11 12 13 14 15 16 17 18 19 20 21 22 23 24 25 26

A B C D E F G H I J K L M N O P Q R S T U V W X Y Z

A B C D E F G H I J K L M N O P Q R S T U V W X Y Z

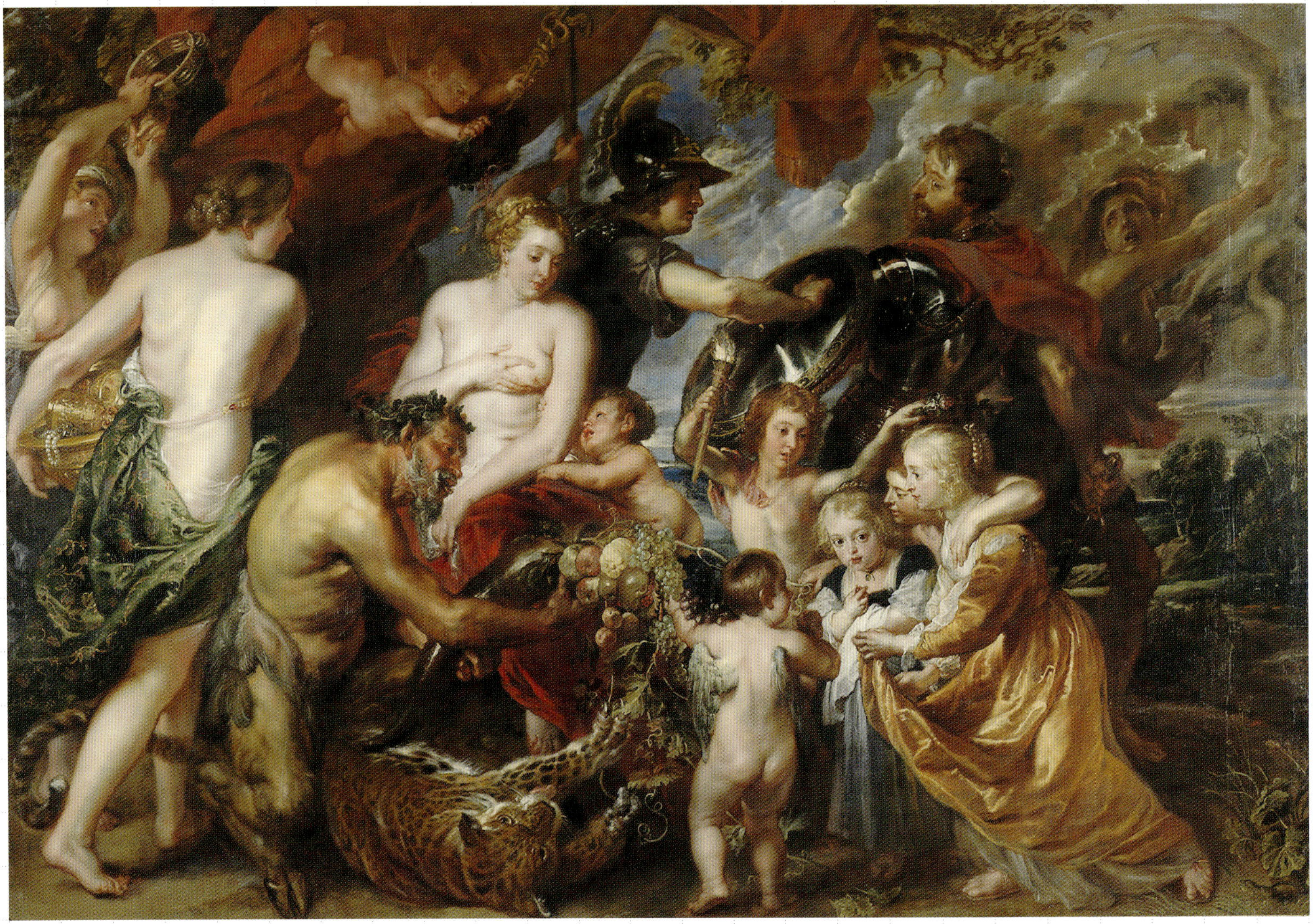

MINERVA PROTECTS PAX FROM MARS ('PEACE AND WAR')

Peter Paul Rubens (1577–1640)
1629–1630
Oil on canvas

As Pax tends to an infant, Minerva, the goddess of wisdom, shields her from Mars, the god of war. A cherub holds an olive wreath, a symbol of peace, above her head. In the foreground are references to Bacchus, the god of fertility, including a satyr, a leopard and a bounty of grapes.

A B C D E F G H I J K L M N O P Q R S T U V W X Y Z

A B C D E F G H I J K L M N O P Q R S T U V W X Y Z

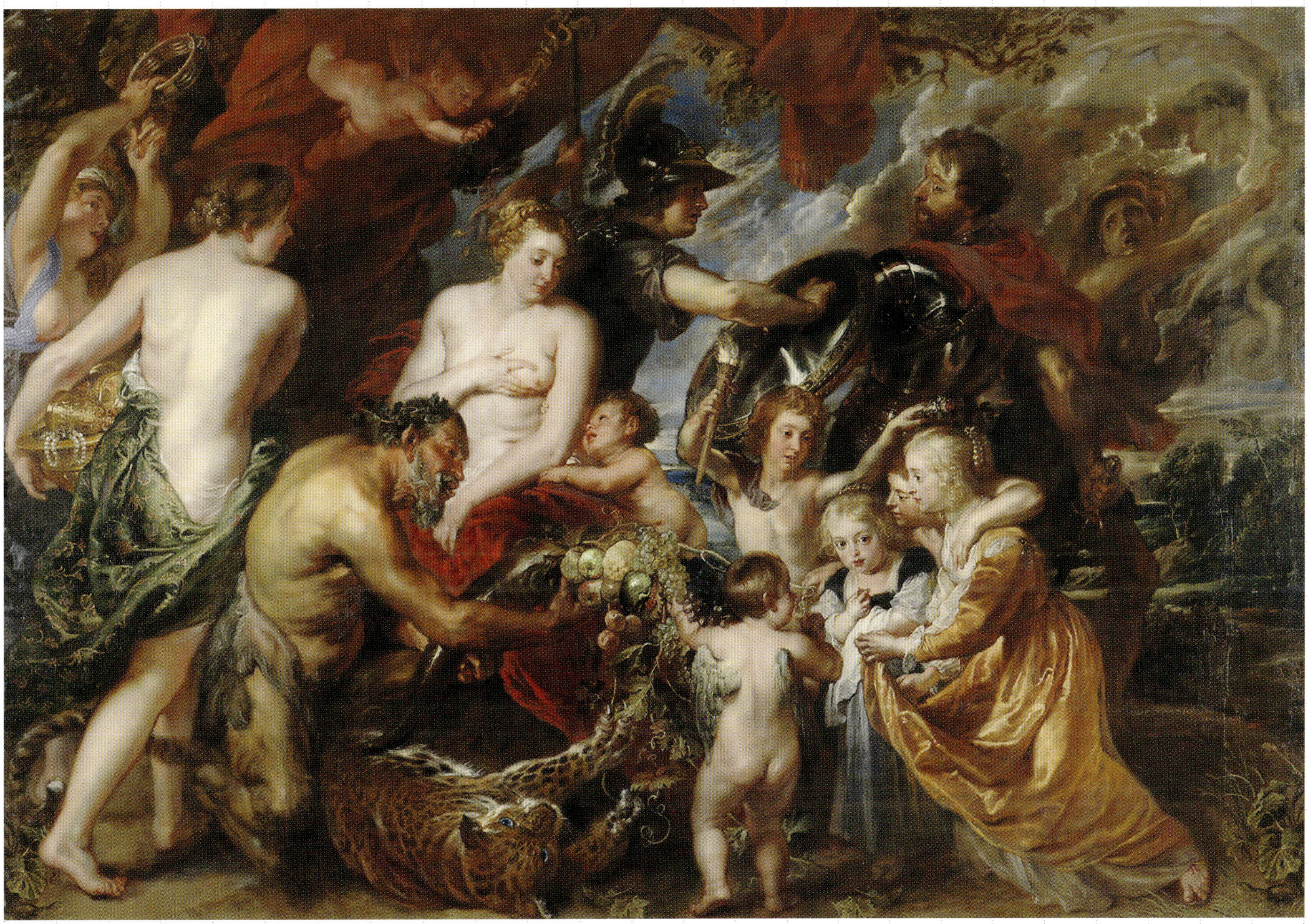

A B C D E F G H I J K L M N O P Q R S T U V W X Y Z

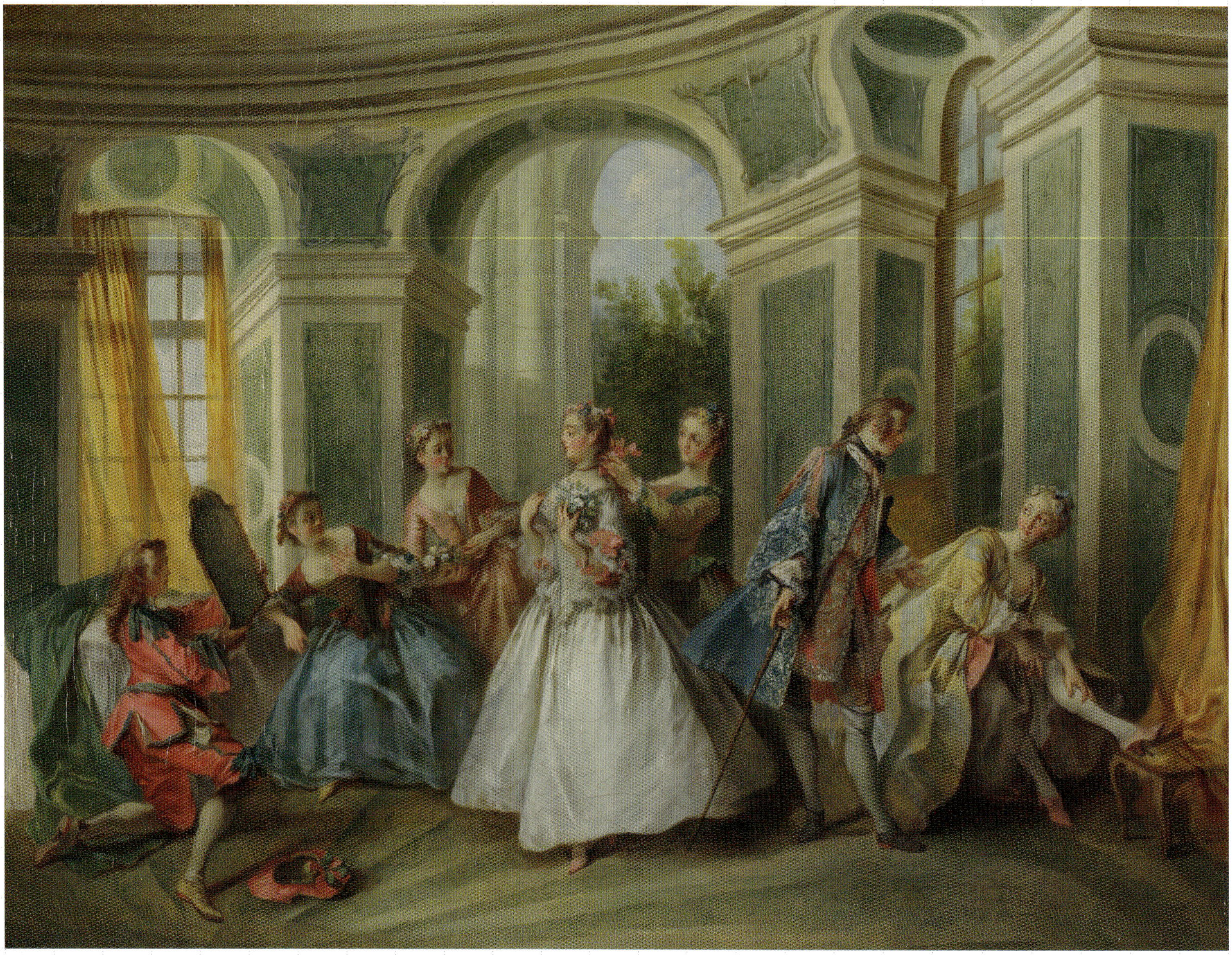

THE FOUR AGES OF MAN: YOUTH

Nicolas Lancret (1690–1743)
by 1735
Oil on canvas

Light streams through a window on the left, illuminating this scene of young women on the cusp of adulthood. It is the second in Lancret's series that depicts the four ages of man: 'Childhood', 'Youth', 'Maturity' and 'Old Age'. A girl being adorned with flowers and admiring her reflection is the focal point. On the right another fingers her stocking and talks to a young man.

A B C D E F G H I J K L M N O P Q R S T U V W X Y Z

1 2 3 4 5 6 7 8 9 10 11 12 13 14 15 16 17 18 19 20 21 22 23 24 25 26

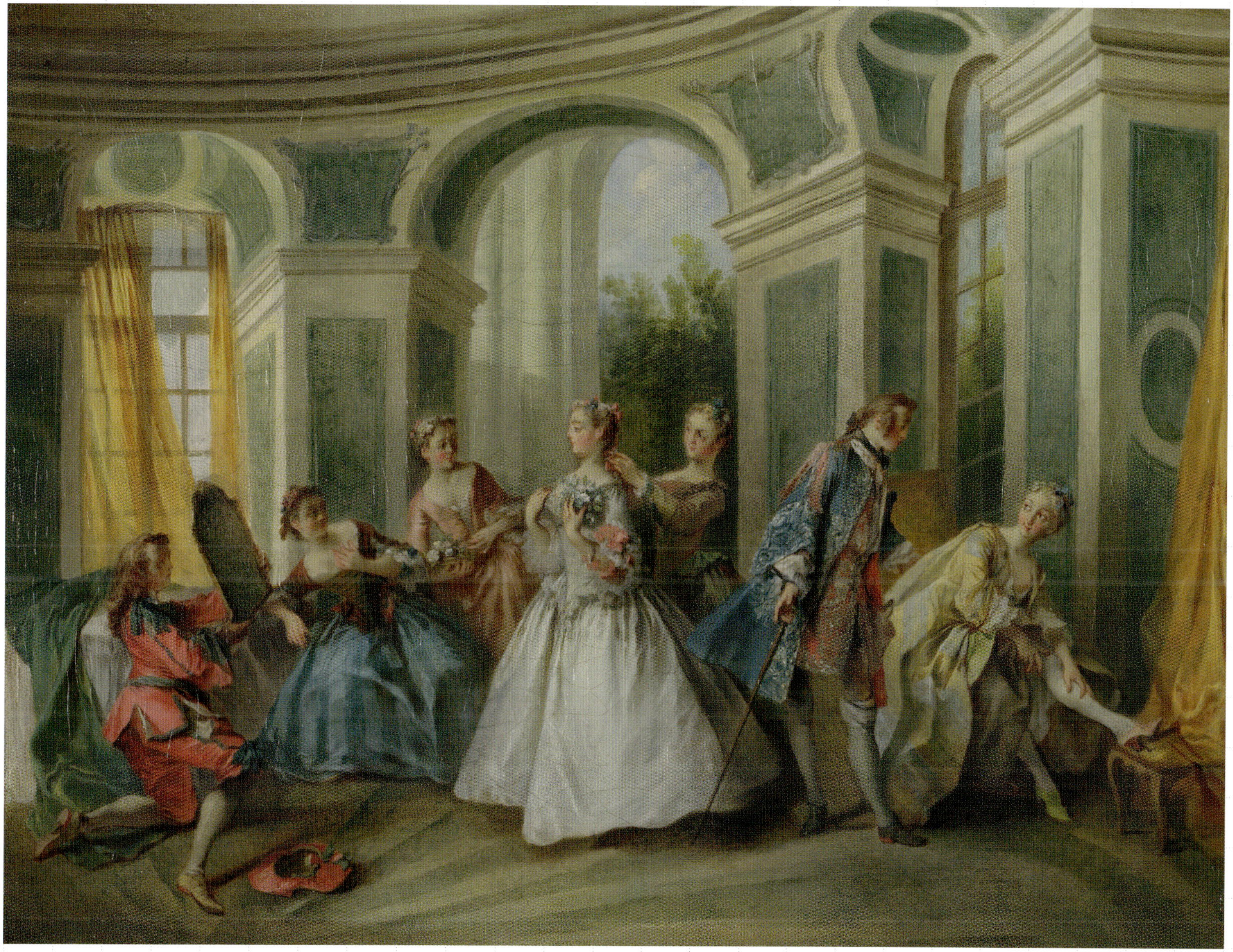

A B C D E F G H I J K L M N O P Q R S T U V W X Y Z

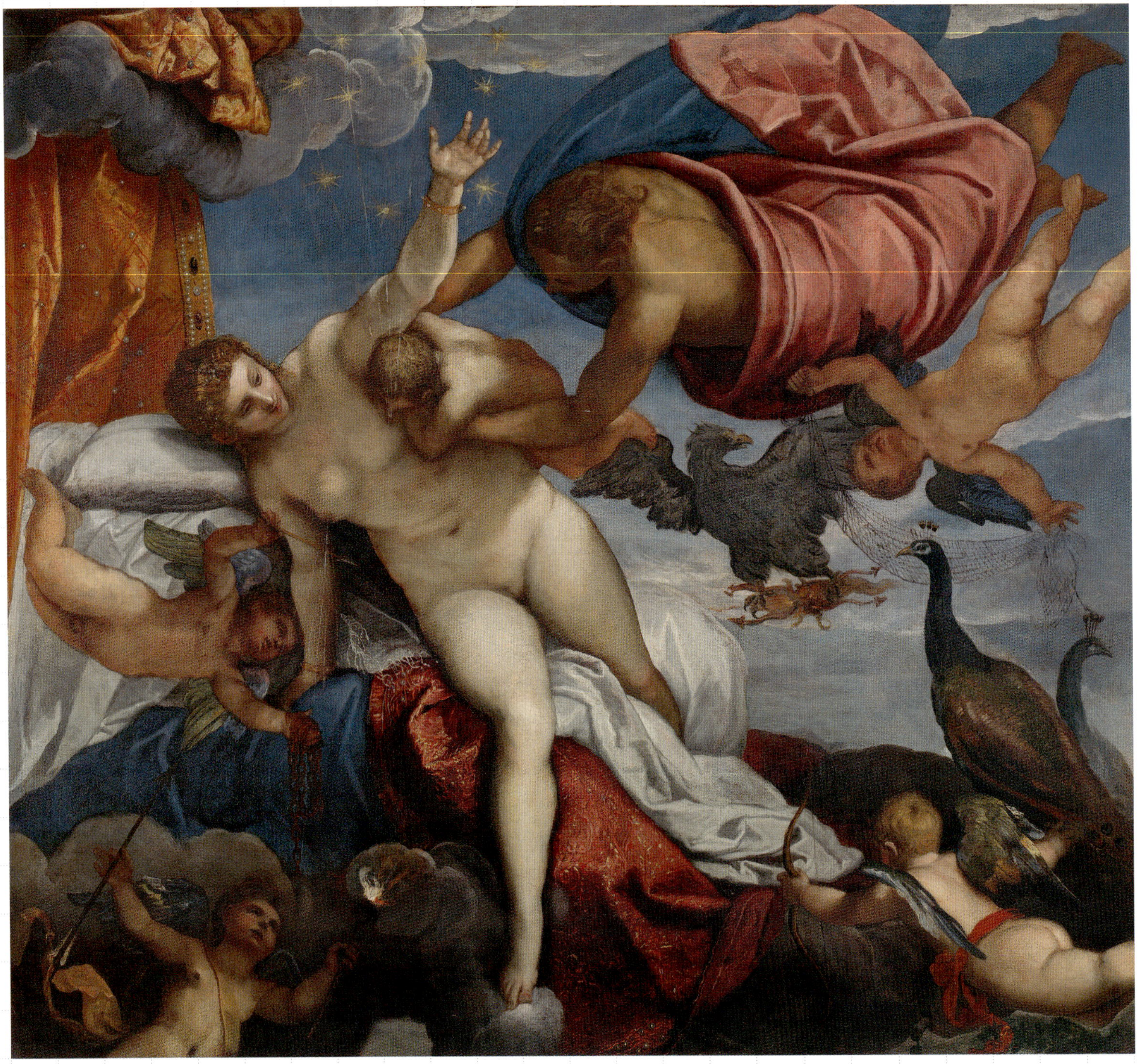

THE ORIGIN OF THE MILKY WAY

Jacopo Tintoretto (about 1518–1594)
about 1575
Oil on canvas

Hoping to immortalise an infant Hercules, the god Jupiter takes the child to feed from the goddess Juno. The milk streaming skywards formed the Milky Way, according to a Roman text. Juno is surrounded by cherubs, an eagle and a pair of peacocks – the latter is often associated with the goddess.

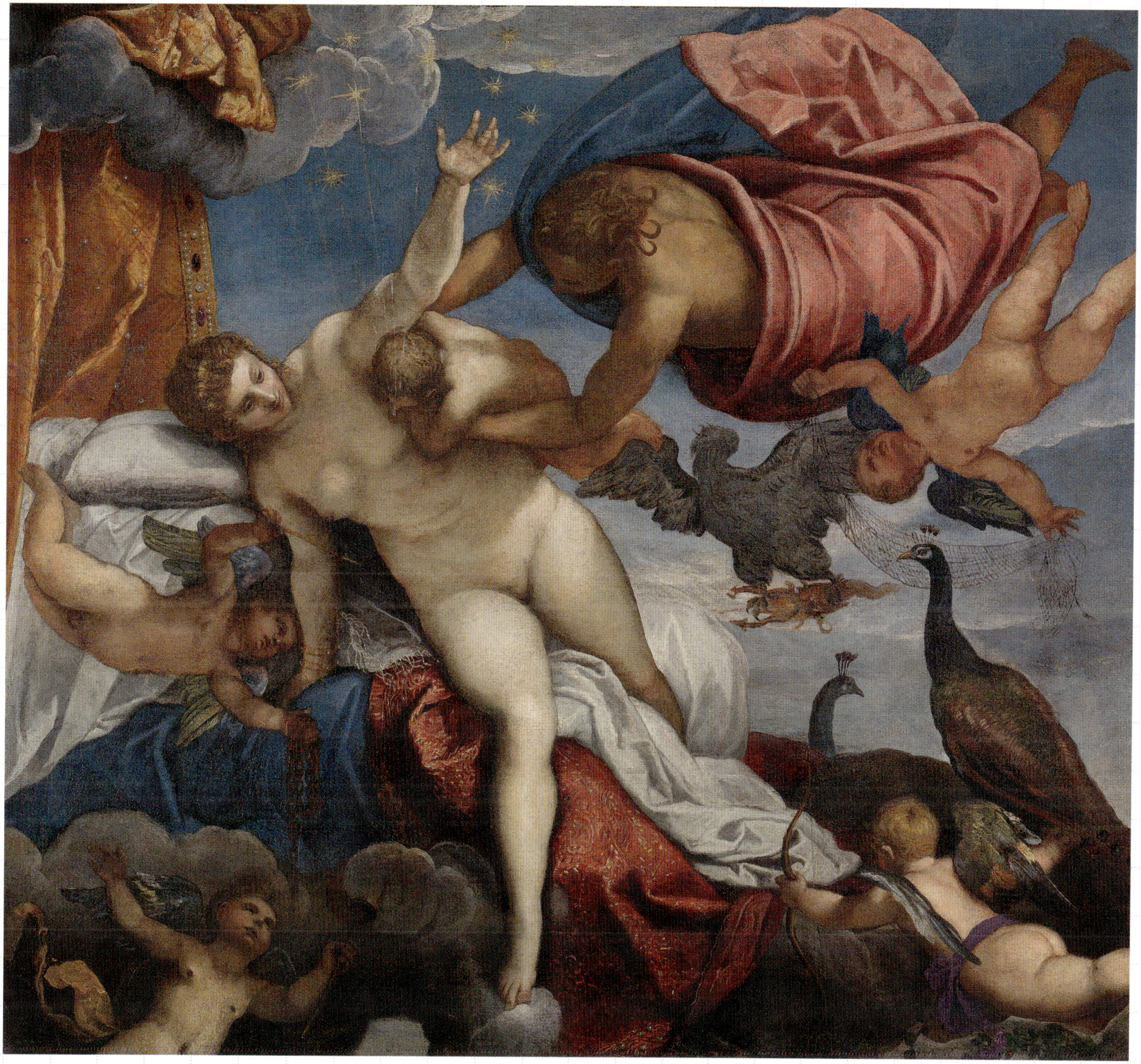

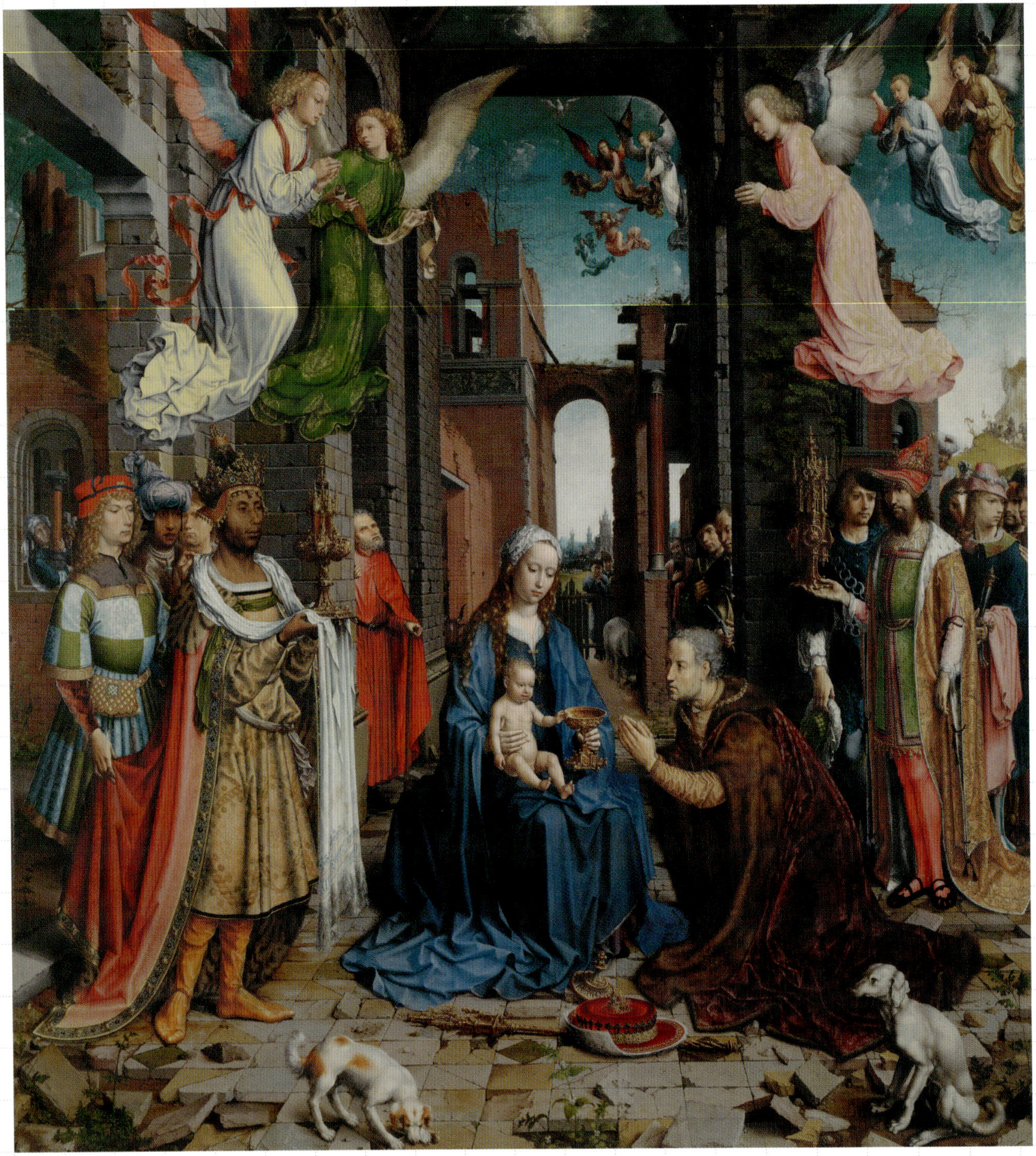

THE ADORATION OF THE KINGS

Jan Gossaert (active 1508–died 1532)

1510–1515

Oil on oak

In this rich and elaborate painting, baby Jesus is presented with gifts from the Three Kings. The ruins of the building contrast with the elegant and colourful finery of the Kings and attendants; Caspar's golden staff and exquisite hat rest on crumbling paving stones. Fans of the artist Dürer may recognise the copy of his dog bottom right.

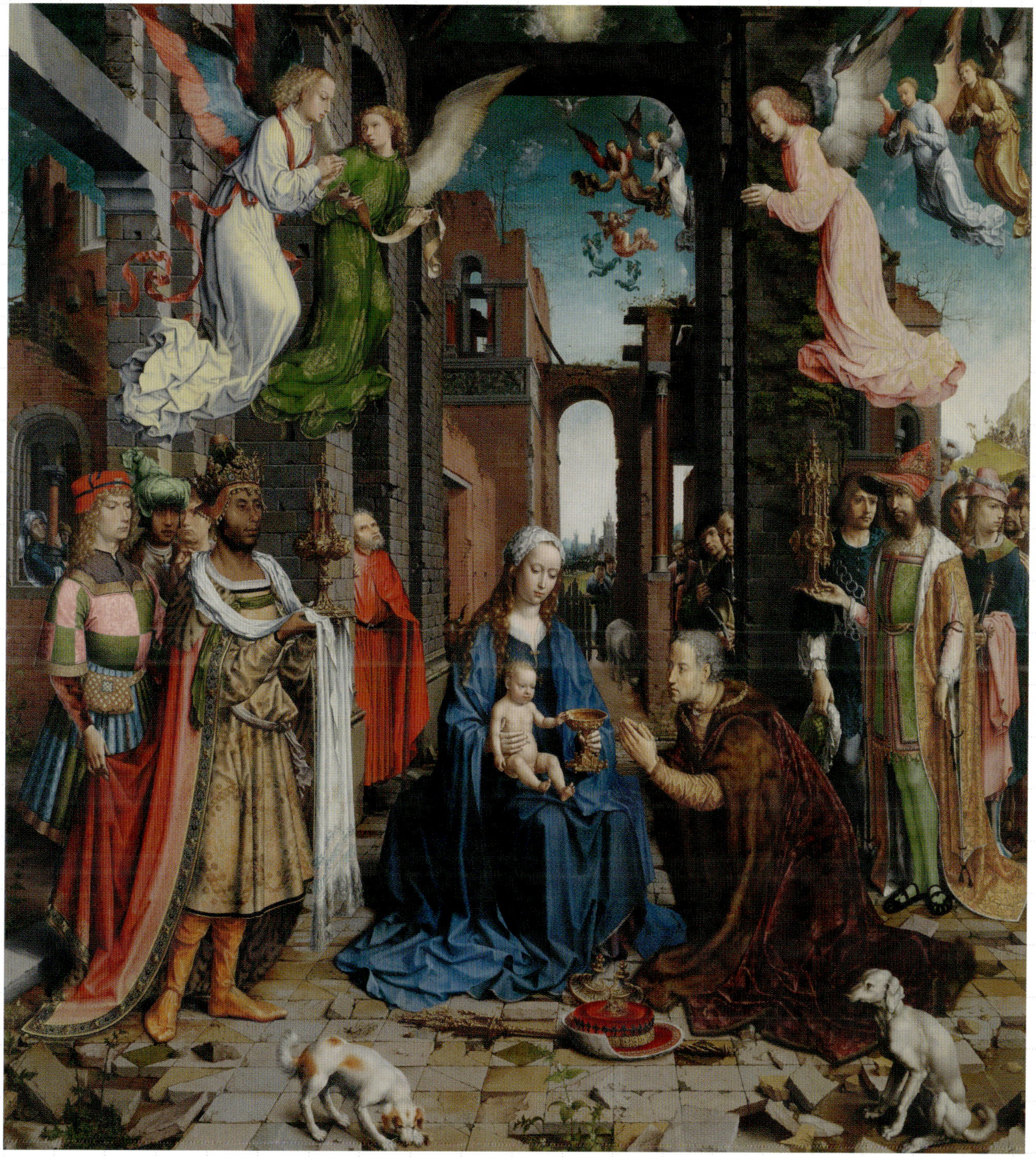

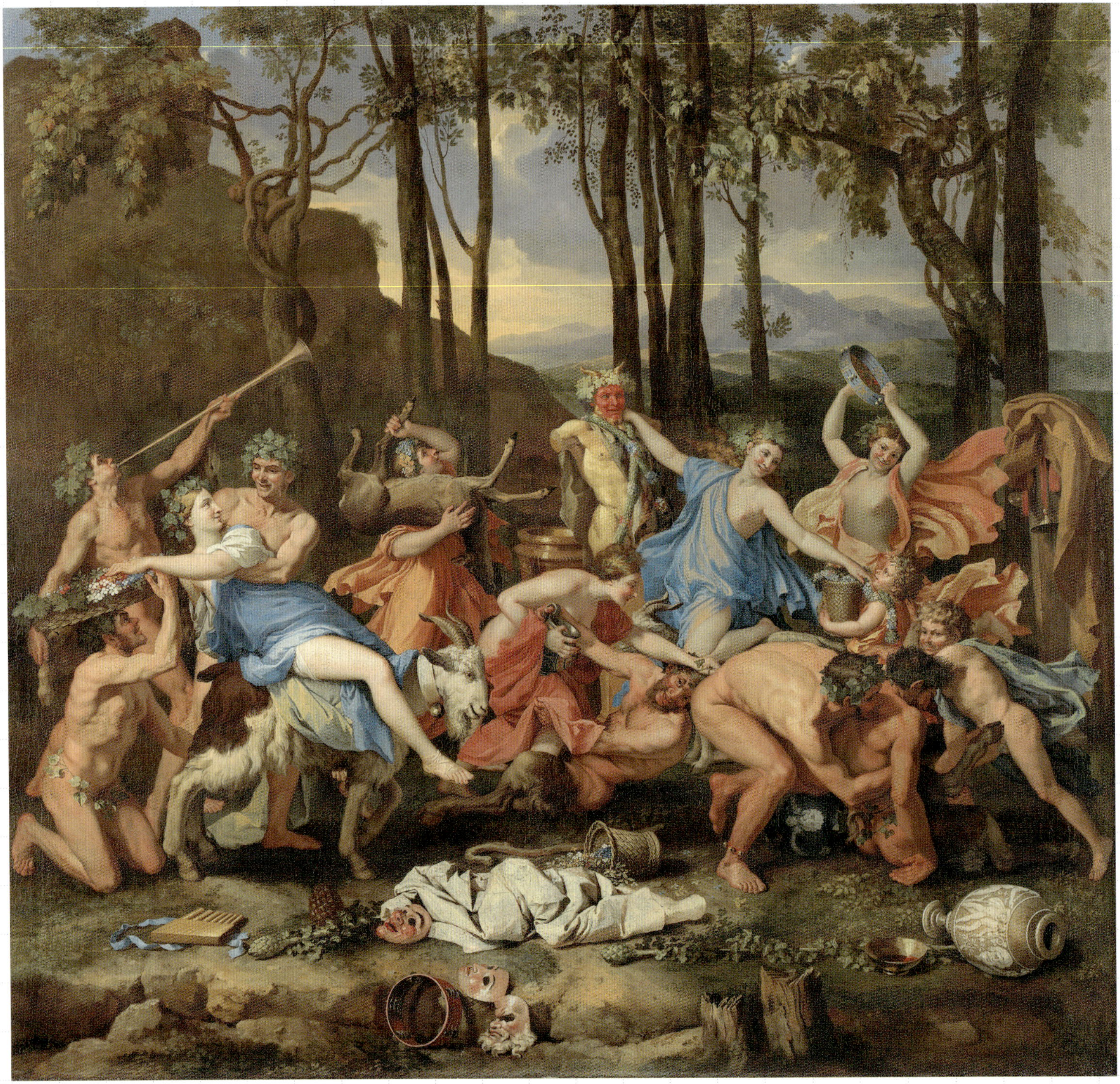

THE TRIUMPH OF PAN

Nicolas Poussin (1594–1665)
1636
Oil on canvas

This raucous mythical scene is littered with literary and visual references to the satyr Pan, god of the woods and fields, from panpipes and sacrificial deer to theatrical masks and a shepherd's staff.

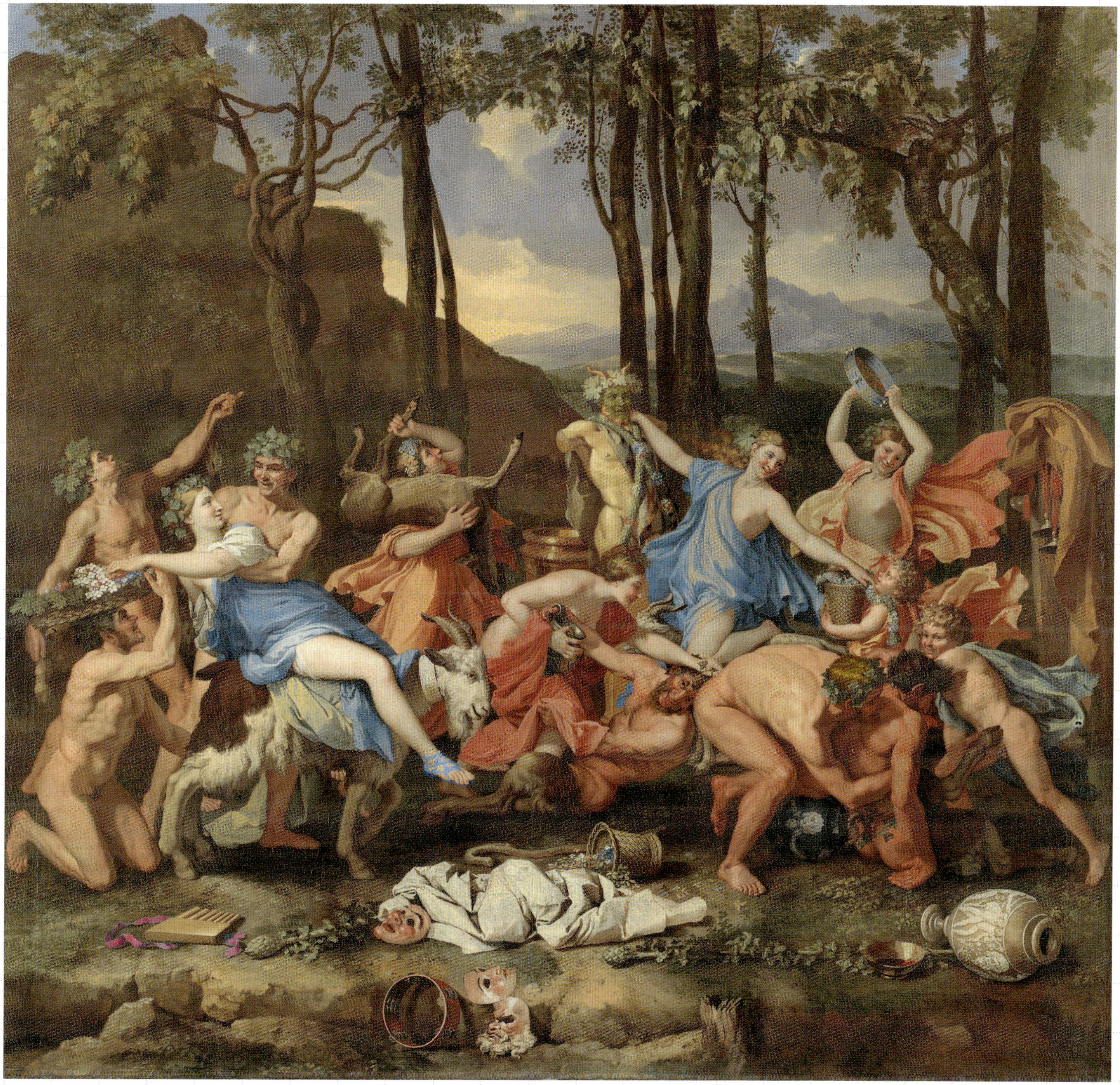

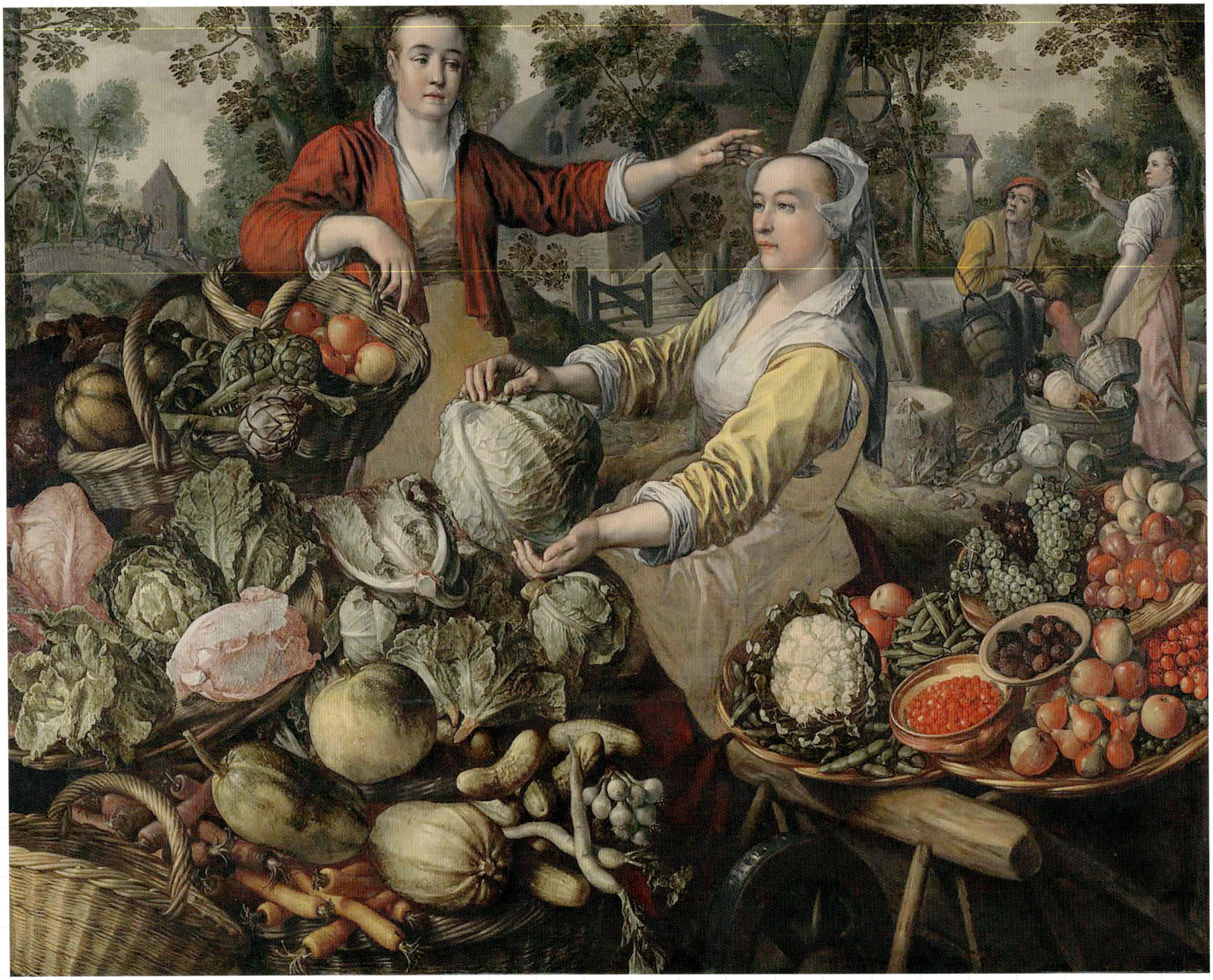

THE FOUR ELEMENTS: EARTH

Joachim Beuckelaer (probably 1535–died 1575)
1569
Oil on canvas

One of a set of paintings that link everyday scenes to the four elements and Biblical episodes. 'Earth' shows an abundance of natural produce: 16 different varieties of vegetables and fruit can be identified. Can you see the Holy Family crossing the bridge in the background?

A B C D E F G H I J K L M N O P Q R S T U V W X Y Z

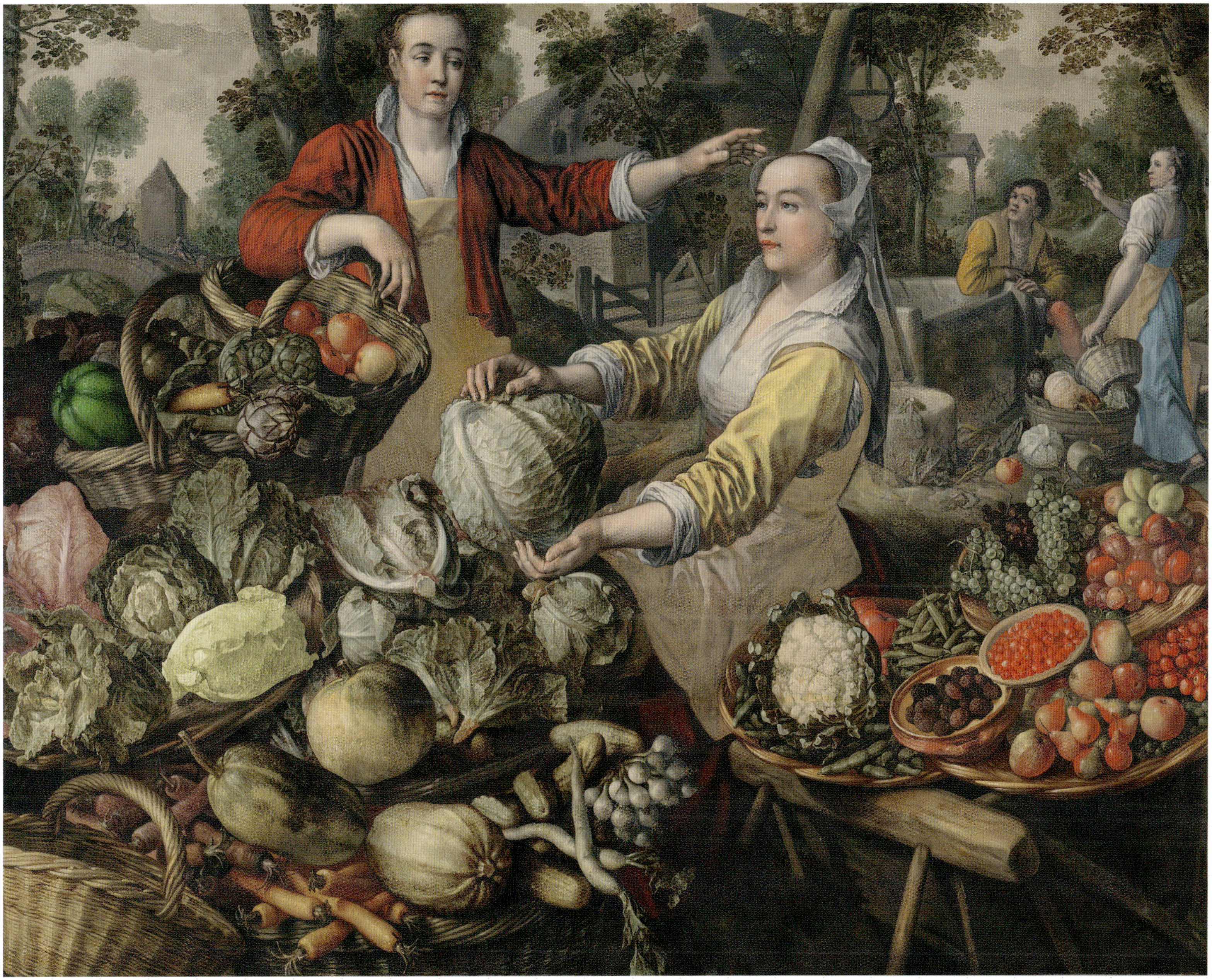

A B C D E F G H I J K L M N O P Q R S T U V W X Y Z

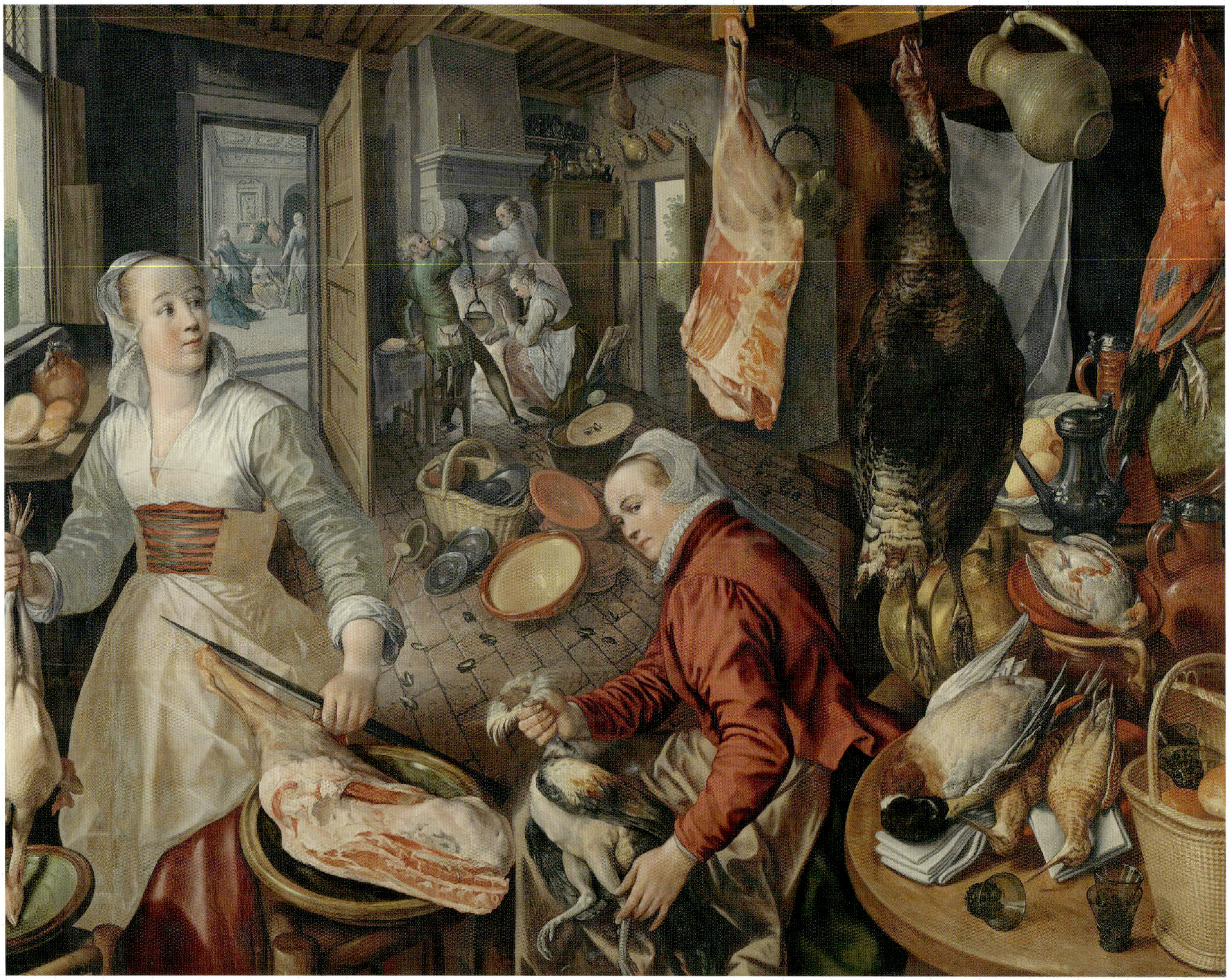

THE FOUR ELEMENTS: FIRE

Joachim Beuckelaer (probably 1535–died 1575)
1570
Oil on canvas

"Fire" is one of Beuckelaer's most ambitious works, combining the still life of haunches of meat and poultry being prepared for cooking on the fire beyond with a dramatic use of perspective. Beyond the kitchen, Christ is shown seated with Martha and Mary.

A B C D E F G H I J K L M N O P Q R S T U V W X Y Z

1

2

3

4

5

6

7

8

9

10

11

12

13

14

15

16

17

18

19

20

21

22

23

24

25

26

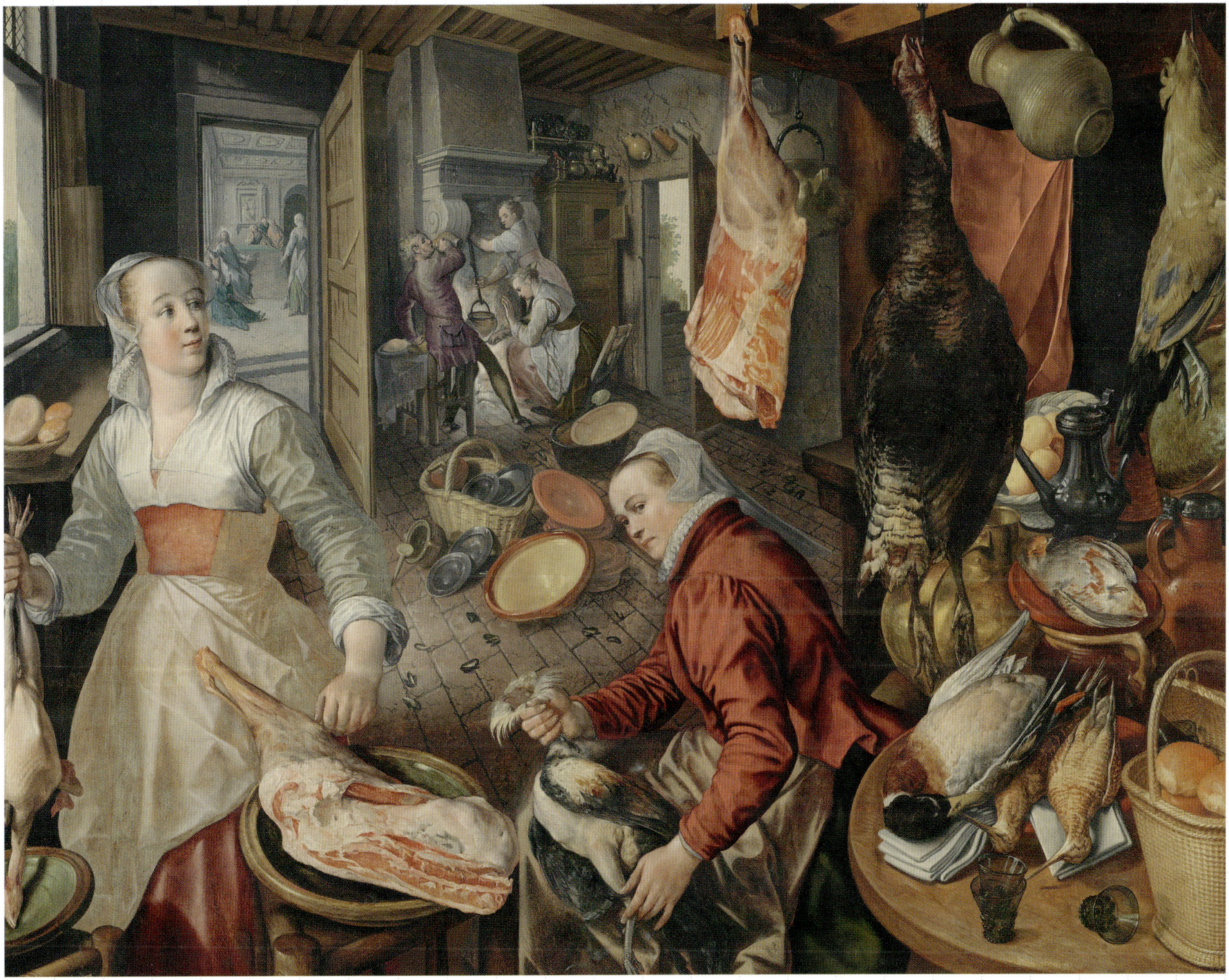

A B C D E F G H I J K L M N O P Q R S T U V W X Y Z

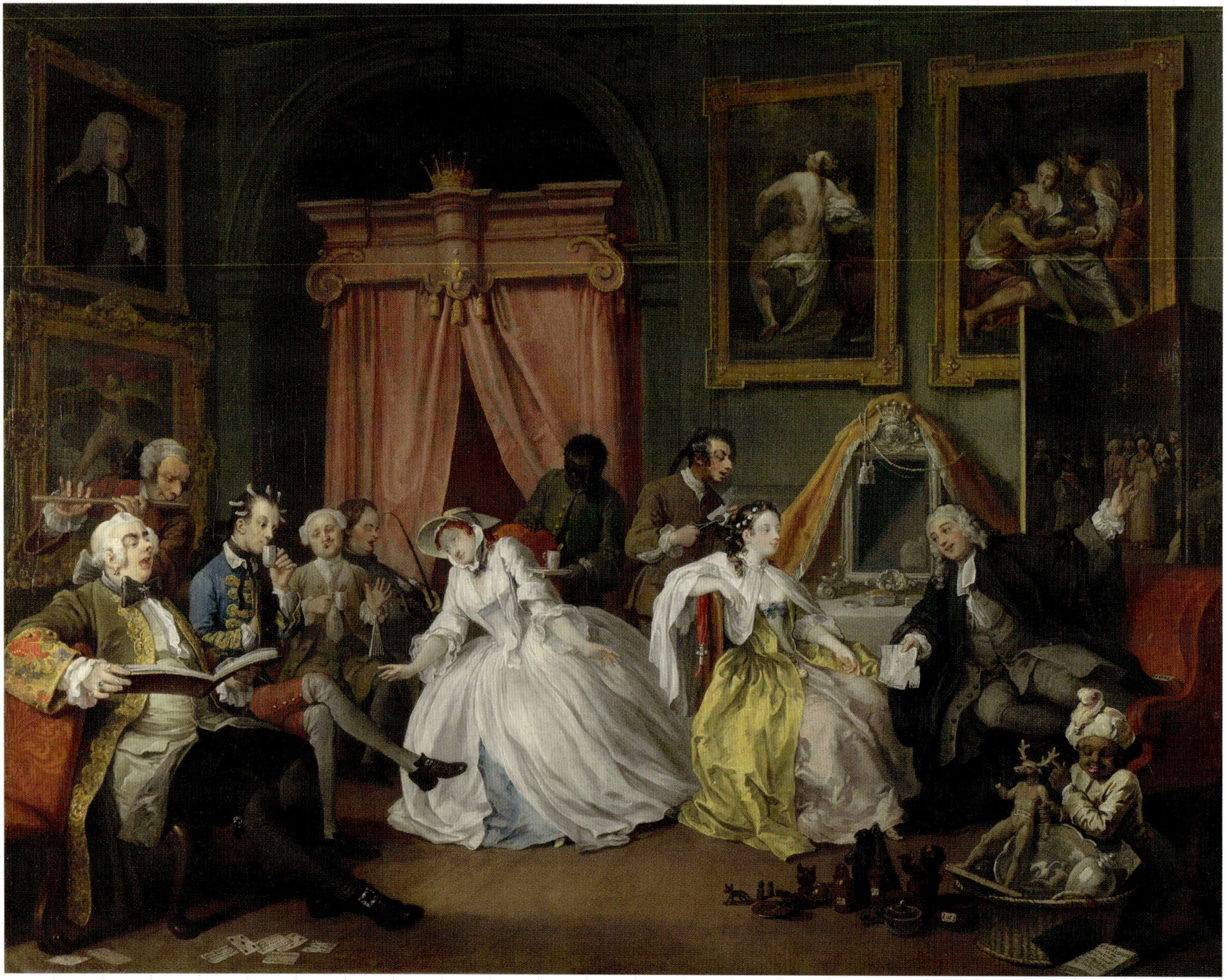

MARRIAGE A-LA-MODE: 4, THE TOILETTE

William Hogarth (1697–1764)
about 1743
Oil on canvas

Hogarth created many engravings satirising high society. Here, the newly appointed Countess receives guests. Can you spot two crowns highlighting her new status? The lawyer Silvertongue, also depicted in a portrait on the left, invites her to a masquerade, gesturing to a scene of one on a screen.

A B C D E F G H I J K L M N O P Q R S T U V W X Y Z

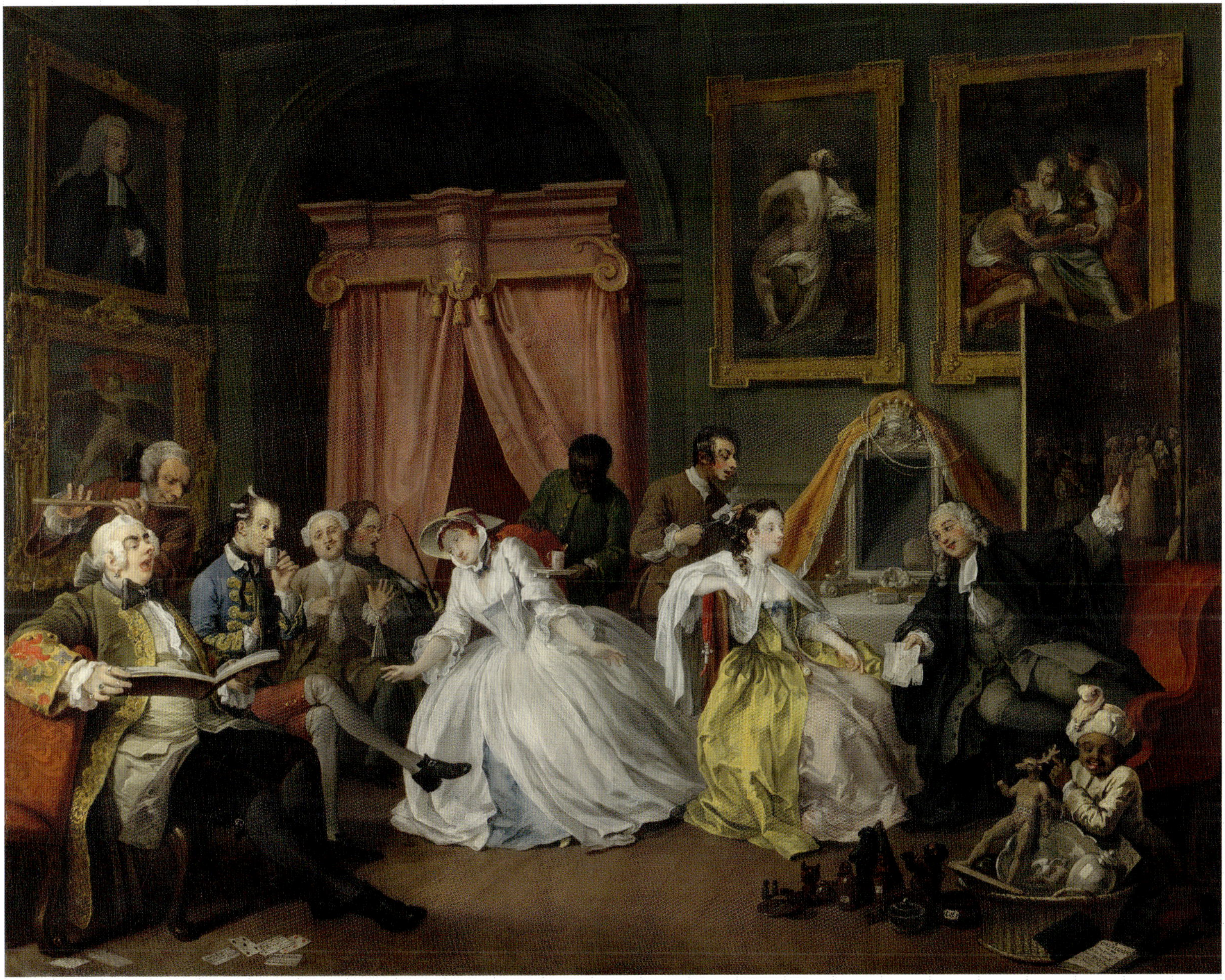

A B C D E F G H I J K L M N O P Q R S T U V W X Y Z

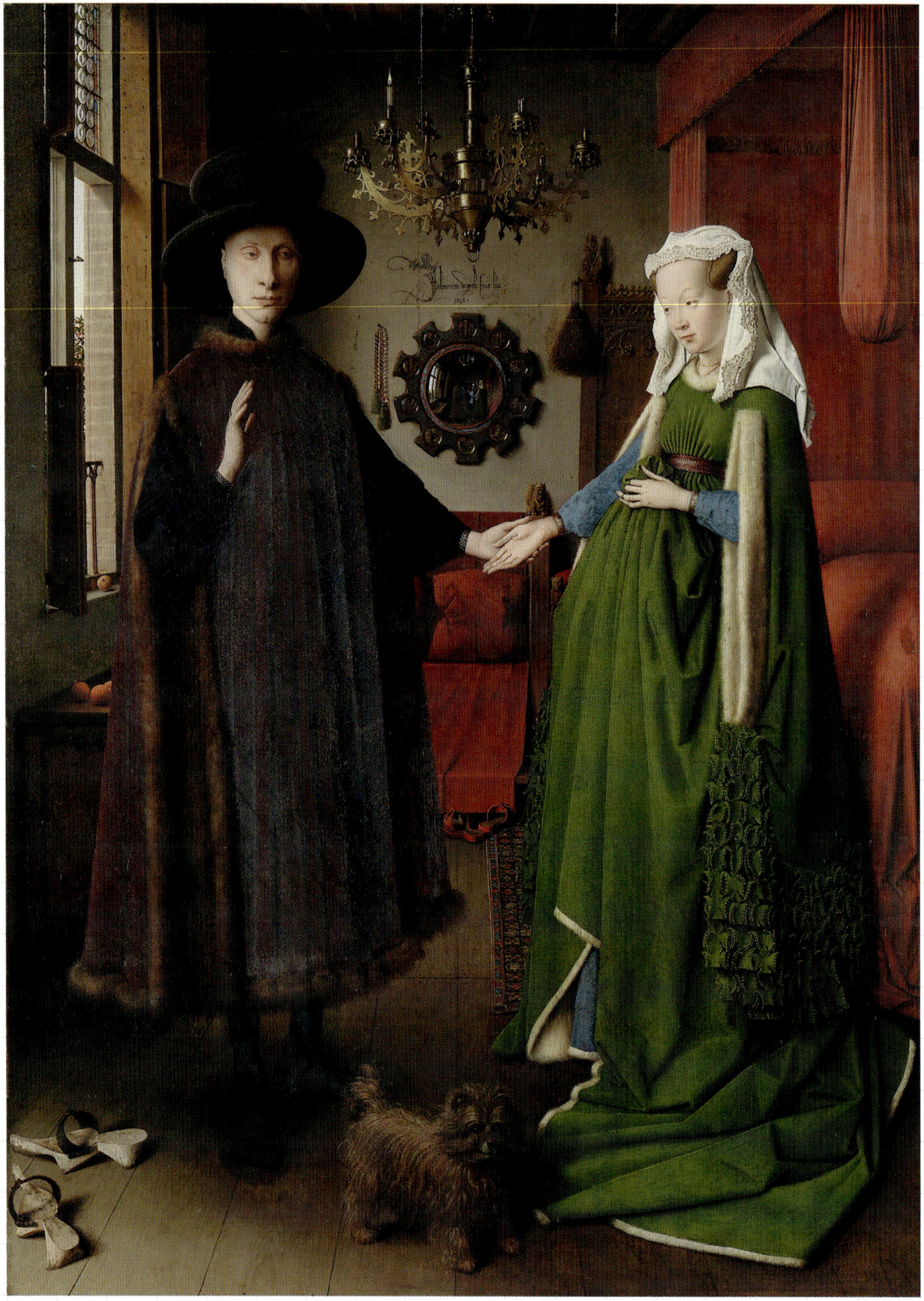

PORTRAIT OF GIOVANNI(?) ARNOLFINI AND HIS WIFE

Jan van Eyck (active 1422–died 1441)
1434
Oil on oak

This portrait is a clever study of light using oils. Van Eyck describes different textures, such as the fine hairs of the dog, the brass of the chandelier and the convex glass of the mirror. Religious symbolism abounds – the mirror is embellished with scenes from the Passion of Christ, while prayer beads hang on its left. Can you spot the artist in the reflection?

A B C D E F G H I J K L M N O P Q R S T U V W X Y Z

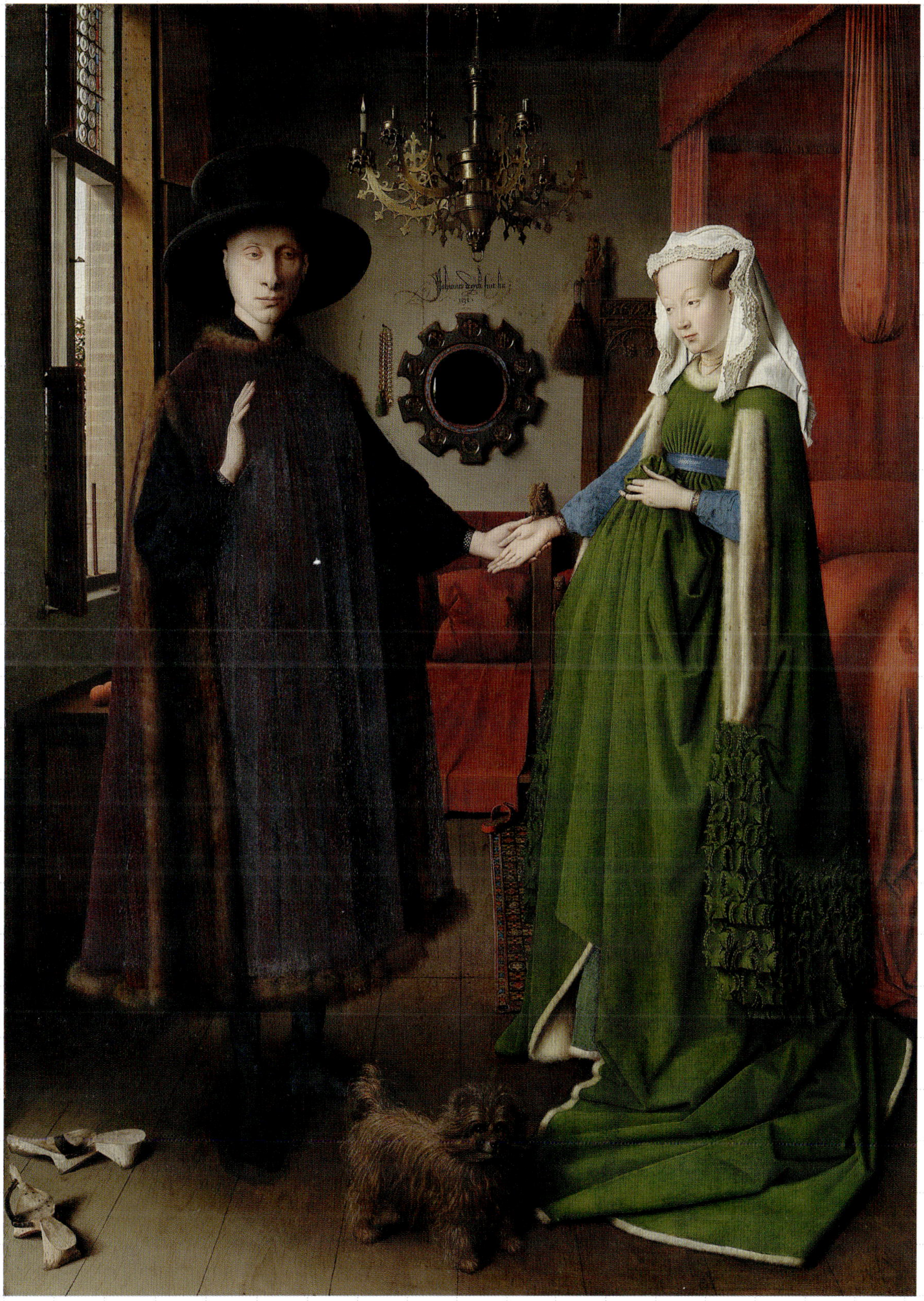

1 2 3 4 5 6 7 8 9 10 11 12 13 14 15 16 17 18 19 20 21 22 23 24 25 26

A B C D E F G H I J K L M N O P Q R S T U V W X Y Z

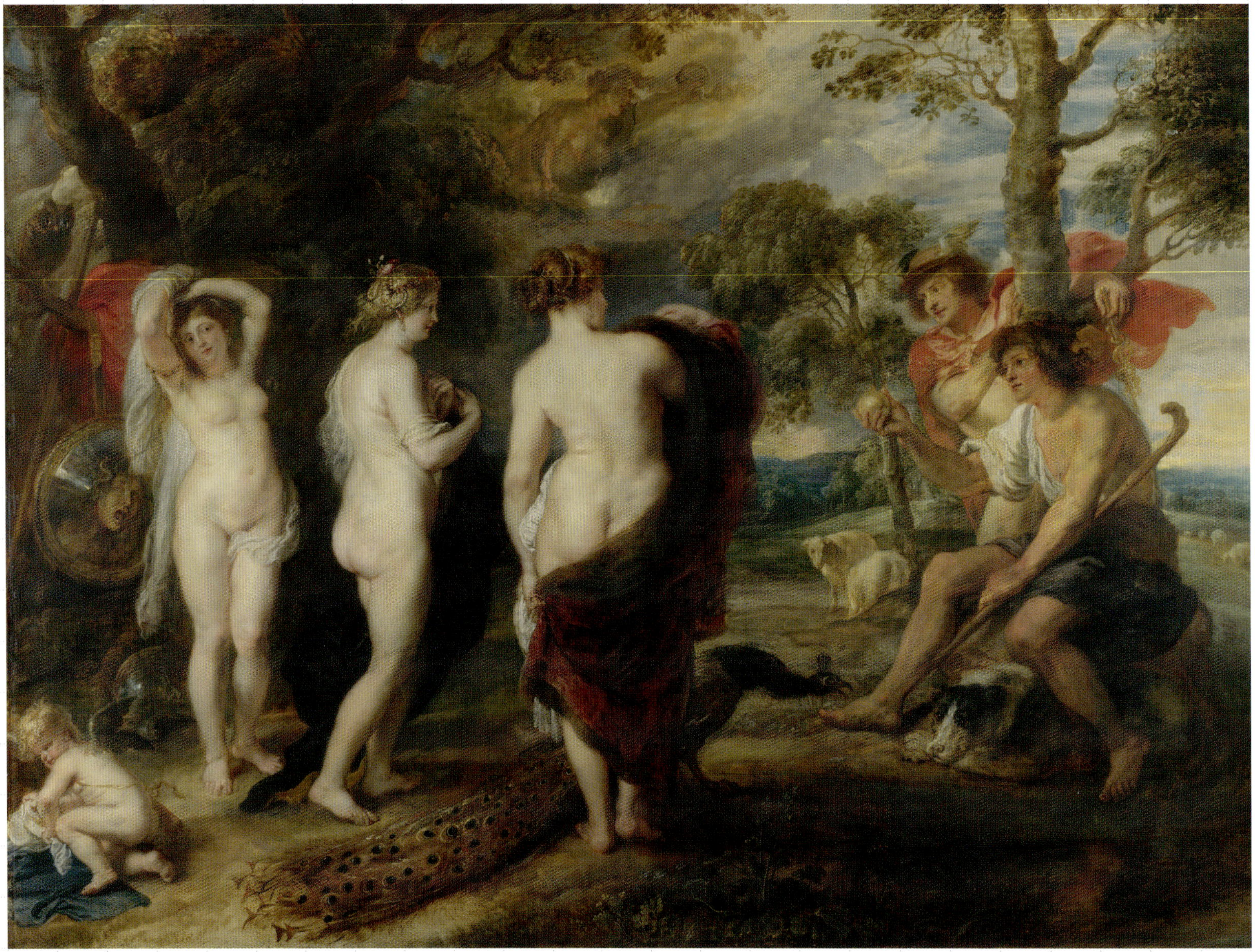

THE JUDGEMENT OF PARIS

Peter Paul Rubens (1577–1640)
about 1632–1635
Oil on oak

The goddesses Minerva (far left), Venus (middle) and Juno, stand before Paris, who, after judging their beauty, awards Venus with the golden apple. The animals in the scene link to the figures – Minerva, goddess of wisdom, with the owl, Juno with the peacock, and Paris, the mortal shepherd prince, with the dog and sheep.

A B C D E F G H I J K L M N O P Q R S T U V W X Y Z

1

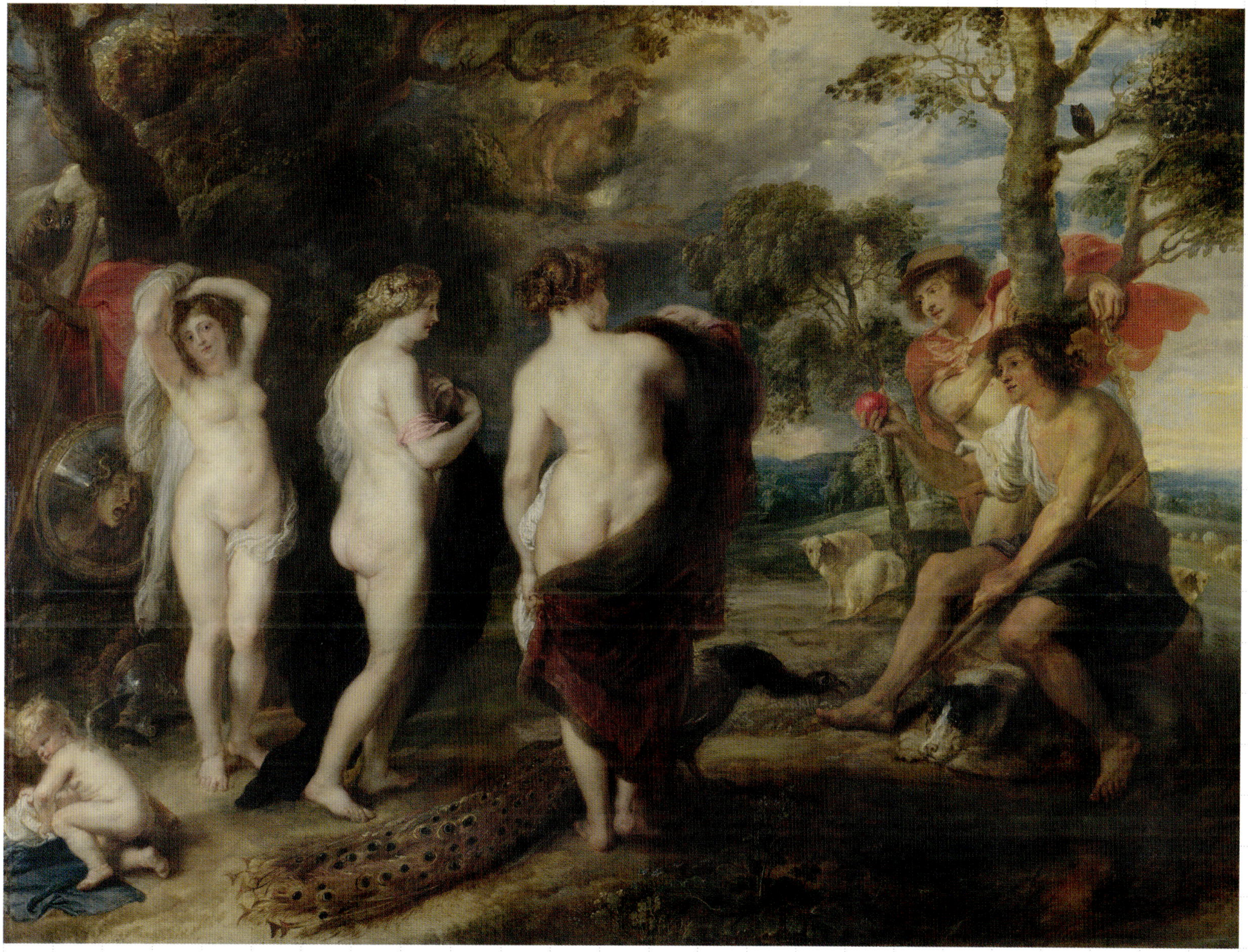

2 3 4 5 6 7 8 9 10 11 12 13 14 15 16 17 18 19 20 21 22 23 24 25 26

A B C D E F G H I J K L M N O P Q R S T U V W X Y Z

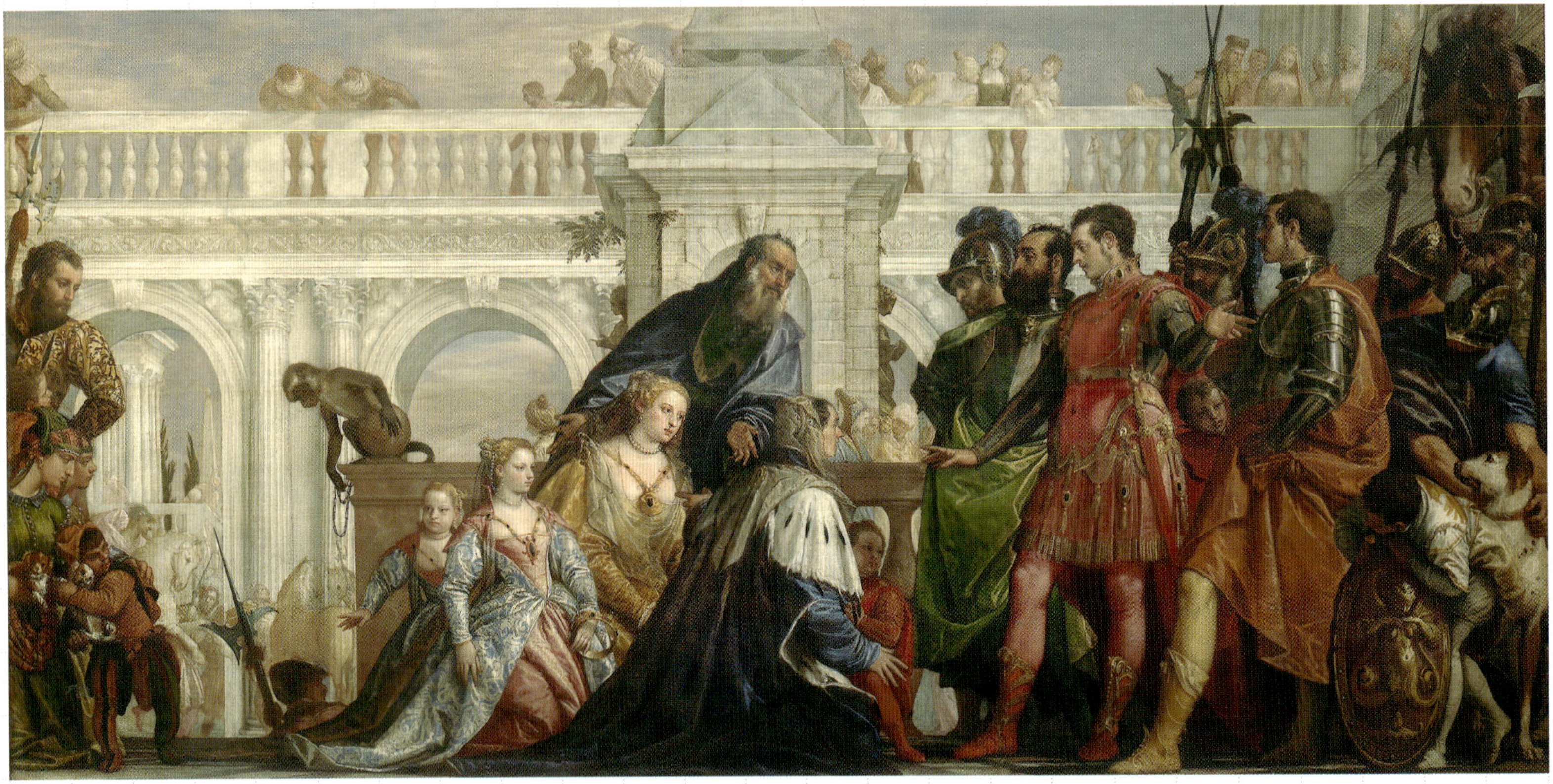

THE FAMILY OF DARIUS BEFORE ALEXANDER

Paolo Veronese (1528–1588)
1565–1567
Oil on canvas

In this painting, the family of the defeated Persian Emperor Darius are spared by the victorious Alexander. Darius's mother (dressed in blue) submits to the conquerer, but mistakenly proffers herself to his general Hephaestion instead. Veronese deliberately confuses the viewer too – is Alexander the figure dressed in imperial red finery or battle-fresh armour and gold cloak?

A B C D E F G H I J K L M N O P Q R S T U V W X Y Z

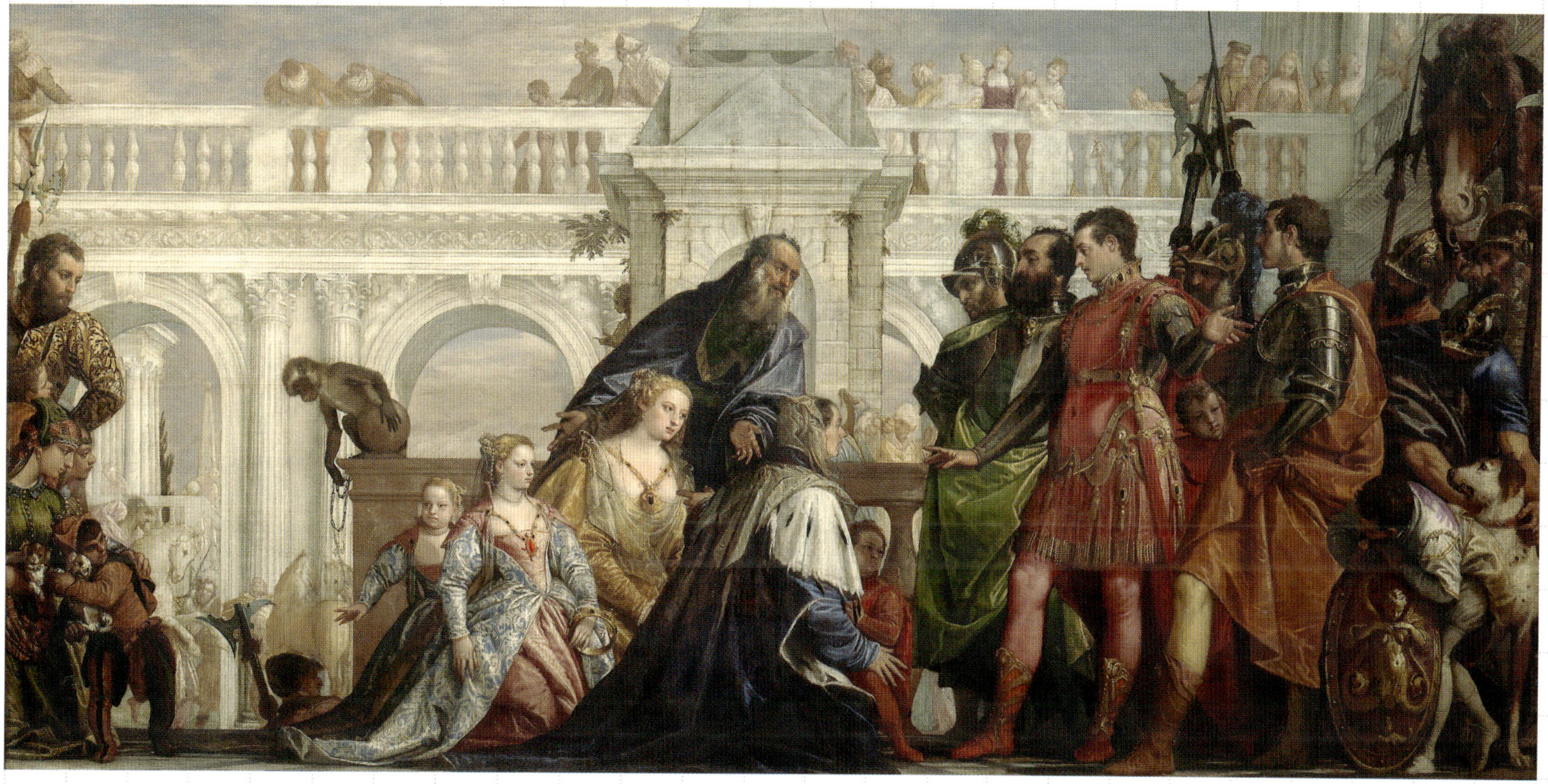

A B C D E F G H I J K L M N O P Q R S T U V W X Y Z

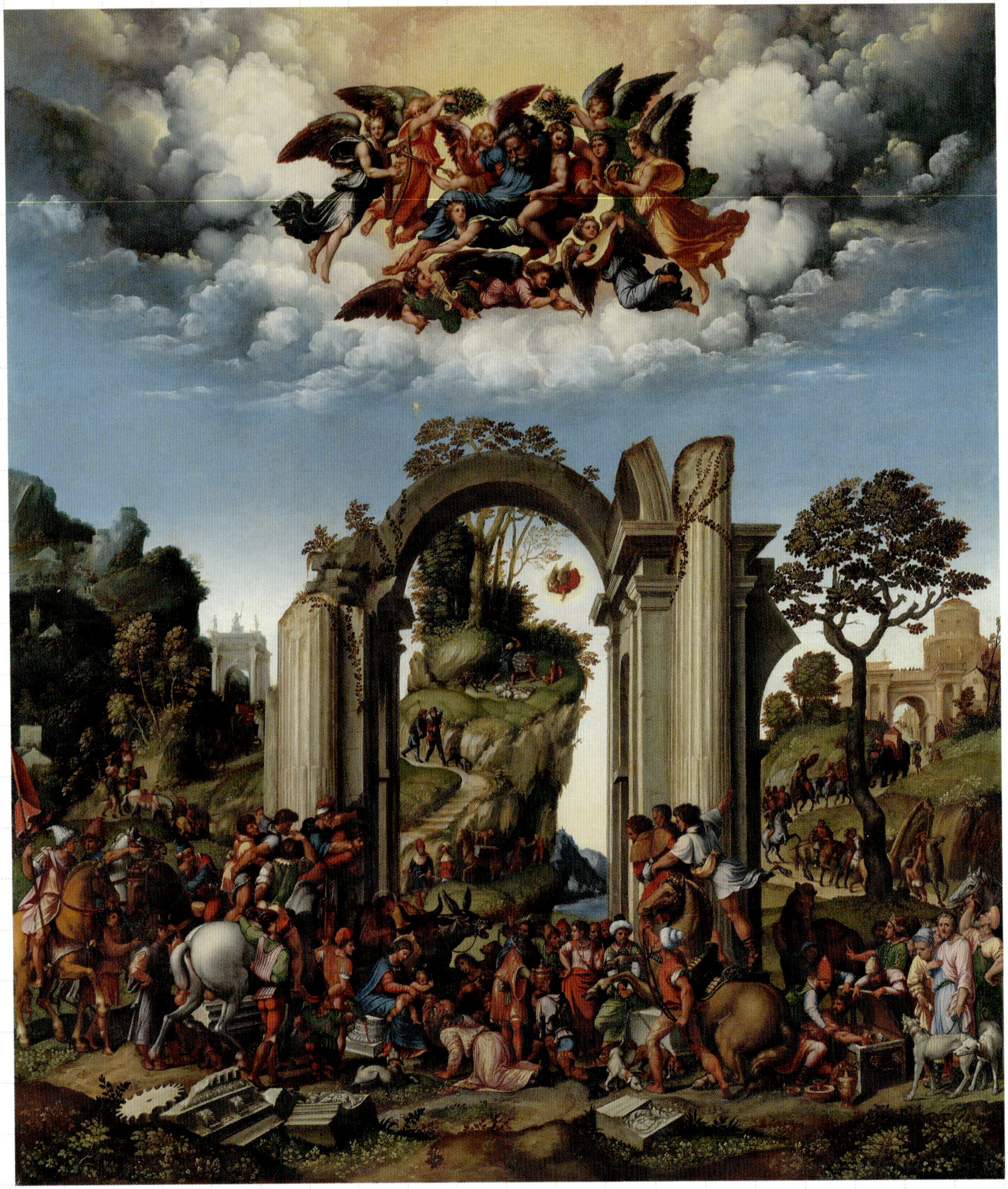

THE ADORATION OF THE KINGS

Girolamo da Treviso (about 1497/8–1544)
about 1524–1525
Oil on wood

Framed beneath the central arches, Baby Jesus is gifted gold, frankincense and myrrh by the Three Kings. Heaven smiles down on them. Devotees stream in winding processions from the left and right. Among the crowds are two elephants, a camel, a giraffe and a parrot. Can you spot them all?

A B C D E F G H I J K L M N O P Q R S T U V W X Y Z

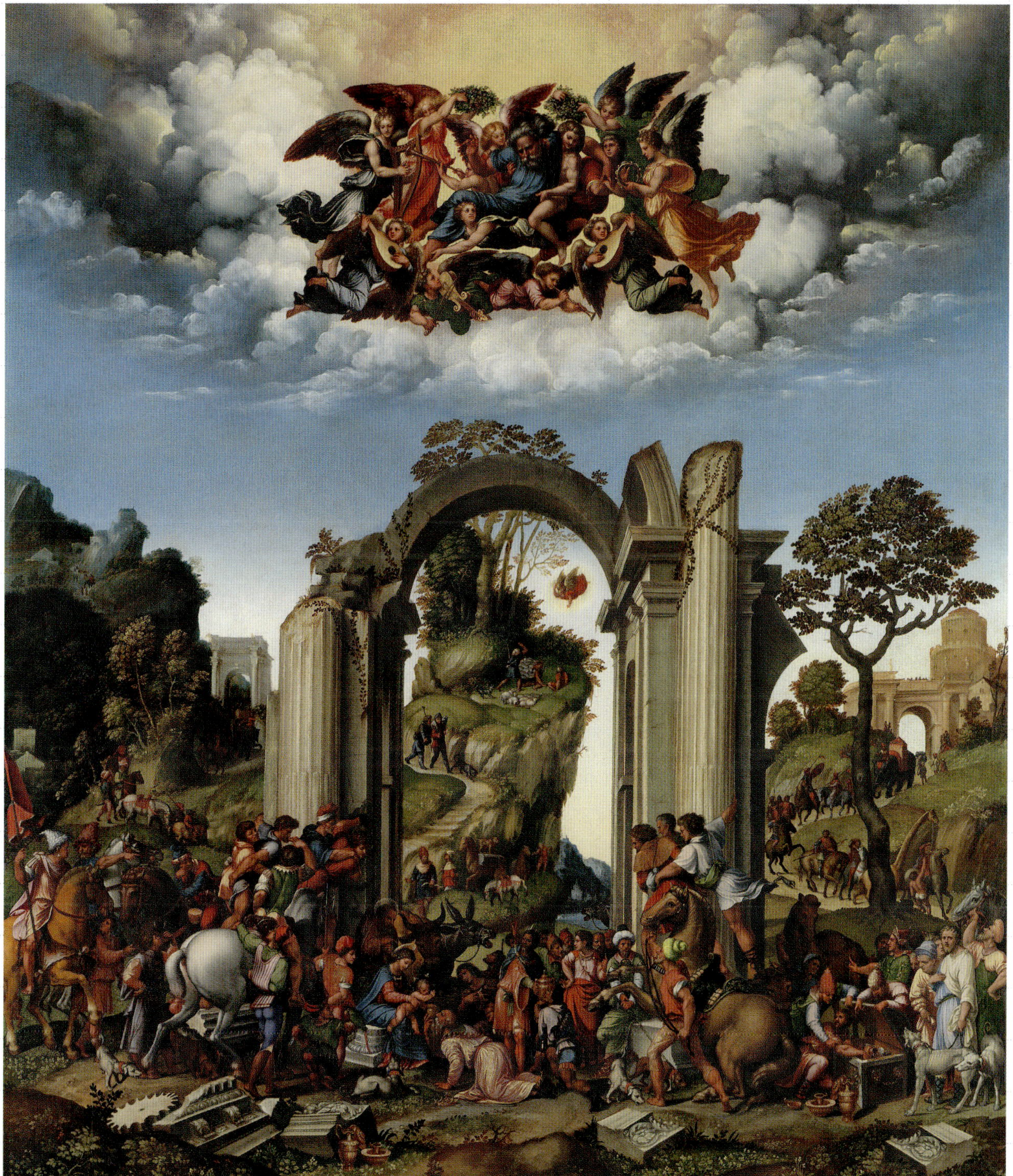

A B C D E F G H I J K L M N O P Q R S T U V W X Y Z

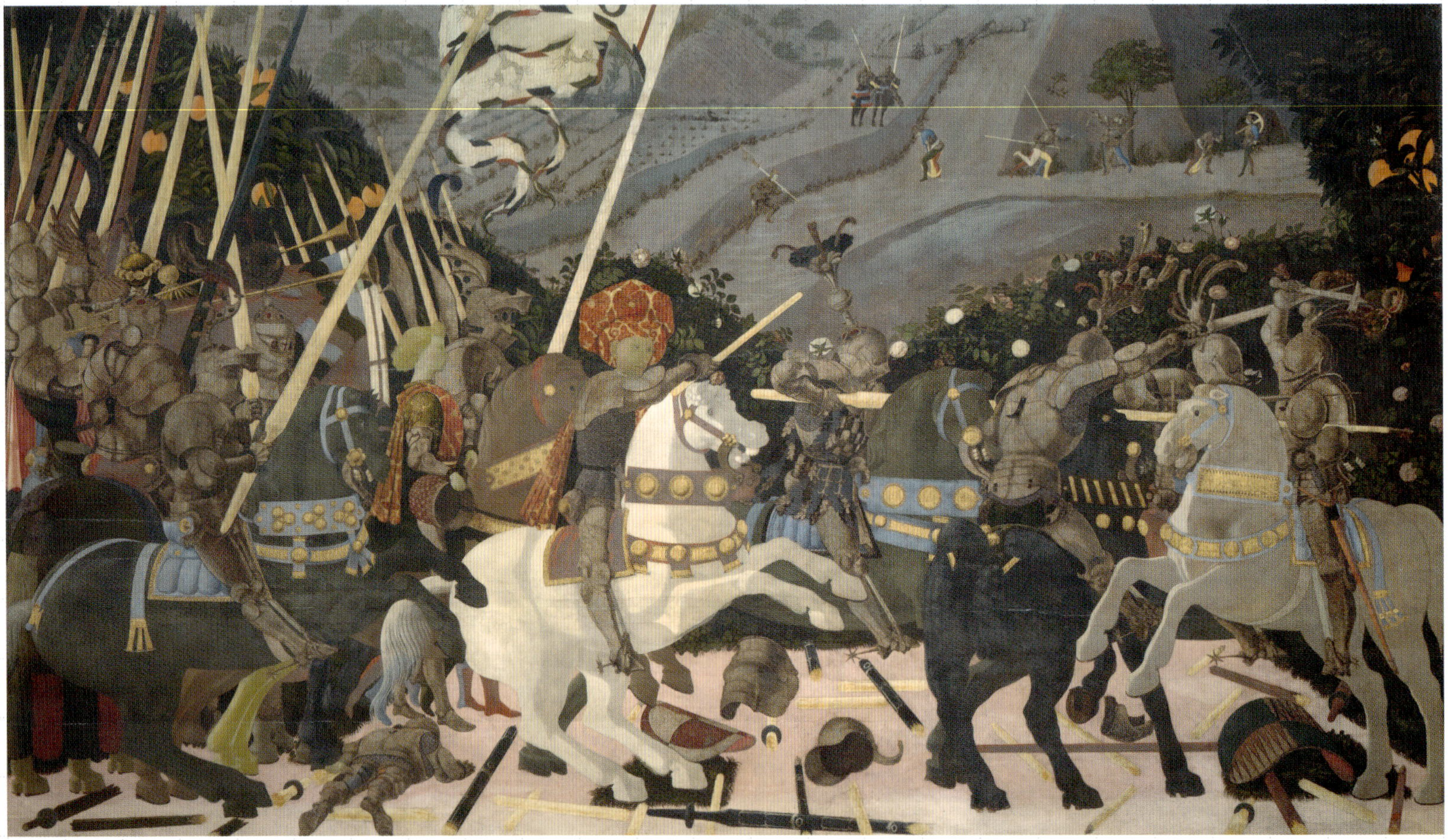

THE BATTLE OF SAN ROMANO

Paolo Uccello (about 1397–1475)
about 1438–1440
Egg tempera with walnut oil and linseed oil on poplar

In this grand battle scene, Florentine forces defeat Sienese troops. Uccello has used gold leaf for the horses' tack and painted in decorative features such as feathers in the soldiers' helmets and roses, pomegranates and oranges in the hedge. The foreshortened broken lances on the floor aid the perspective.

A B C D E F G H I J K L M N O P Q R S T U V W X Y Z

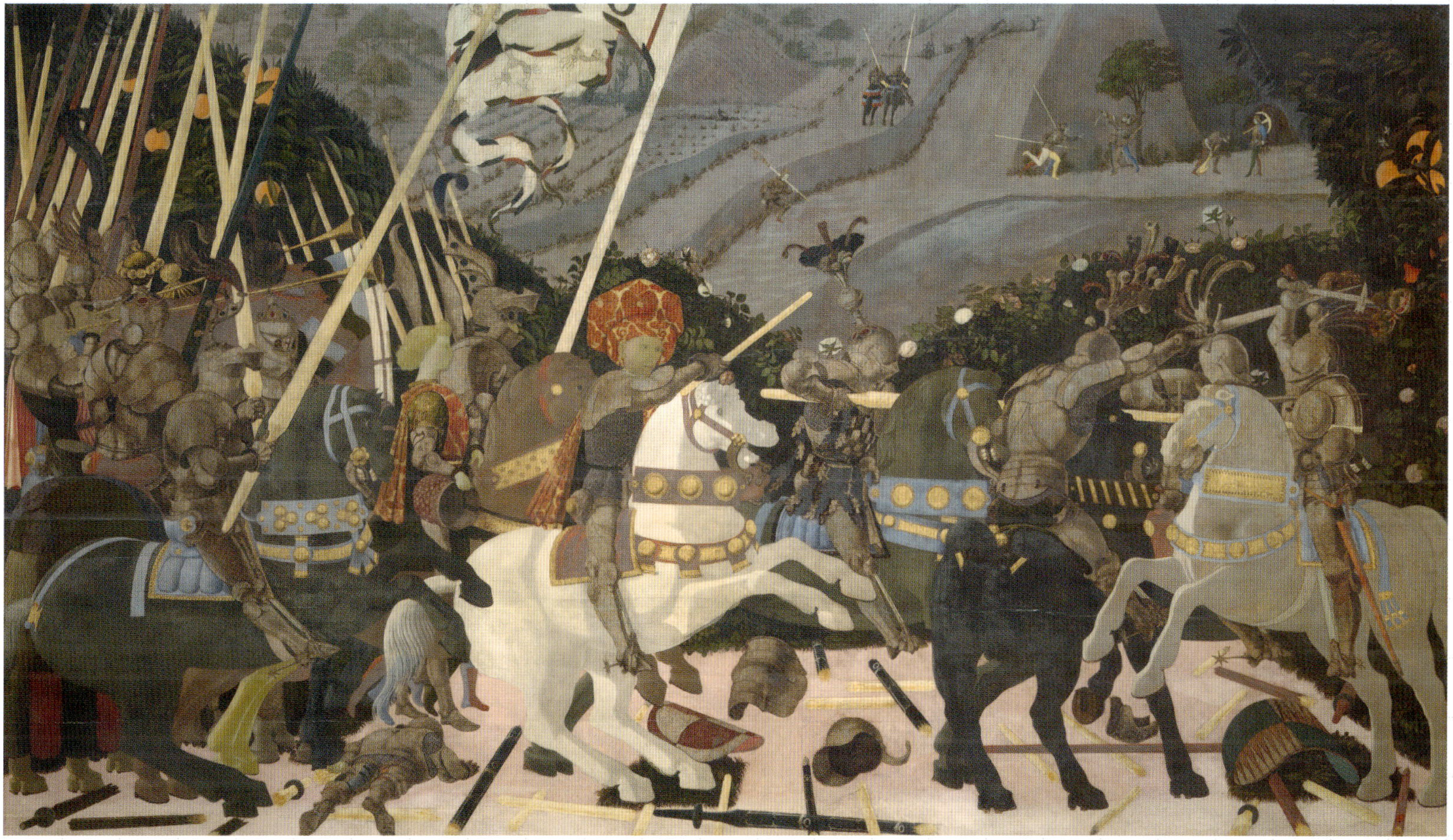

A B C D E F G H I J K L M N O P Q R S T U V W X Y Z

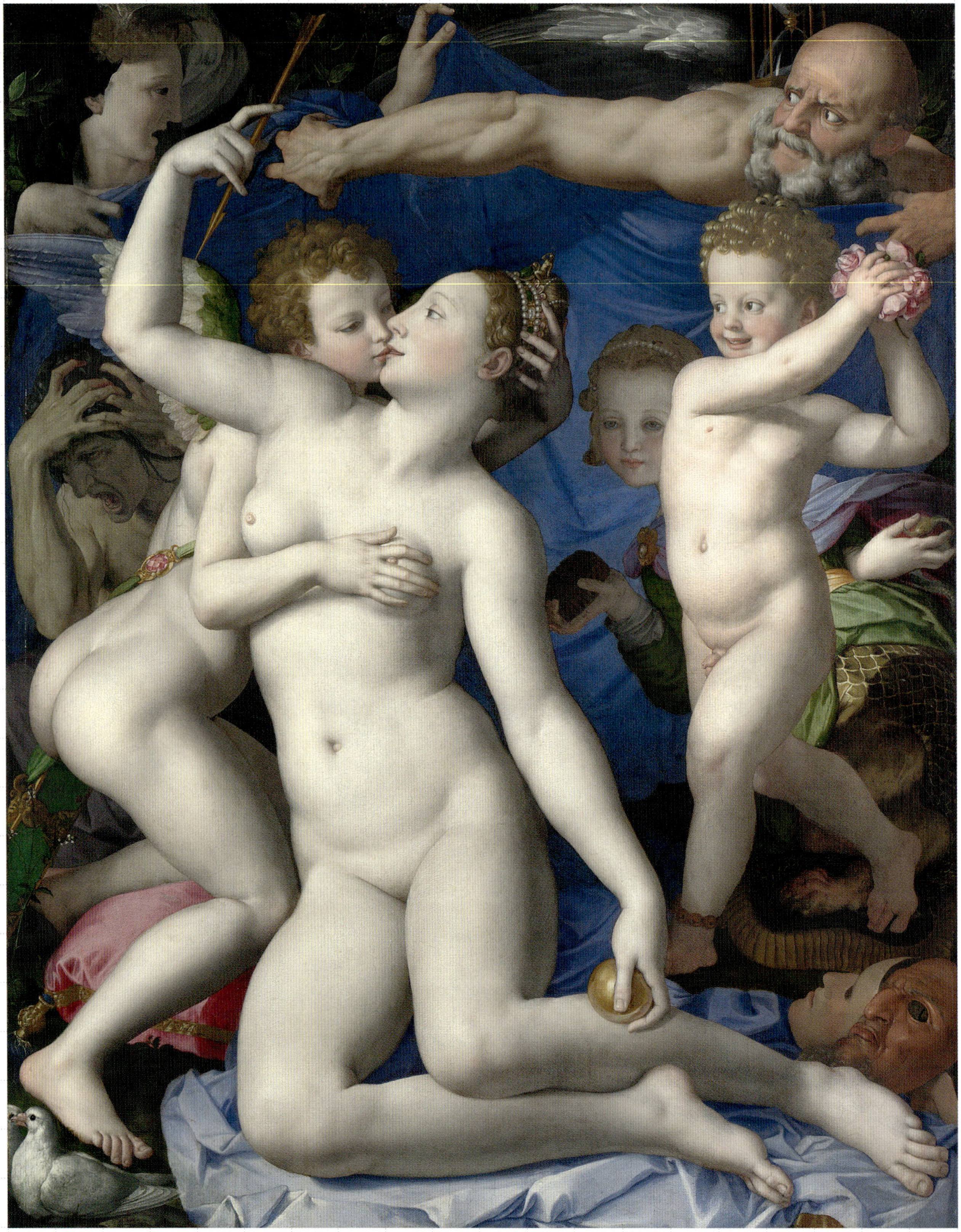

AN ALLEGORY WITH VENUS AND CUPID

Agnolo di Cosimo,
known as Bronzino (1503–1572)
about 1545
Oil on wood

Venus, with her doves and golden apple, is locked into an erotic embrace with Cupid. Pleasure goes to shower them in petals, while Deceit offers up a honeycomb, simultaneously hiding the sting of her tail. Oblivion is missing critical faculties and Jealousy is on the left. The hourglass top right is a clue to the 'Father' figure. Any guesses?

A B C D E F G H I J K L M N O P Q R S T U V W X Y Z

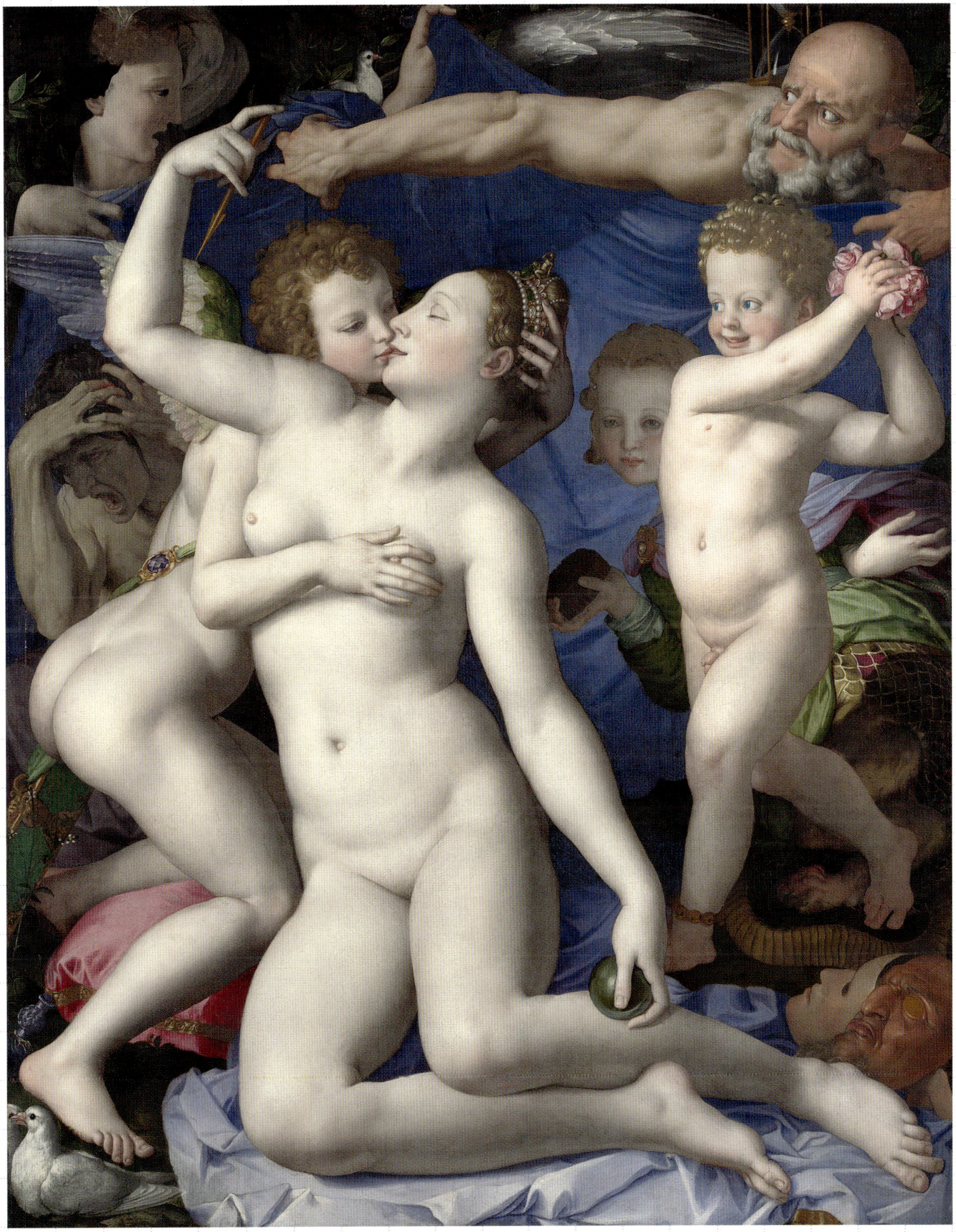

1 2 3 4 5 6 7 8 9 10 11 12 13 14 15 16 17 18 19 20 21 22 23 24 25 26

A B C D E F G H I J K L M N O P Q R S T U V W X Y Z

A B C D E F G H I J K L M N O P Q R S T U V W X Y Z

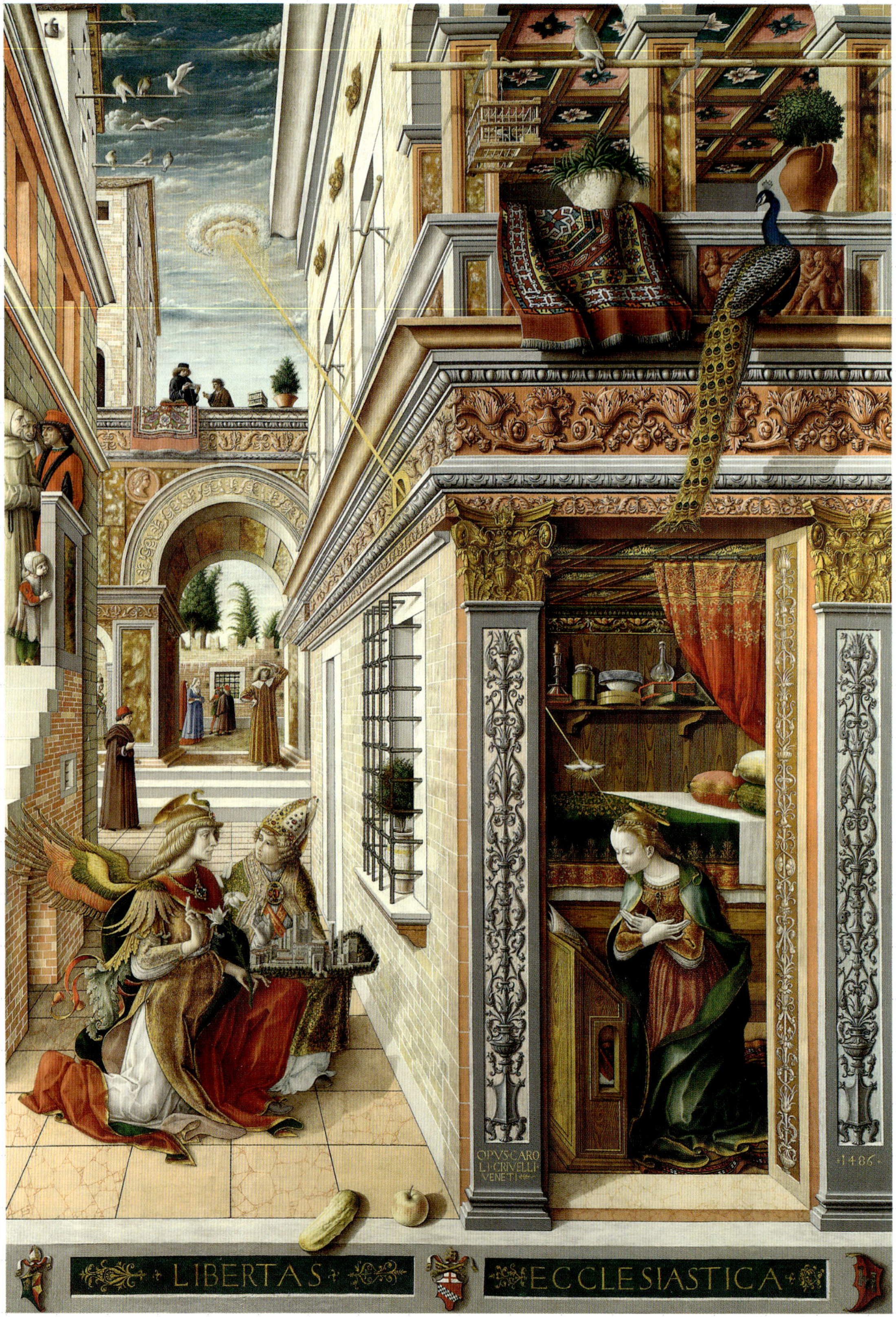

THE ANNUNCIATION, WITH SAINT EMIDIUS

Carlo Crivelli (about 1430/5–about 1494)

1486
Egg and oil on canvas

This painting celebrates the town of Ascoli being granted limited self-government by the Pope. Saint Emidius, alongside the Archangel Gabriel, carries a model of the town. A ray beams down from heaven onto Mary. Carrier pigeons roost top left – can you spot the man reading a recently delivered message?

A B C D E F G H I J K L M N O P Q R S T U V W X Y Z

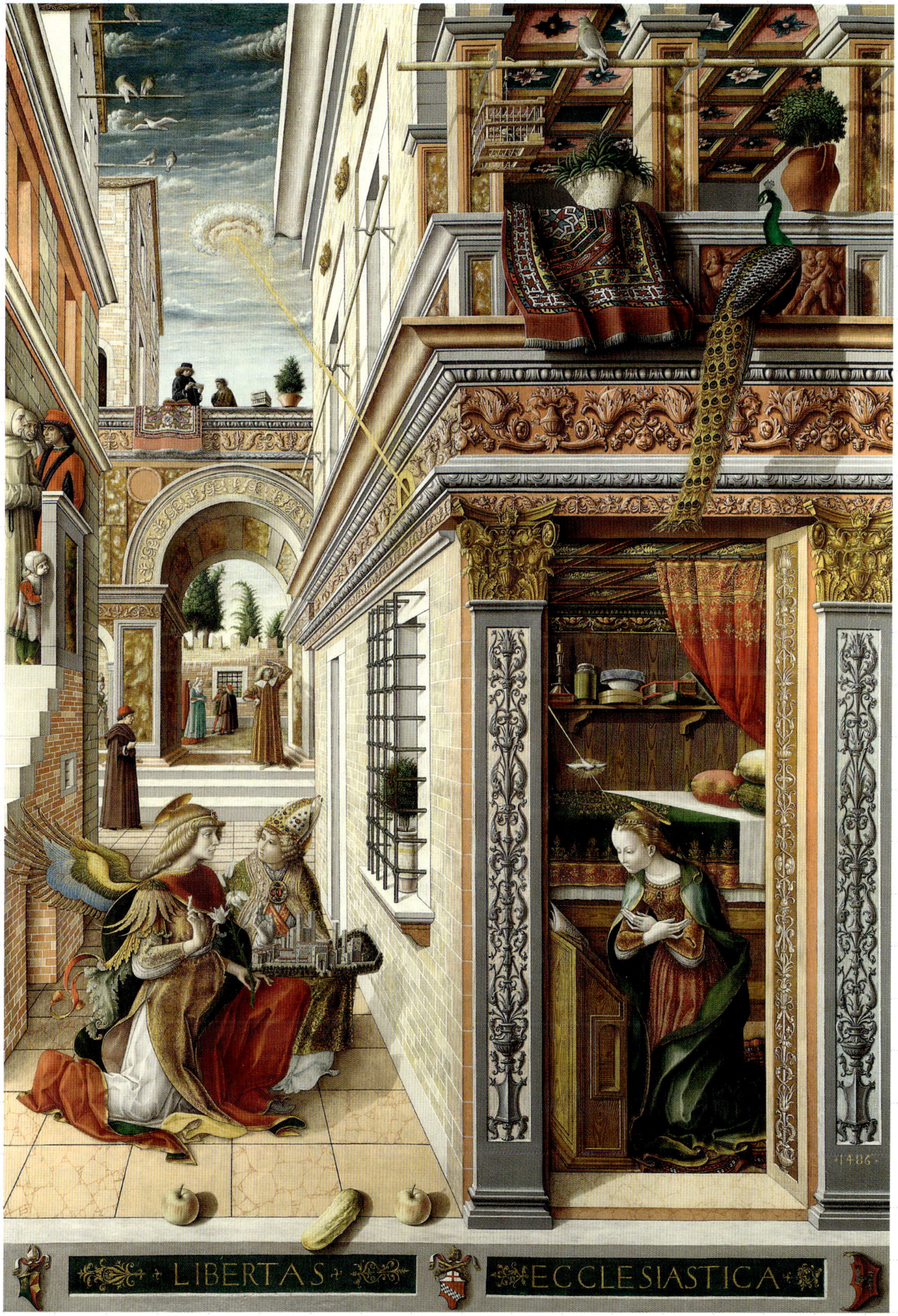

1 2 3 4 5 6 7 8 9 10 11 12 13 14 15 16 17 18 19 20 21 22 23 24 25 26

A B C D E F G H I J K L M N O P Q R S T U V W X Y Z

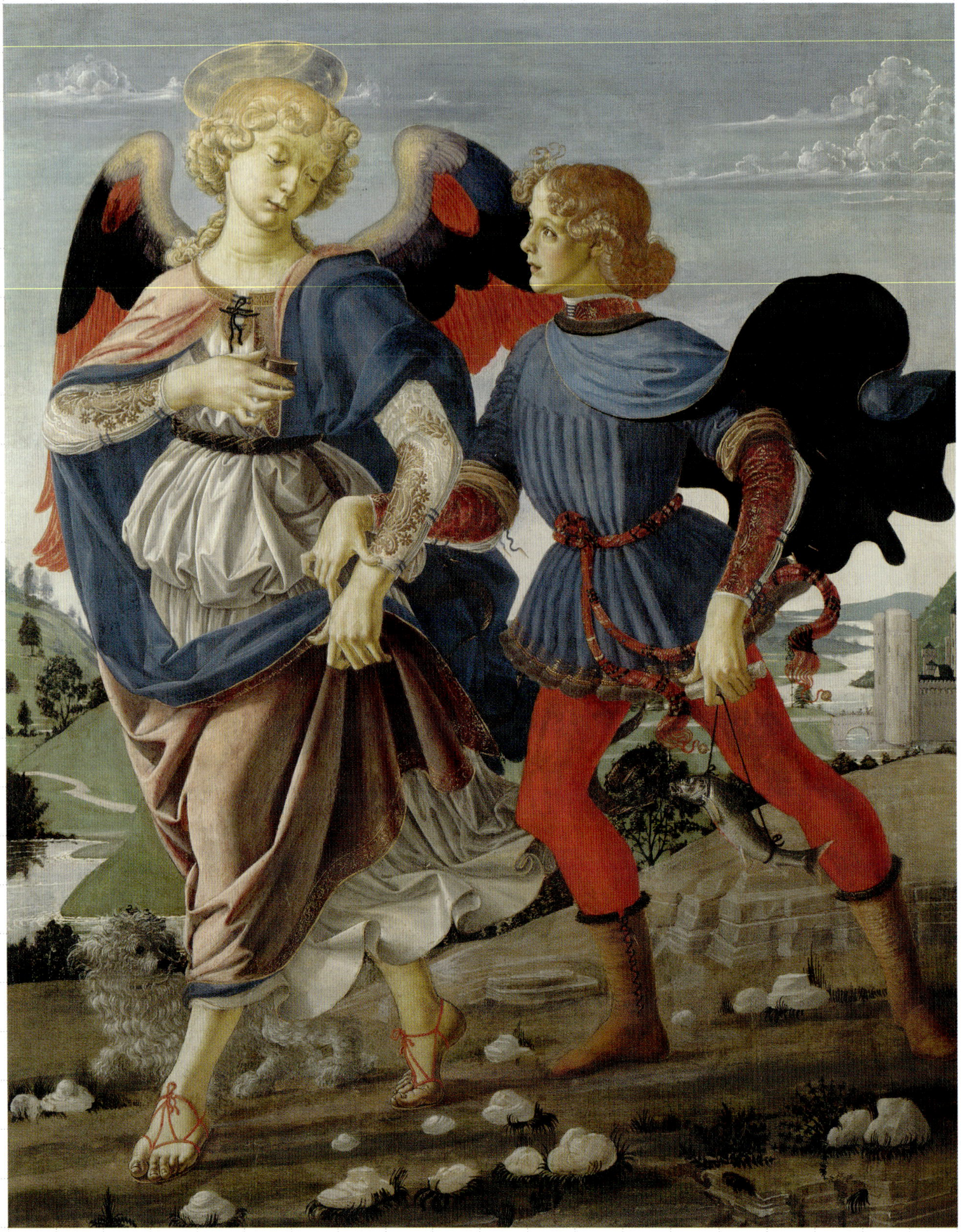

TOBIAS AND THE ANGEL

Workshop of Andrea del Verrocchio (c.1435–1488)
about 1470–1475
Tempera on wood

En route to collect a dept for his blind father, Tobias receives advice from Saint Raphael, a healer, who tells the merchant boy to use the heart, liver and gall from a fish to cure his father. Multiple artists worked on this painting – it is thought Leonardo painted the dog.

A B C D E F G H I J K L M N O P Q R S T U V W X Y Z

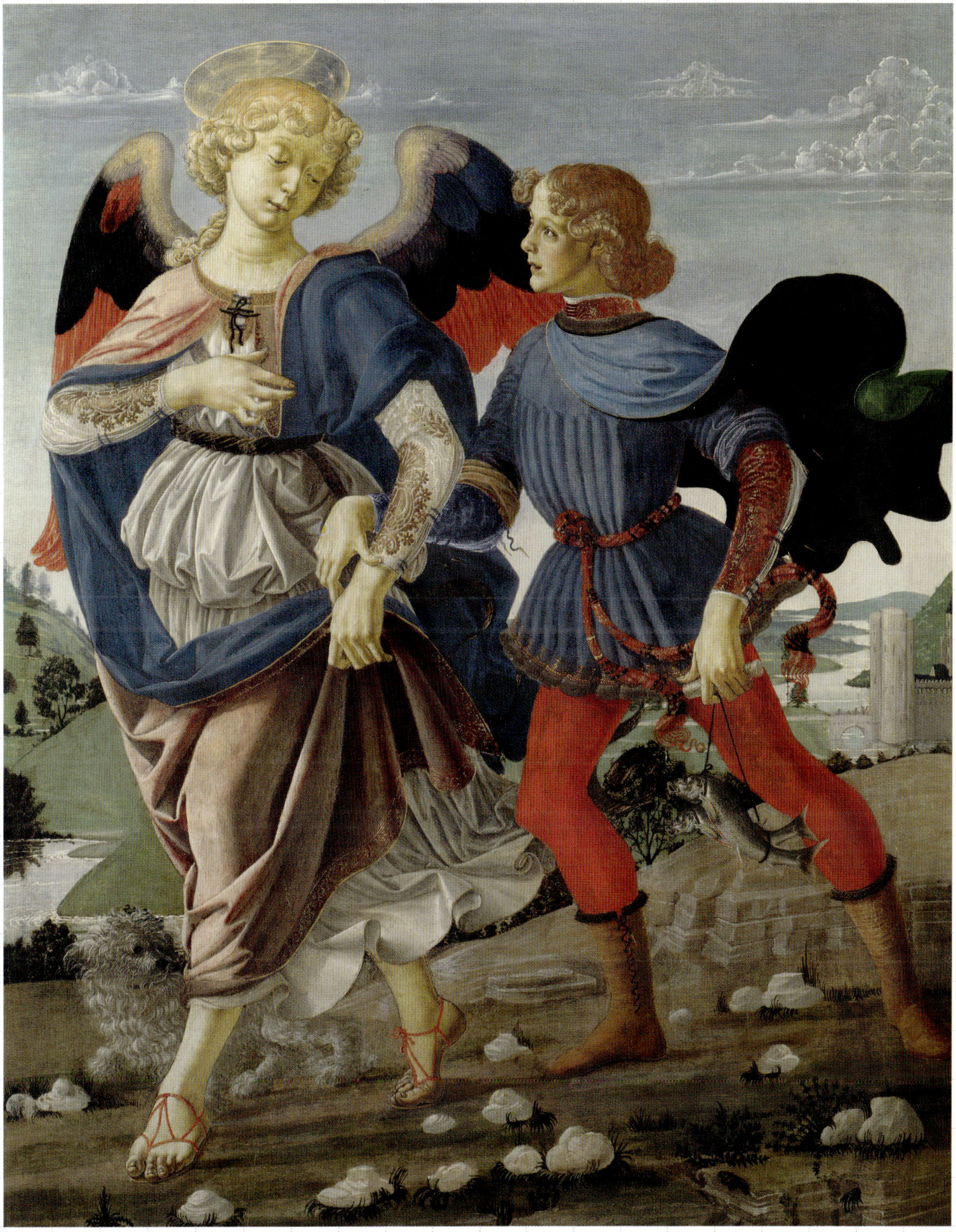

1 2 3 4 5 6 7 8 9 10 11 12 13 14 15 16 17 18 19 20 21 22 23 24 25 26

A B C D E F G H I J K L M N O P Q R S T U V W X Y Z

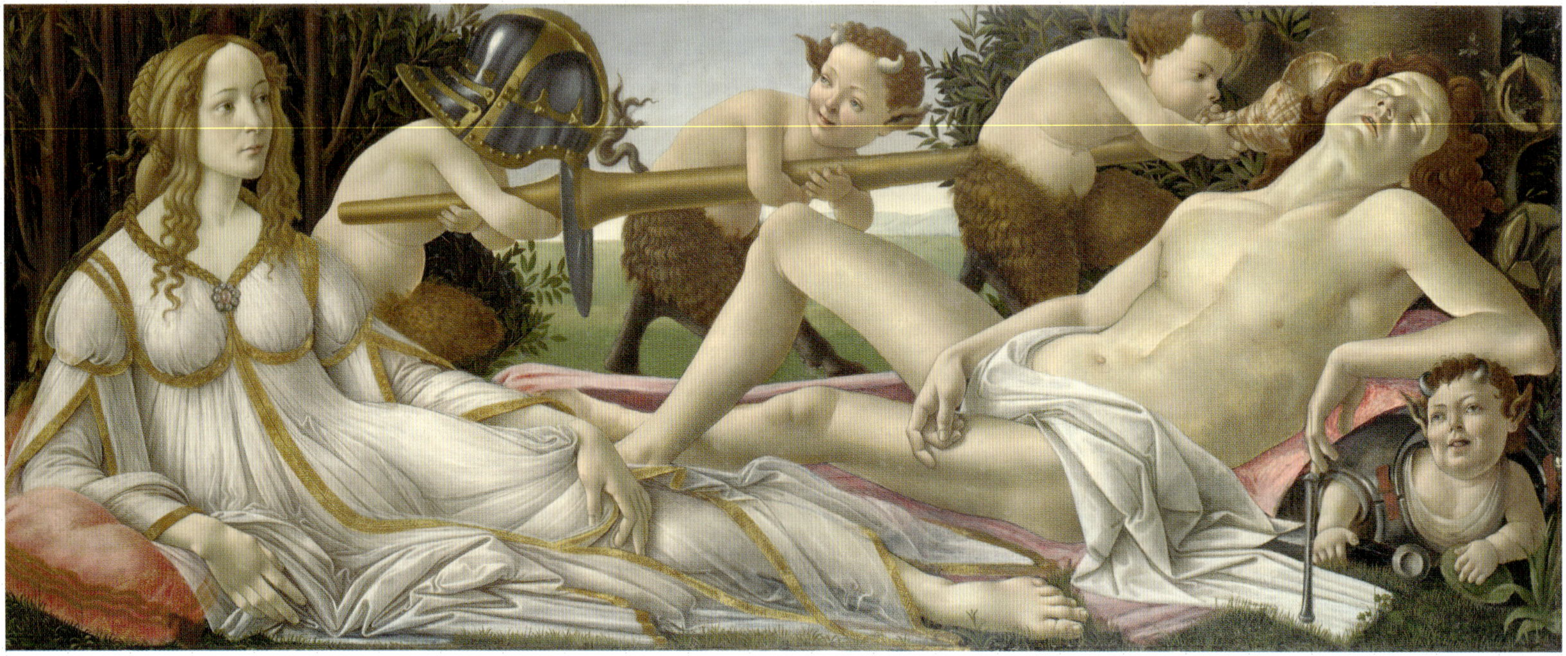

VENUS AND MARS
Sandro Botticelli (1445–1510)
about 1485
Tempera and oil on poplar

Love conquers all is the message here. Venus looks over to her sleeping lover, Mars, the god of war. 'Defeated' and disarmed by the goddess of love, Mars rests while satyrs play with his armour. Not even a conch shell trumpeted in his ear can wake him from his 'little death'.

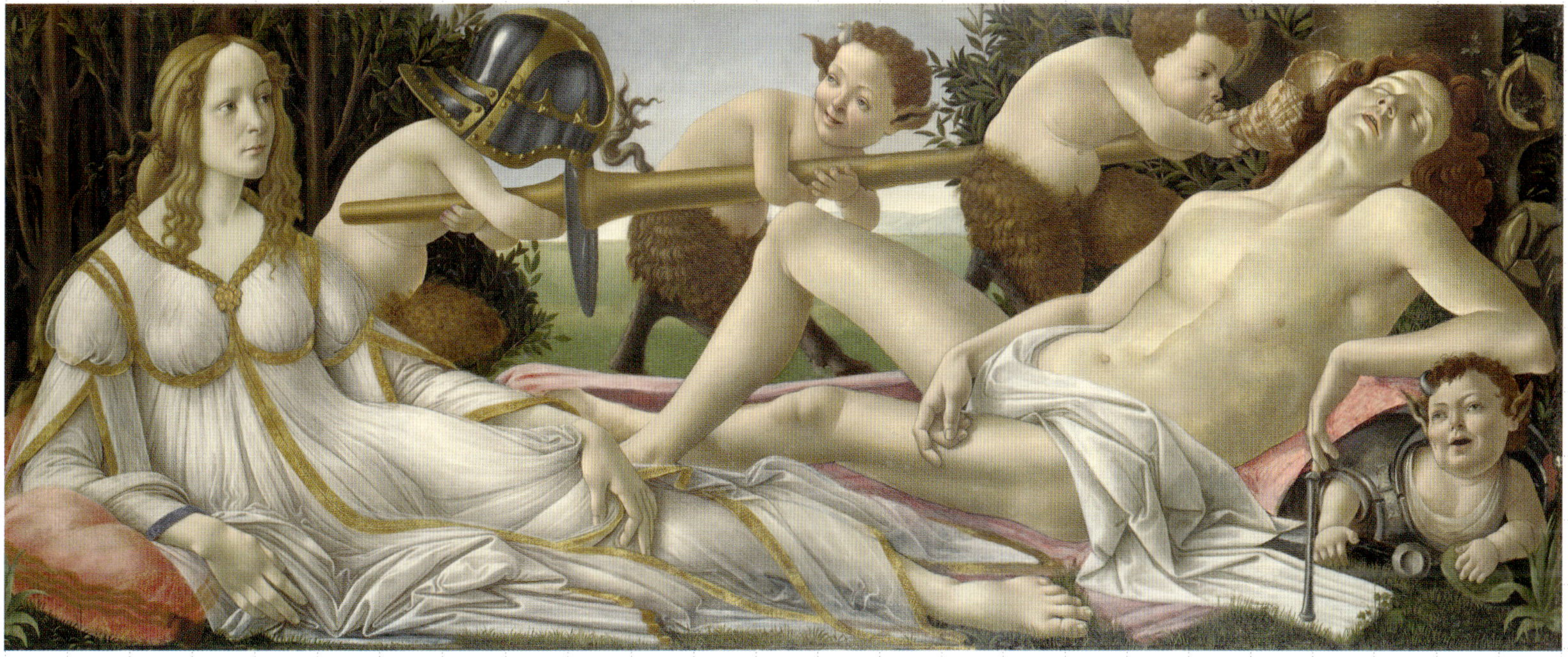

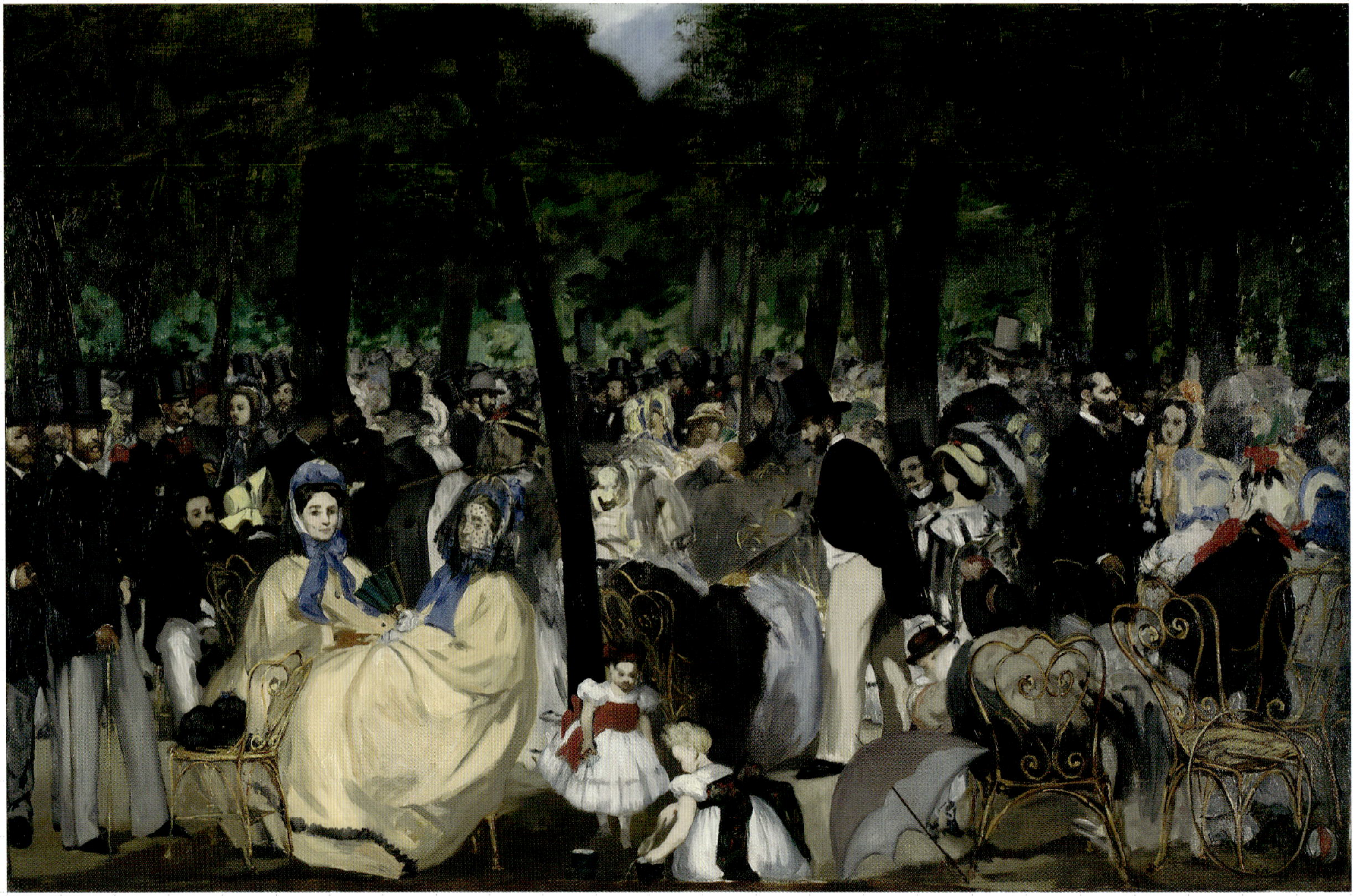

MUSIC IN THE TUILERIES GARDENS

Edouard Manet (1832–1883)

1862

Oil on canvas

Parisians gather in the Tuileries Gardens to listen to music. They wear the fashions of the time – top hats for the men, bonnets and bows for the women. Children play in the foreground, their discarded toys rest bottom right. Can you identify Manet himself peering through his monocle at the viewer?

A B C D E F G H I J K L M N O P Q R S T U V W X Y Z

1
2
3
4
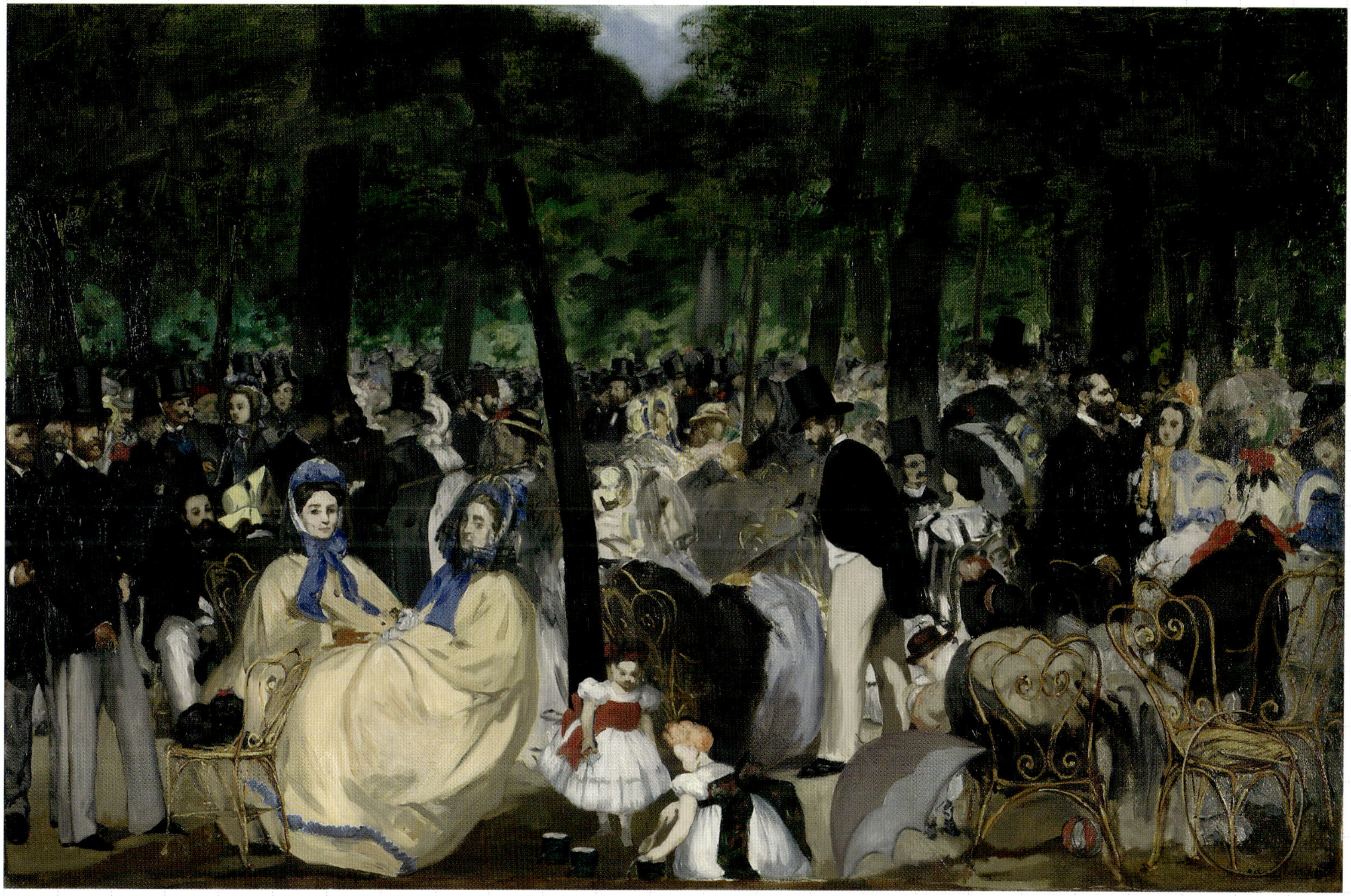
5
6
7
8
9
10
11
12
13
14
15
16
17
18
19
20
21
22
23
24
25
26

A B C D E F G H I J K L M N O P Q R S T U V W X Y Z

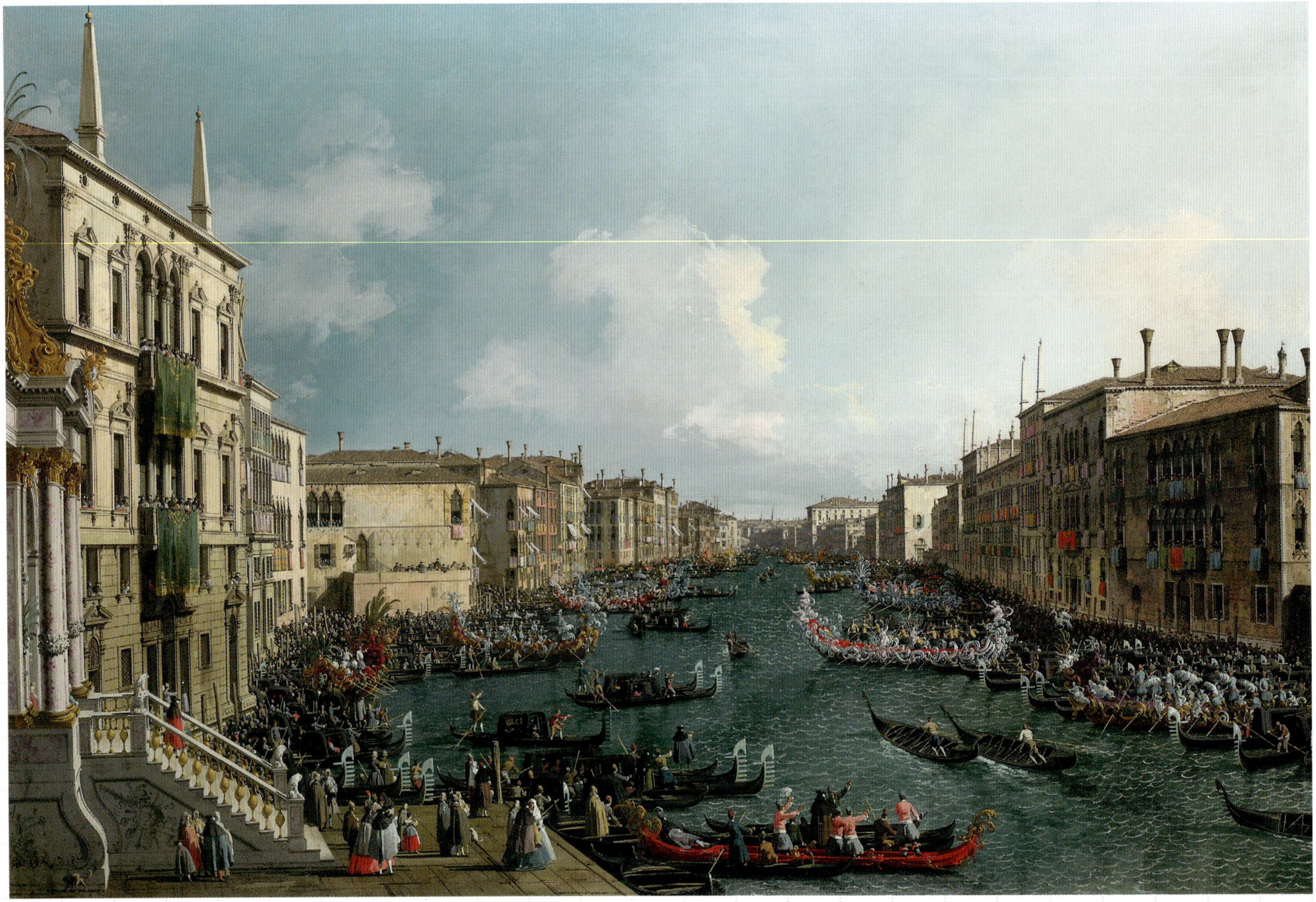

A REGATTA ON THE GRAND CANAL

Canaletto (1697–1768)
about 1740
Oil on canvas

With incredible detail, Canaletto depicts Venice's annual carnival regatta and captures the spirit of the day. Gondolas race up the Grand Canal, while onlookers crowd the streets or spill from windows and balconies adorned in colourful banners. Some spectators can be seen wearing the traditional Venetian white mask and black cape.

A B C D E F G H I J K L M N O P Q R S T U V W X Y Z

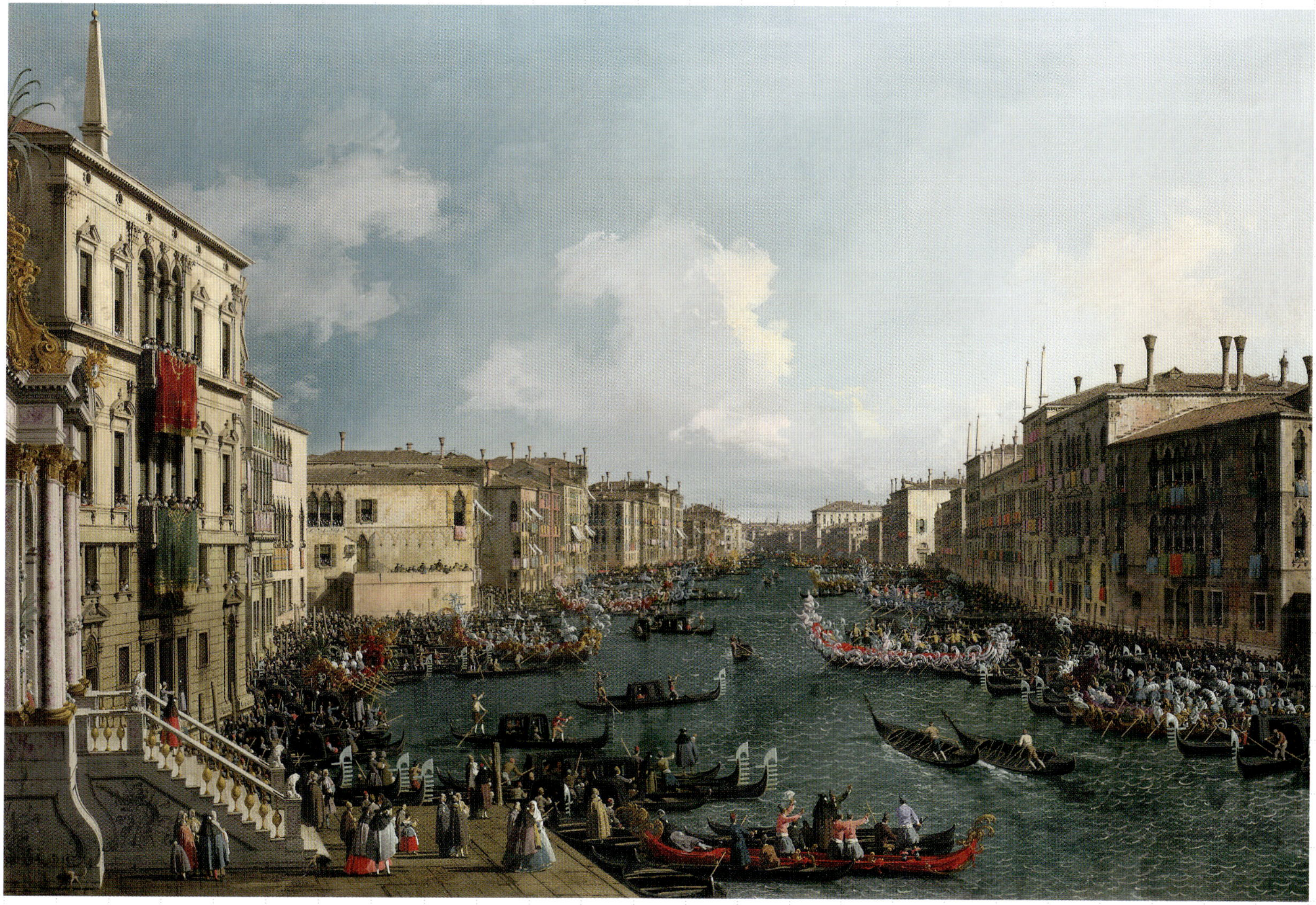

A B C D E F G H I J K L M N O P Q R S T U V W X Y Z

A B C D E F G H I J K L M N O P Q R S T U V W X Y Z

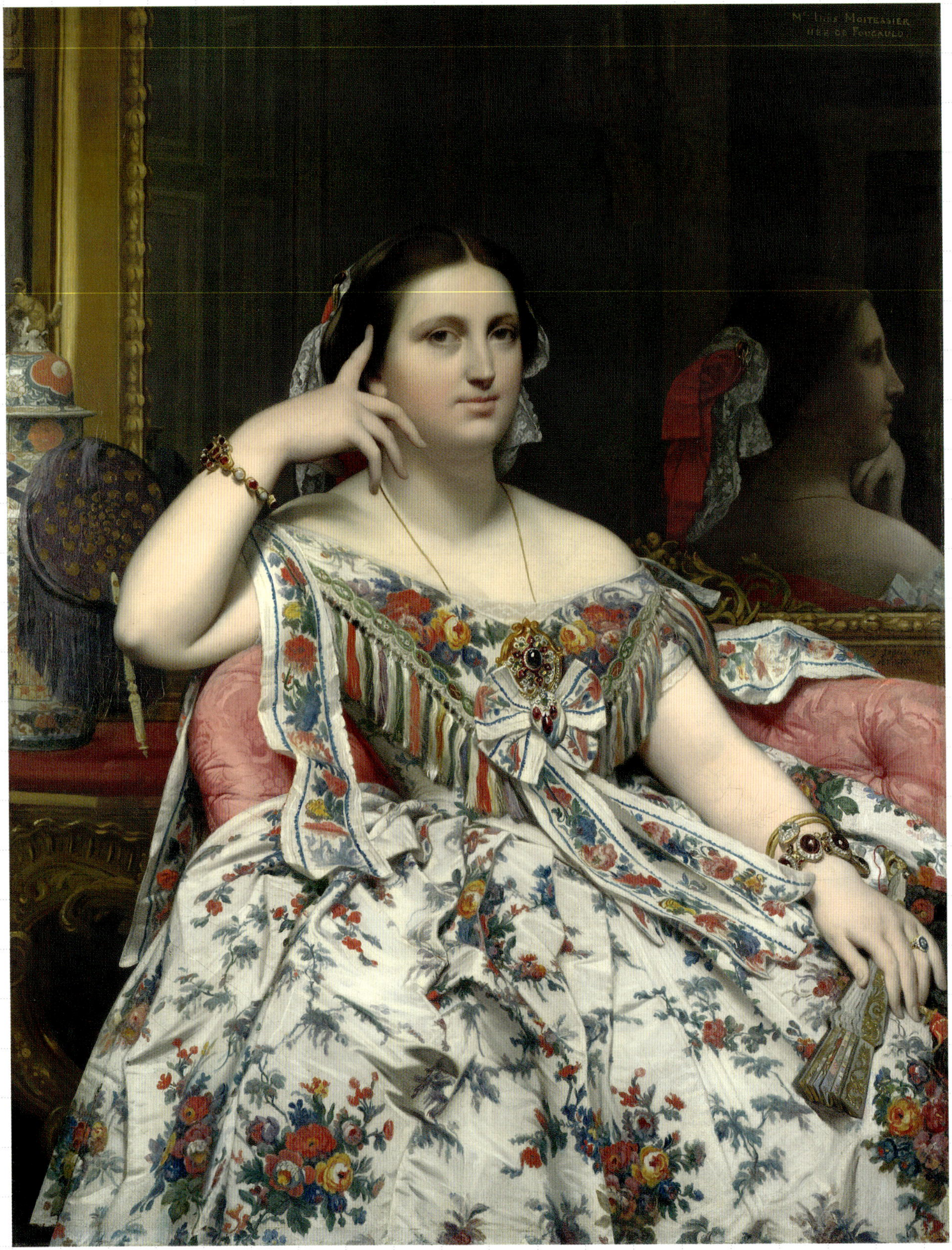

MADAME MOITESSIER

Jean-Auguste-Dominique Ingres (1780–1867)
1856
Oil on Canvas

It was Madame Moitessier's beauty that convinced Ingres to paint her. The artist had little respect for portraiture. He has posed her as if a goddess, and there is great attention to detail – the fine floral-patterned dress, the individual fibres of its tassels, the sparkling jewellery and the intricate decoration on the vase.

A B C D E F G H I J K L M N O P Q R S T U V W X Y Z

A B C D E F G H I J K L M N O P Q R S T U V W X Y Z

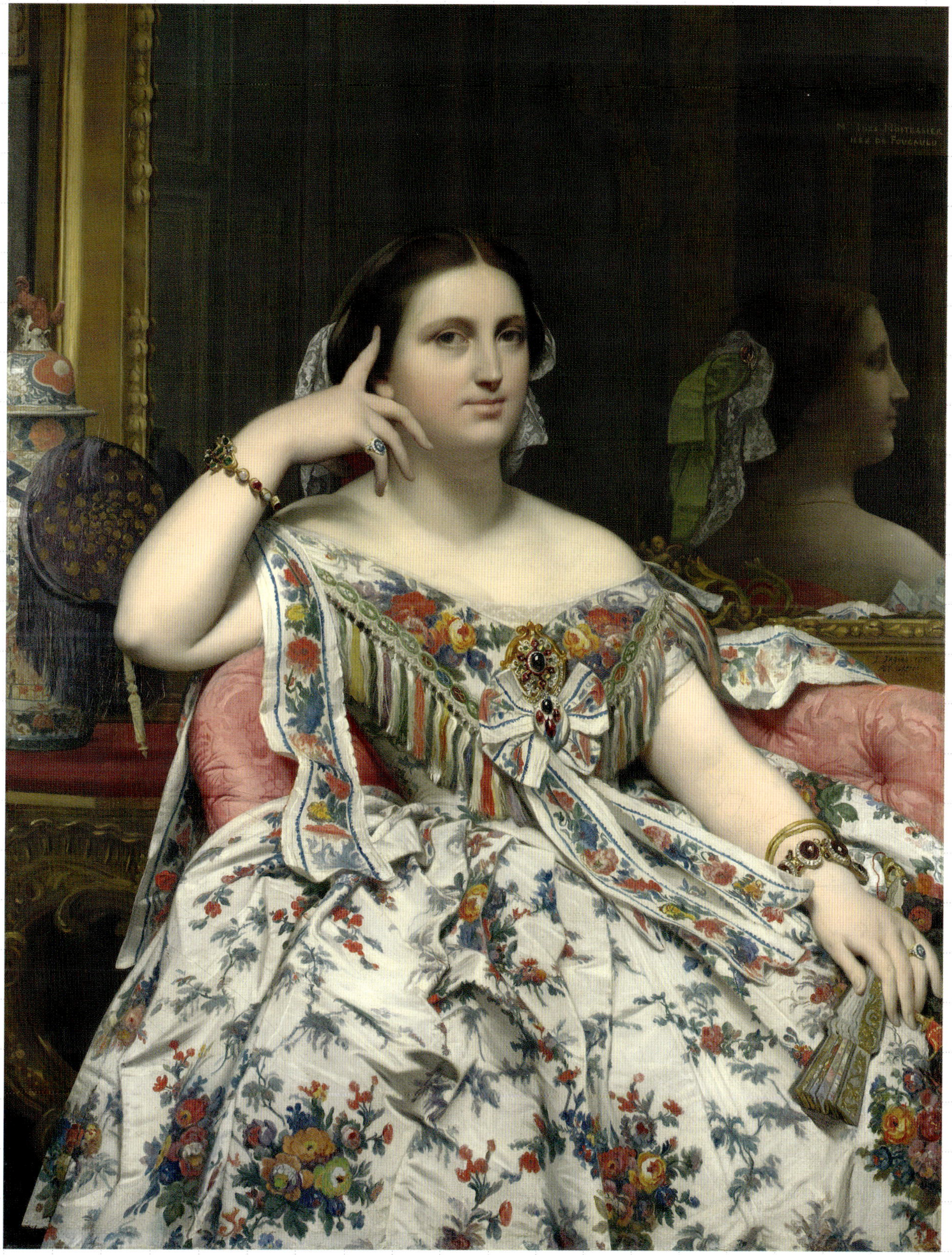

1 2 3 4 5 6 7 8 9 10 11 12 13 14 15 16 17 18 19 20 21 22 23 24 25 26

A B C D E F G H I J K L M N O P Q R S T U V W X Y Z

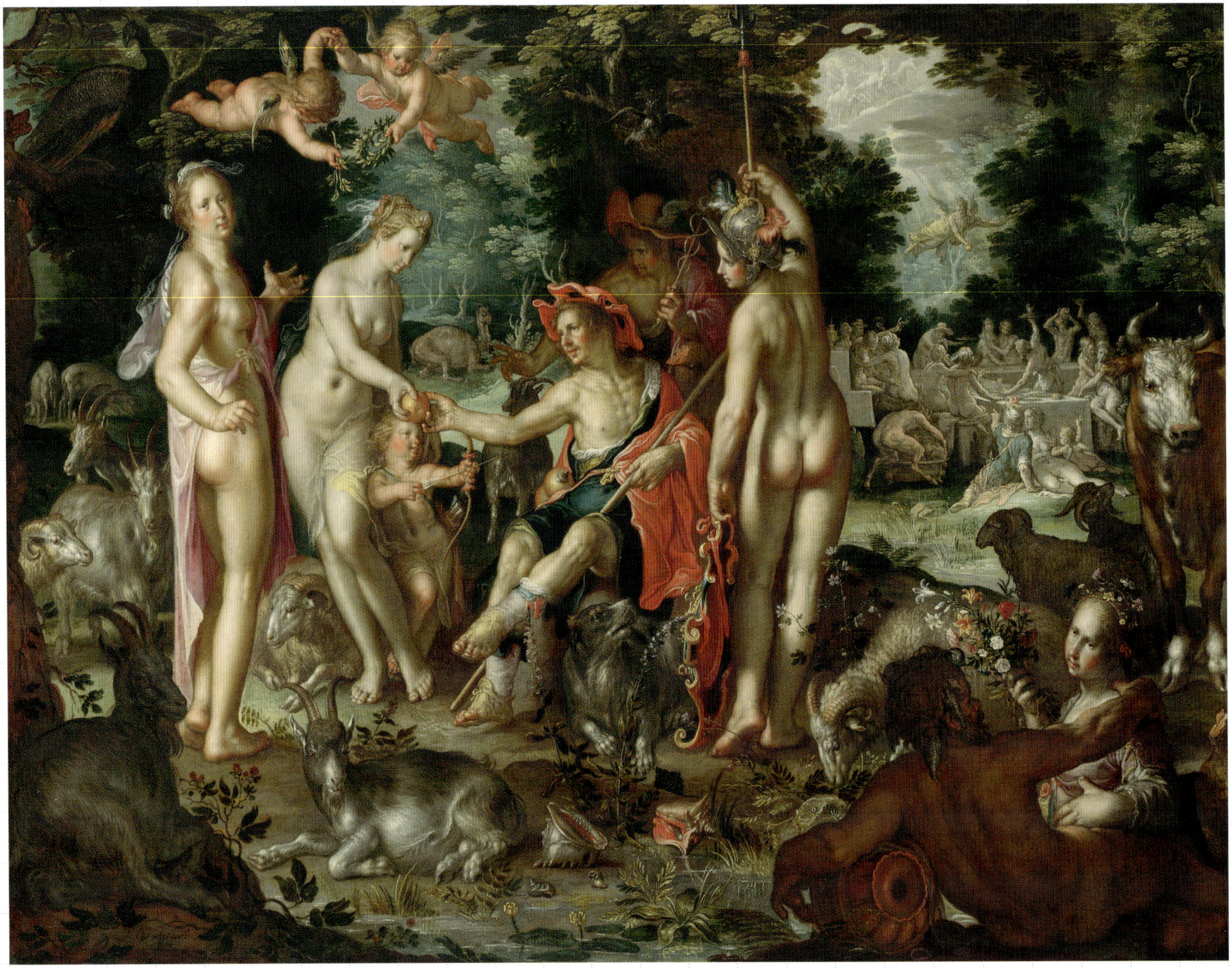

THE JUDGEMENT OF PARIS

Joachim Wtewael (1566–1638)
1615
Oil on oak

Paris hands Venus a golden apple, having judged her to be more beautiful than Juno (left) and Minerva. Mercury, with his serpent-entwined staff, stands behind Paris, whose dog and cattle litter the foreground. In the background, Peleus's wedding party unfolds. Can you find Juno's peacock and Minerva's owl?

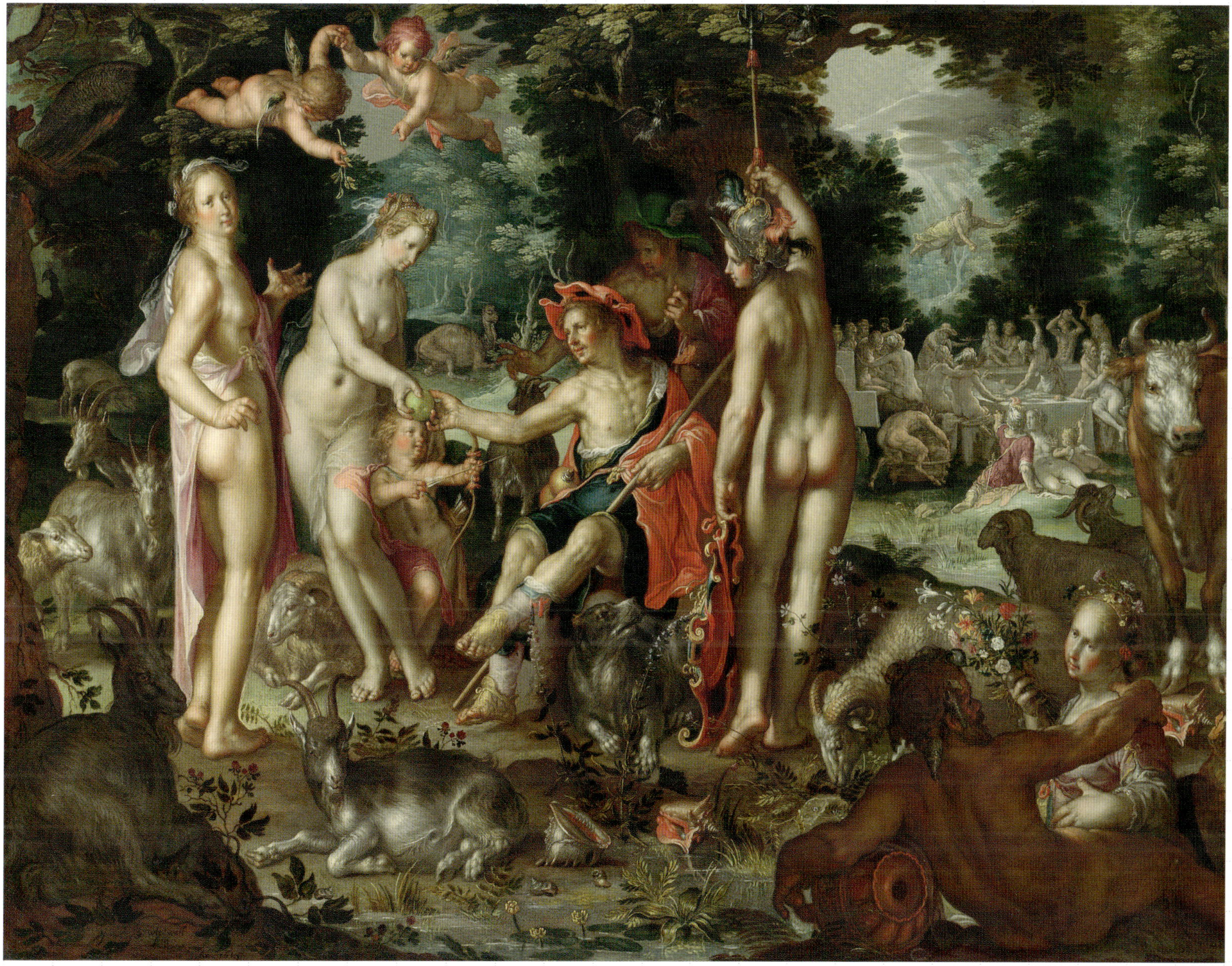

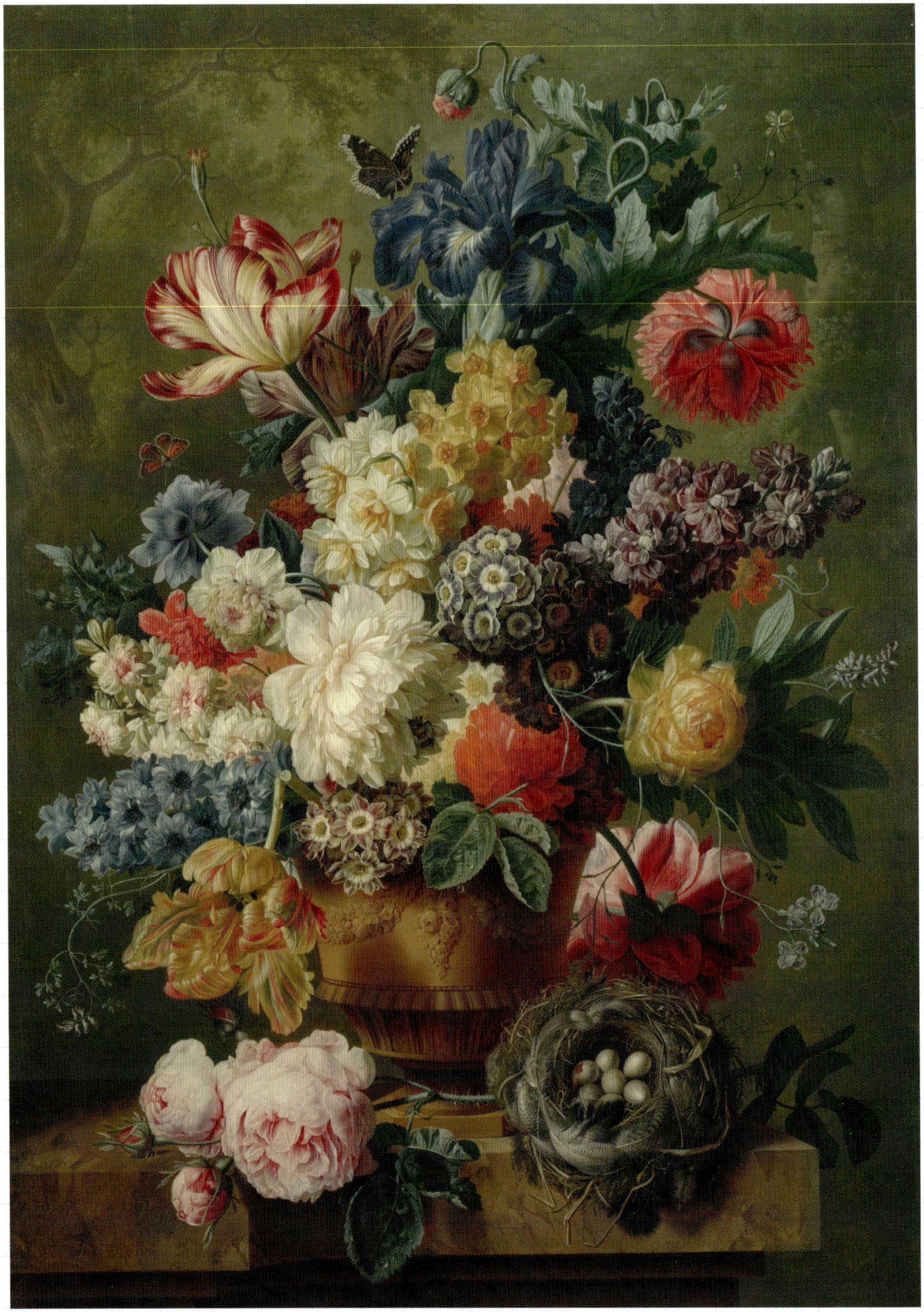

FLOWERS IN A VASE

Paulus Theodorus van Brussel (1754–1795)
1792
Oil on mahogany

This still life bursts with life and colour – butterflies skirt around the flowers; tulips, poppies, narcissi and peonies protrude from the vase. On the table lie roses and a feathery bird's nest filled with eggs. There are faint trees in the green background.

A B C D E F G H I J K L M N O P Q R S T U V W X Y Z

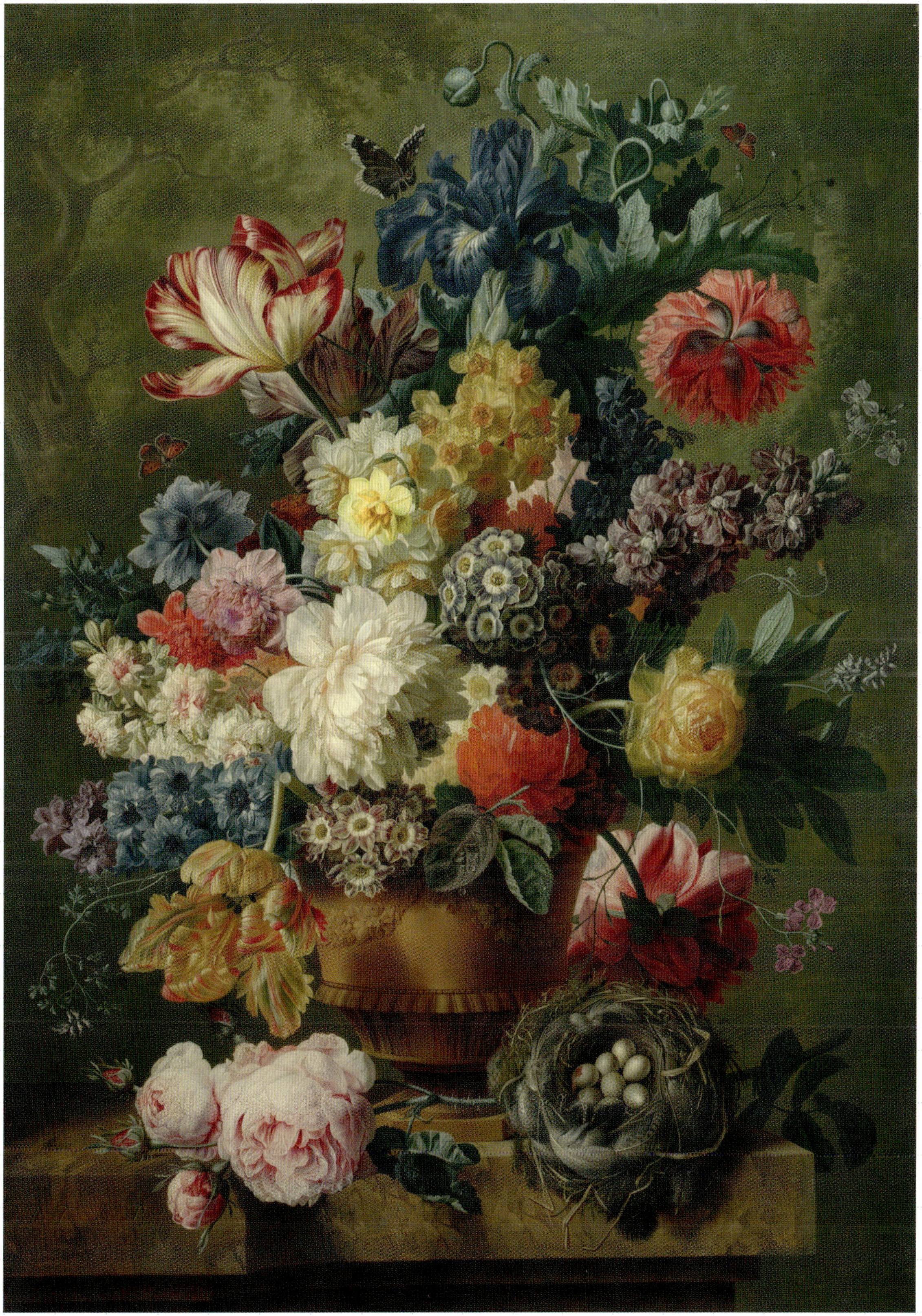

1 2 3 4 5 6 7 8 9 10 11 12 13 14 15 16 17 18 19 20 21 22 23 24 25 26

A B C D E F G H I J K L M N O P Q R S T U V W X Y Z

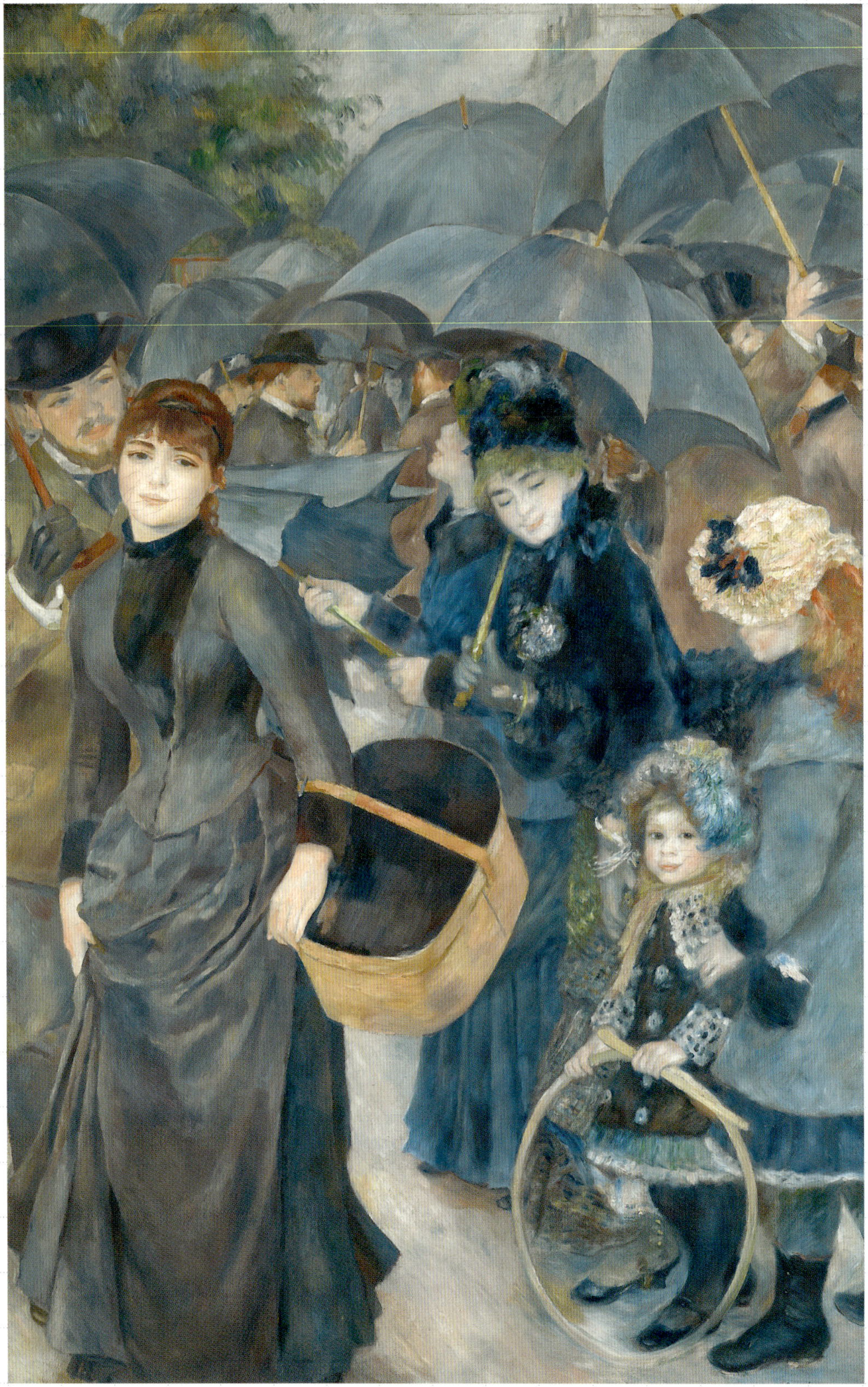

THE UMBRELLAS

Pierre-Auguste Renoir (1841–1919)

about 1881–1886

Oil on canvas

Fashionable Parisians attempt to keep dry in this bustling scene, save for the nearest, most prominent figure on the left, who looks at the viewer as she continues about her business. The little girl holding a hoop also looks towards the viewer, distracted, as the woman behind appears to urge her on.

A B C D E F G H I J K L M N O P Q R S T U V W X Y Z

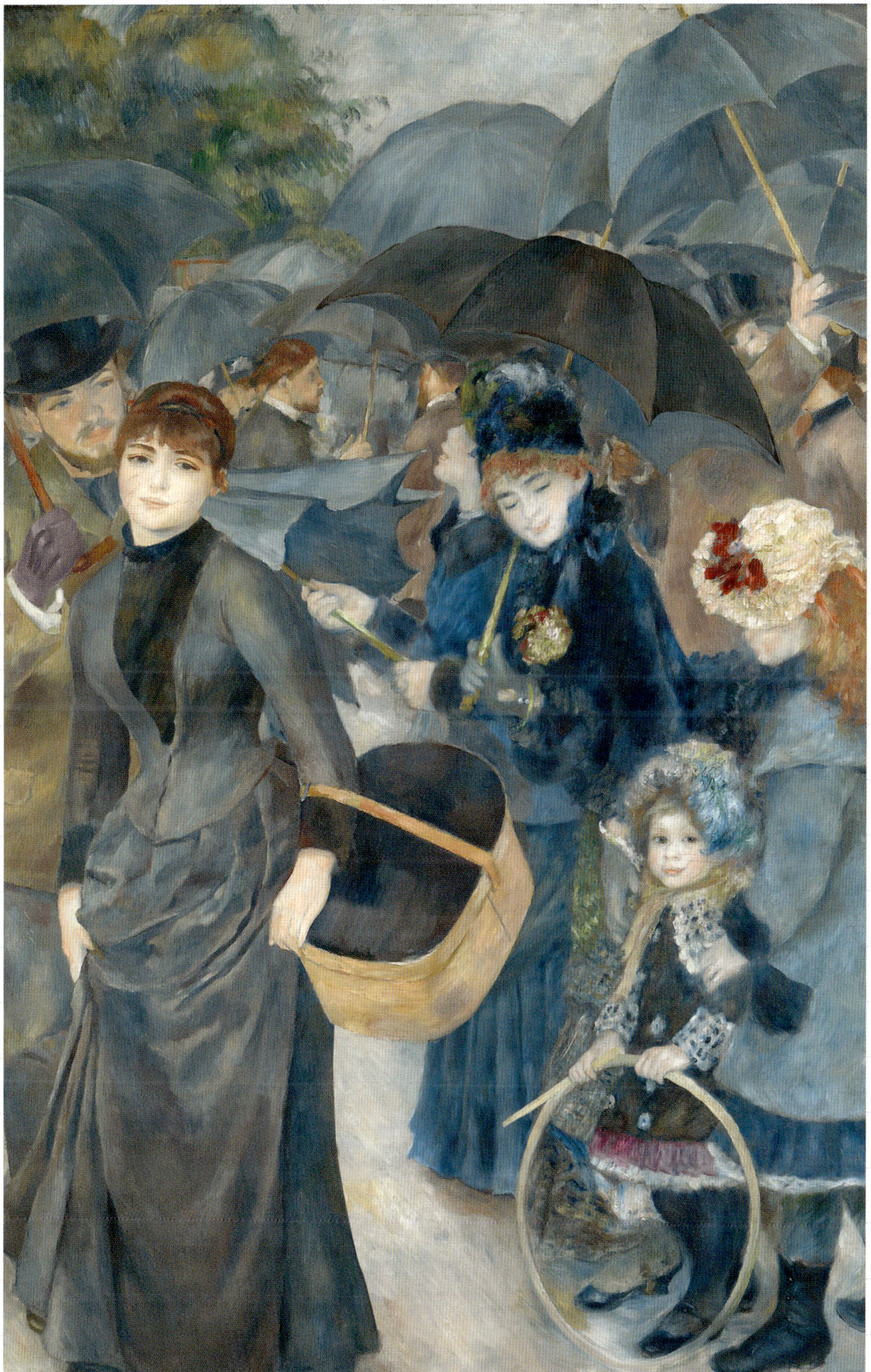

1 2 3 4 5 6 7 8 9 10 11 12 13 14 15 16 17 18 19 20 21 22 23 24 25 26

A B C D E F G H I J K L M N O P Q R S T U V W X Y Z

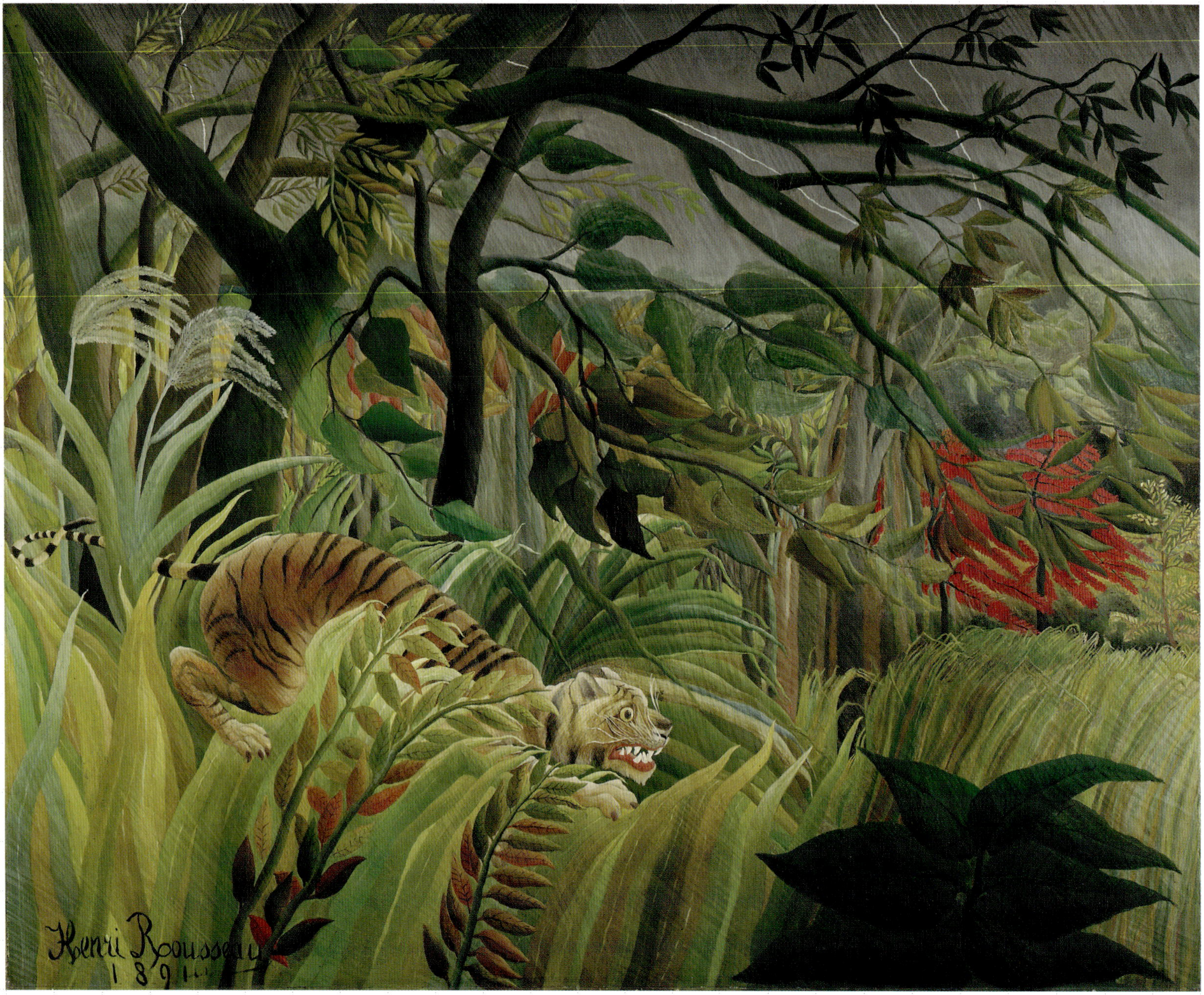

SURPRISED!

Henri Rousseau (1844–1910)
1891
Oil on canvas

In the first of Rousseau's famous jungle scenes, a storm breaks out while a tiger, deep in foliage, is on the hunt. There is a great sense of atmosphere, the forks of lightning cracking in the moody grey sky, and of movement – the sprawling foreground vegetation, the bending branches and diagonal streaks of rain.

A B C D E F G H I J K L M N O P Q R S T U V W X Y Z

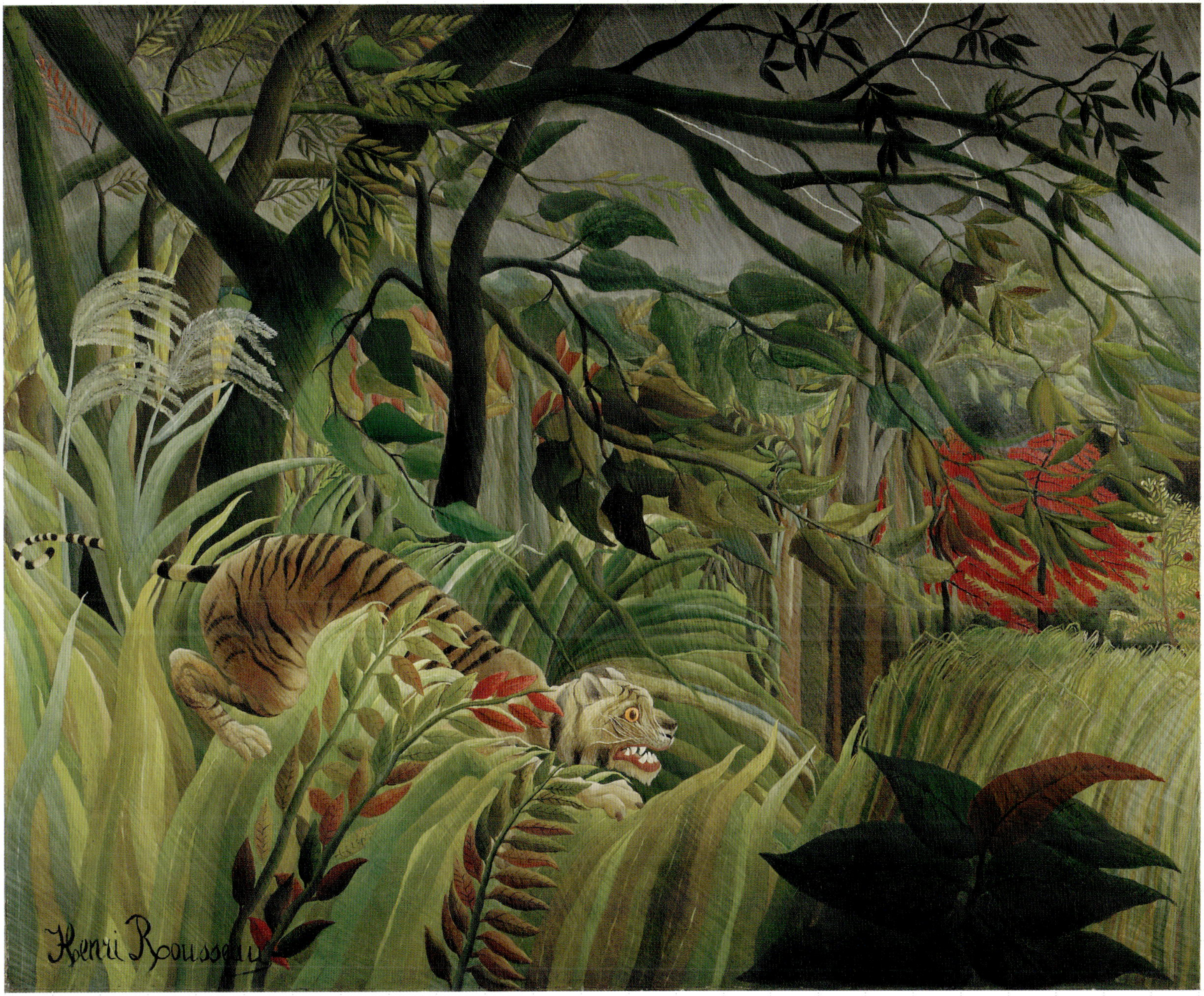

1 2 3 4 5 6 7 8 9 10 11 12 13 14 15 16 17 18 19 20 21 22 23 24 25 26

A B C D E F G H I J K L M N O P Q R S T U V W X Y Z

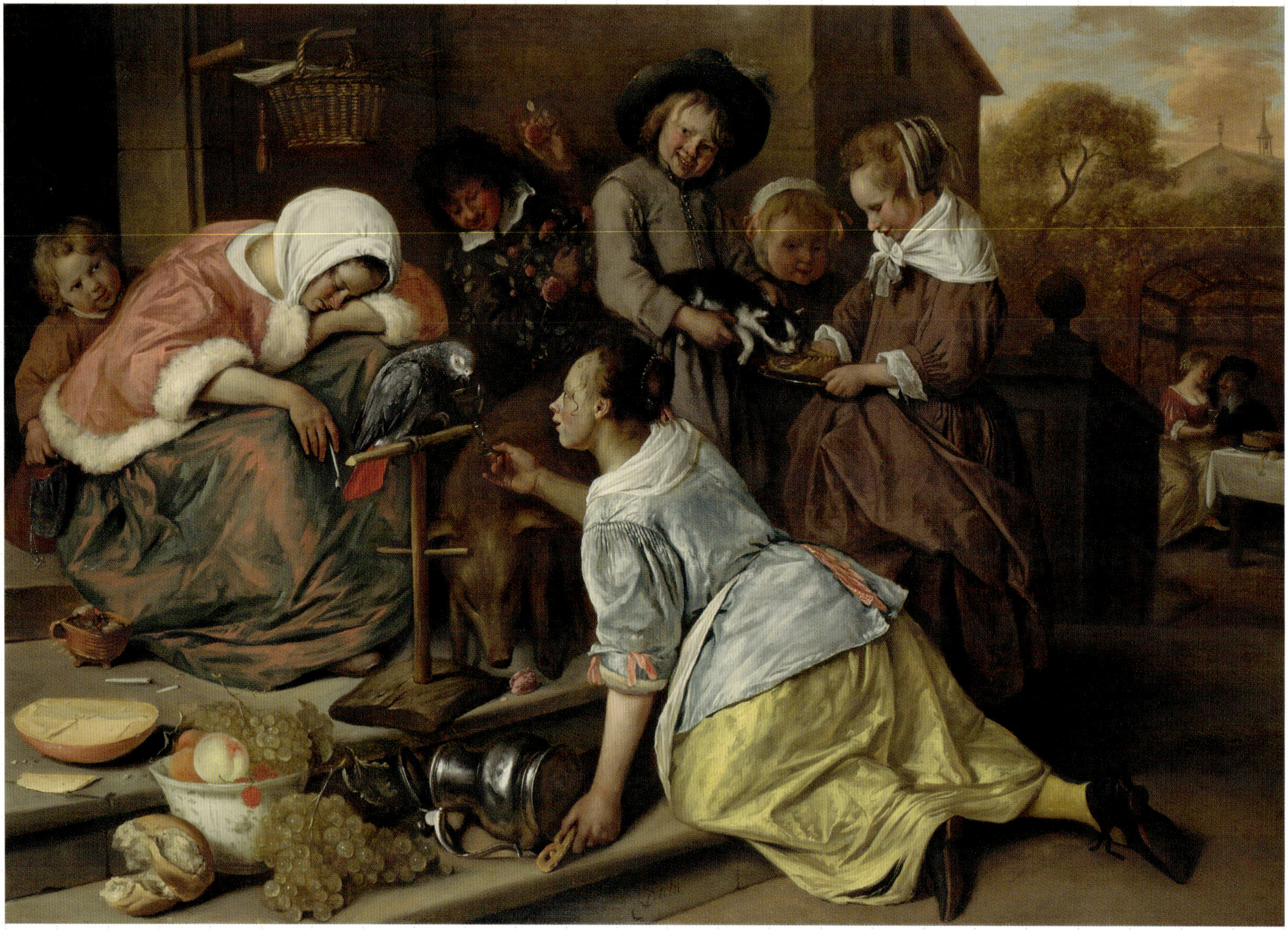

THE EFFECTS OF INTEMPERANCE

Jan Steen (1626–1679)
about 1663–1665
Oil on wood

While a mother sleeps off the effects of alcohol, her children misbehave, following her bad example. One picks her pocket, another wastes meat on a cat, and another 'throws roses before a swine'. Find the two items that hint at a dim future for them – a beggar's crutch and a whip made of birch branches.

A B C D E F G H I J K L M N O P Q R S T U V W X Y Z

1 2 3 4 5 6 7 8 9 10 11 12 13 14 15 16 17 18 19 20 21 22 23 24 25 26

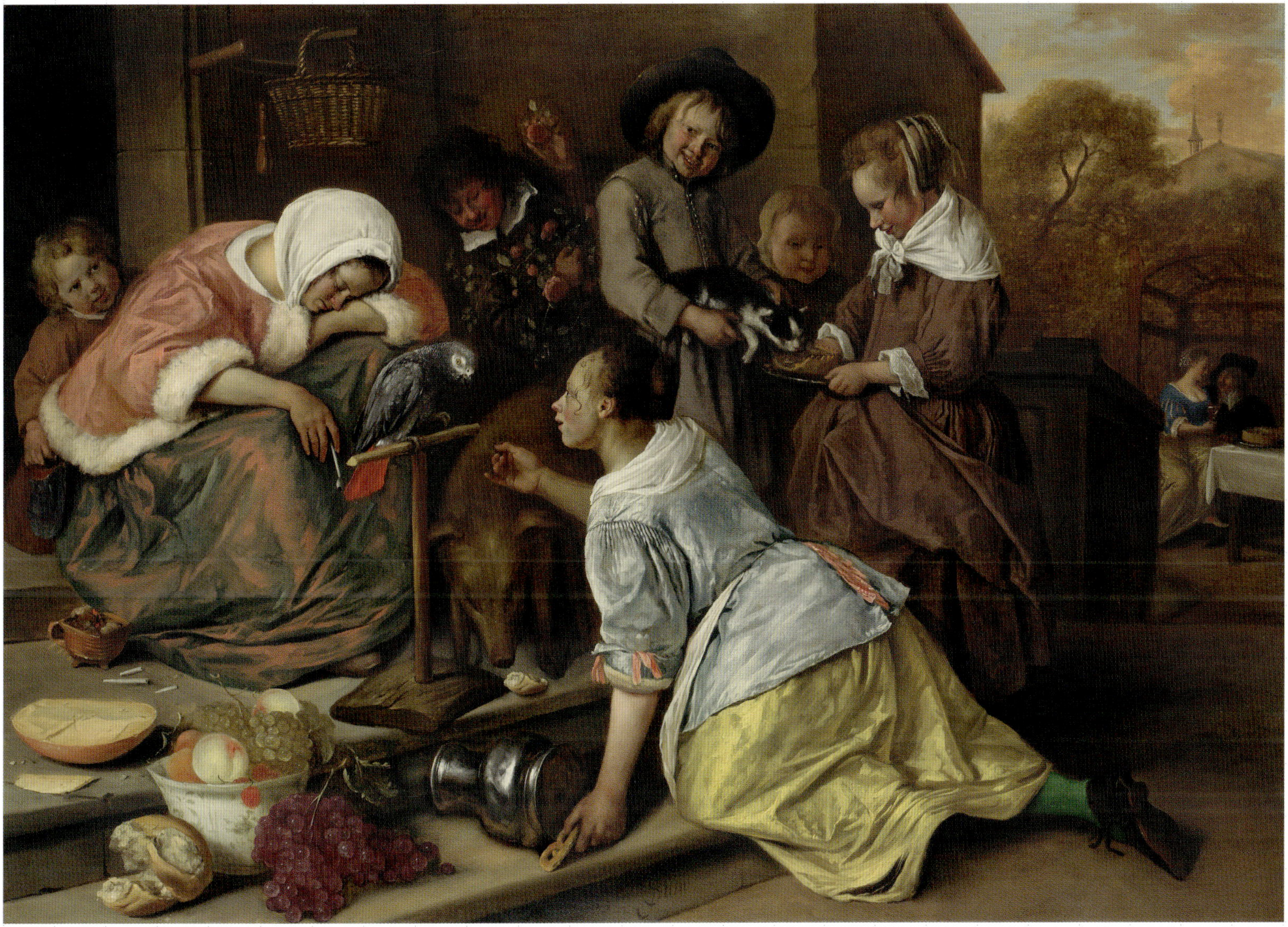

A B C D E F G H I J K L M N O P Q R S T U V W X Y Z

A B C D E F G H I J K L M N O P Q R S T U V W X Y Z

1 2 3 4 5 6 7 8 9 10 11 12 13 14 15 16 17 18 19 20 21

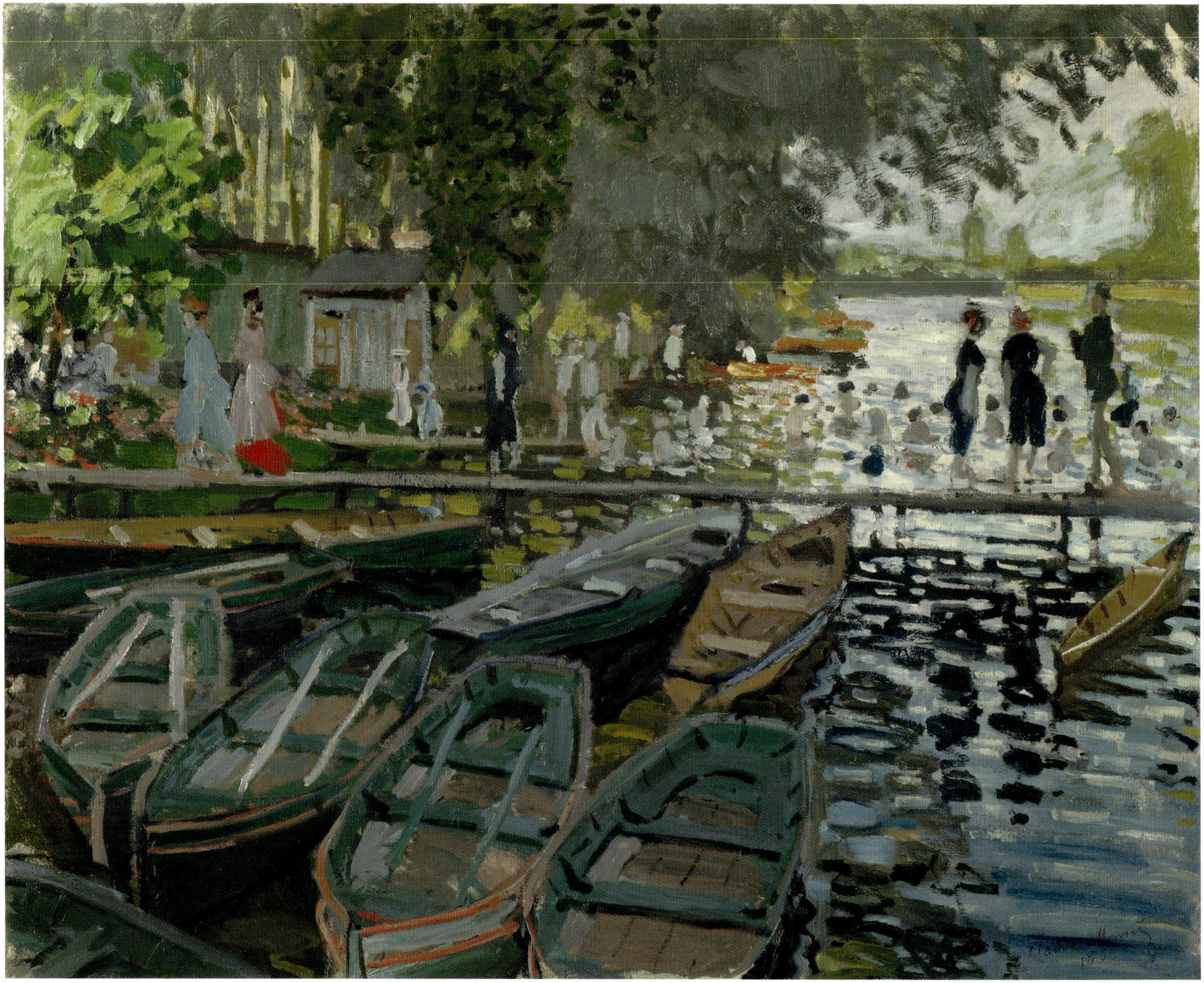

22 23 24 25 26

BATHERS AT LA GRENOUILLÈRE

Claude Monet (1840–1926)
1869
Oil on canvas

This idyllic scene shows bathers at a popular swimming and boating lake outside Paris. Can you find all 20 differences among the thick, painterly brushstrokes of the master Impressionist? Monet's free, but descriptive marks capture the forms and gestures of the figures. Light is expertly modelled on the lake through use of colour.

 A B C D E F G H I J K L M N O P Q R S T U V W X Y Z

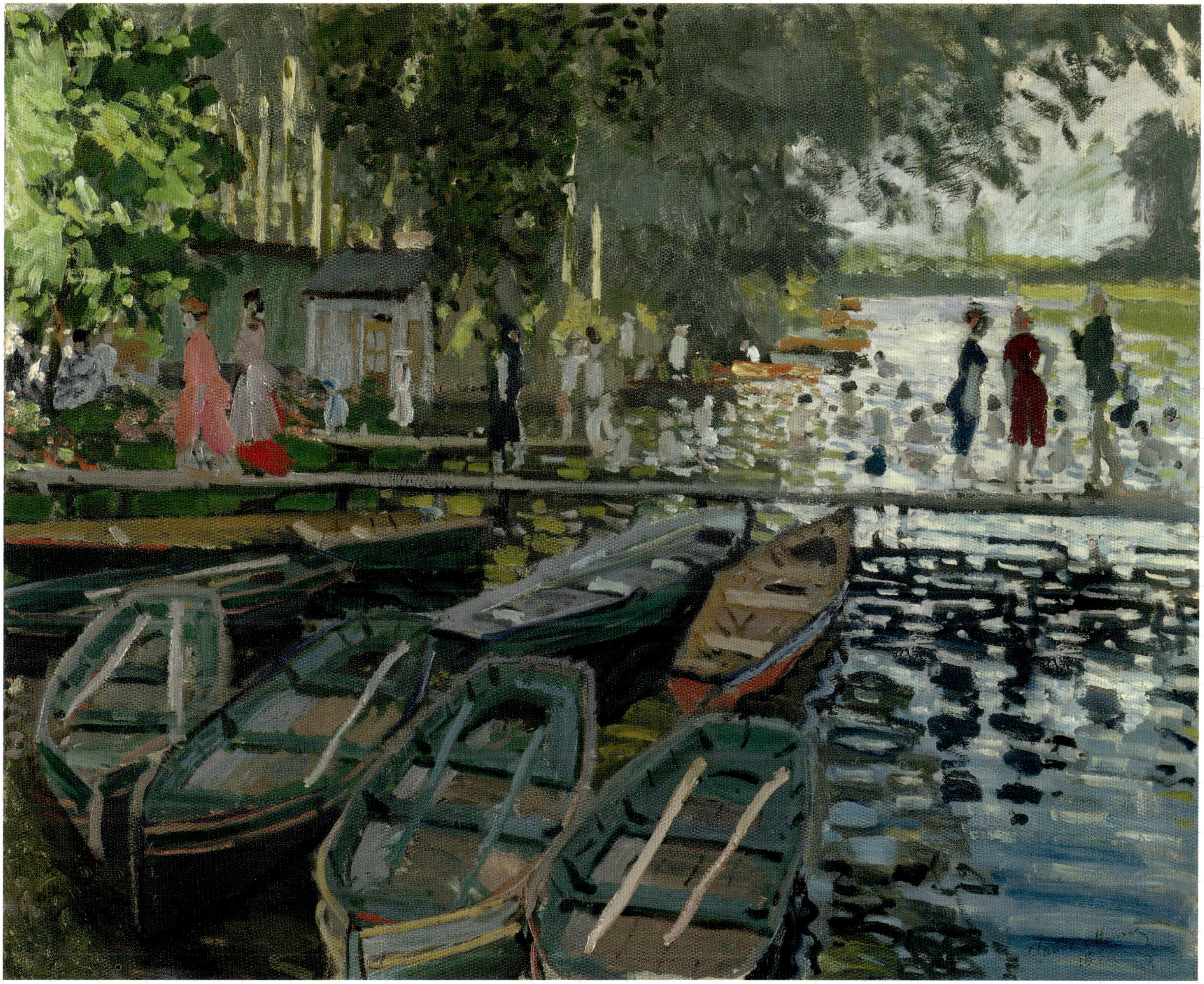

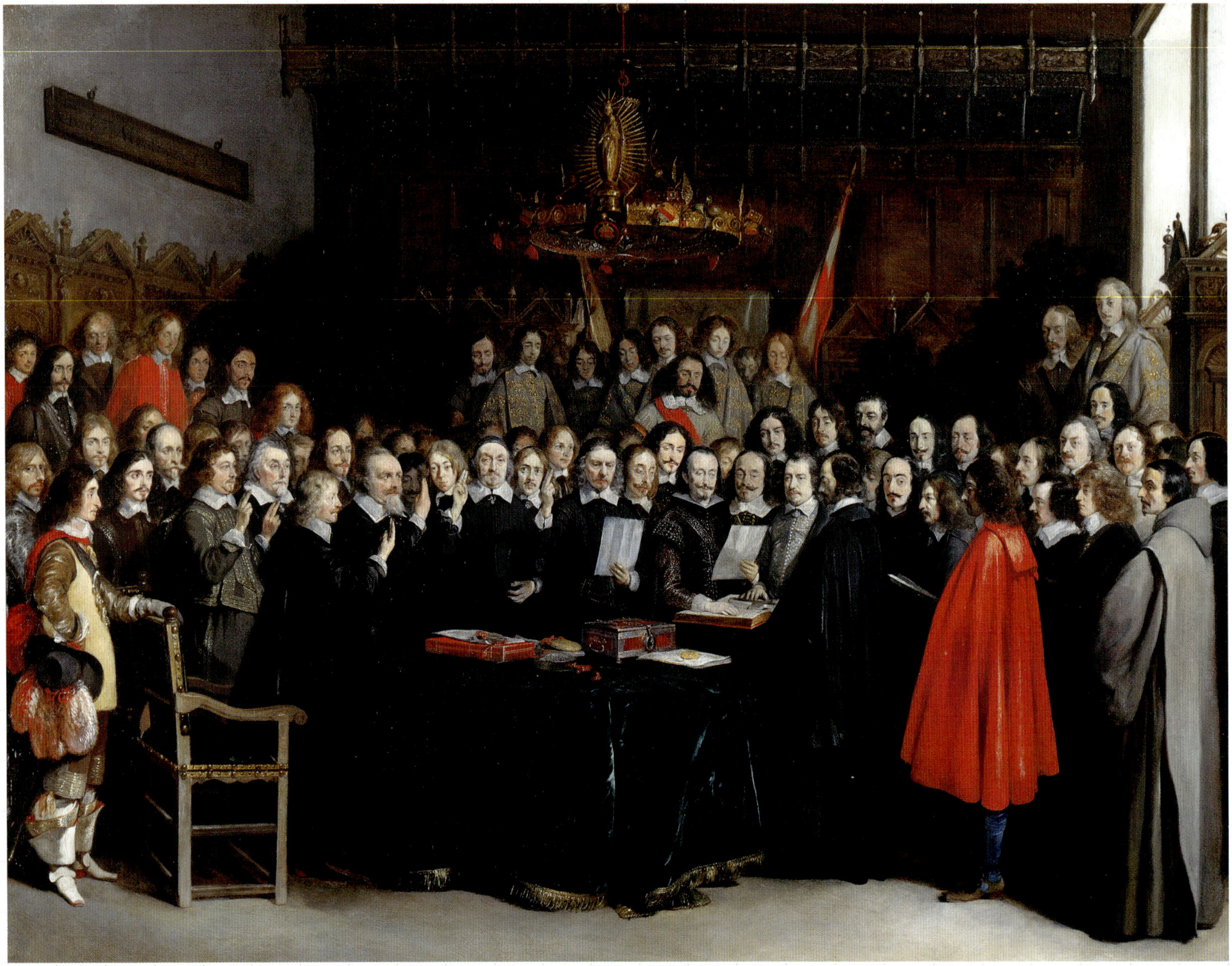

THE RATIFICATION OF THE TREATY OF MÜNSTER

Gerard ter Borch (1617–1681)
1648
Oil on copper

This painting illustrates the Münster treaty being ratified, bringing an end to the Netherlands' eighty-year conflict with Spain. Seventy-seven figures are present. Can you count them all? The men holding their hands up in oath are Dutch delegates. Two Spanish delegates stand right of the table.

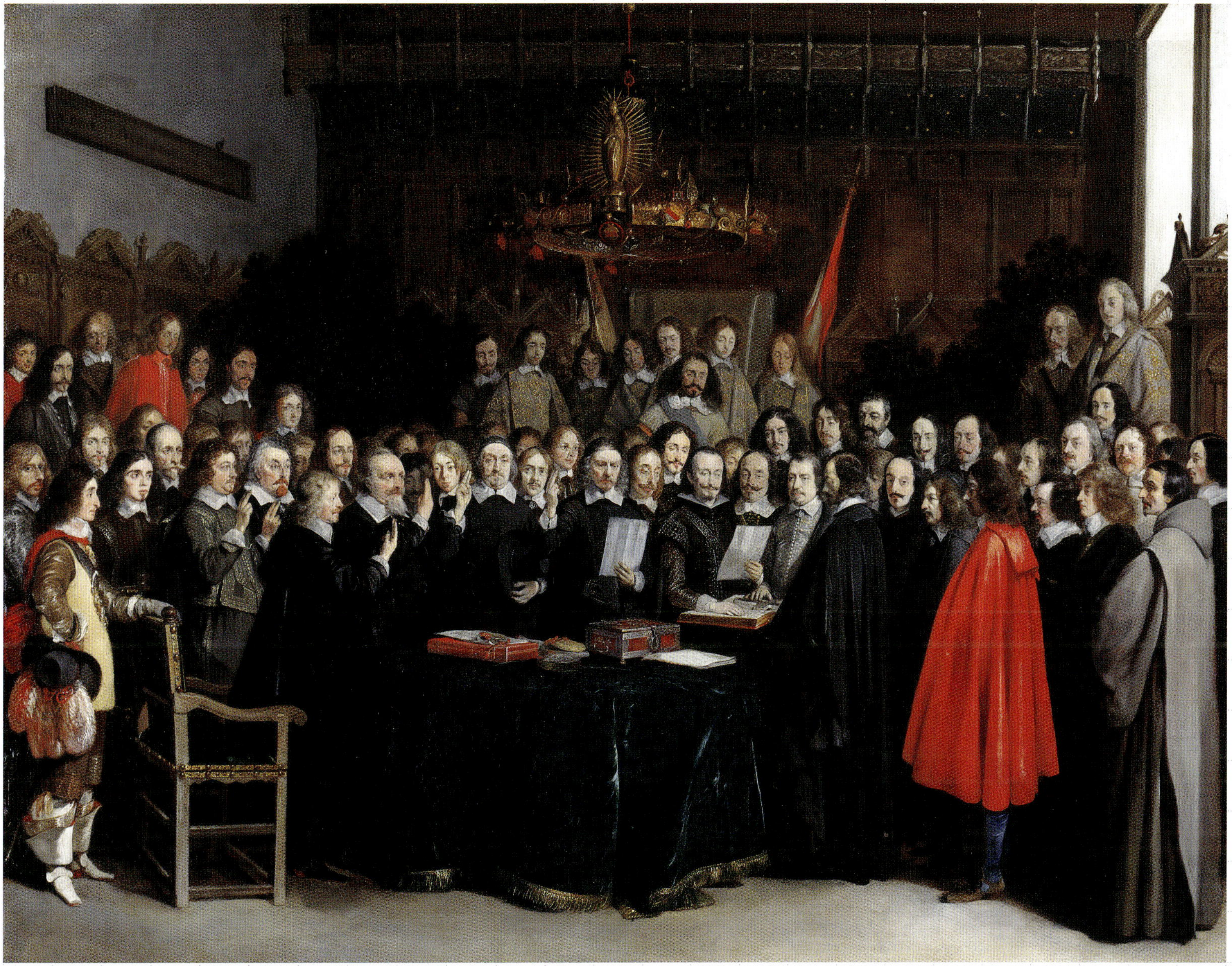

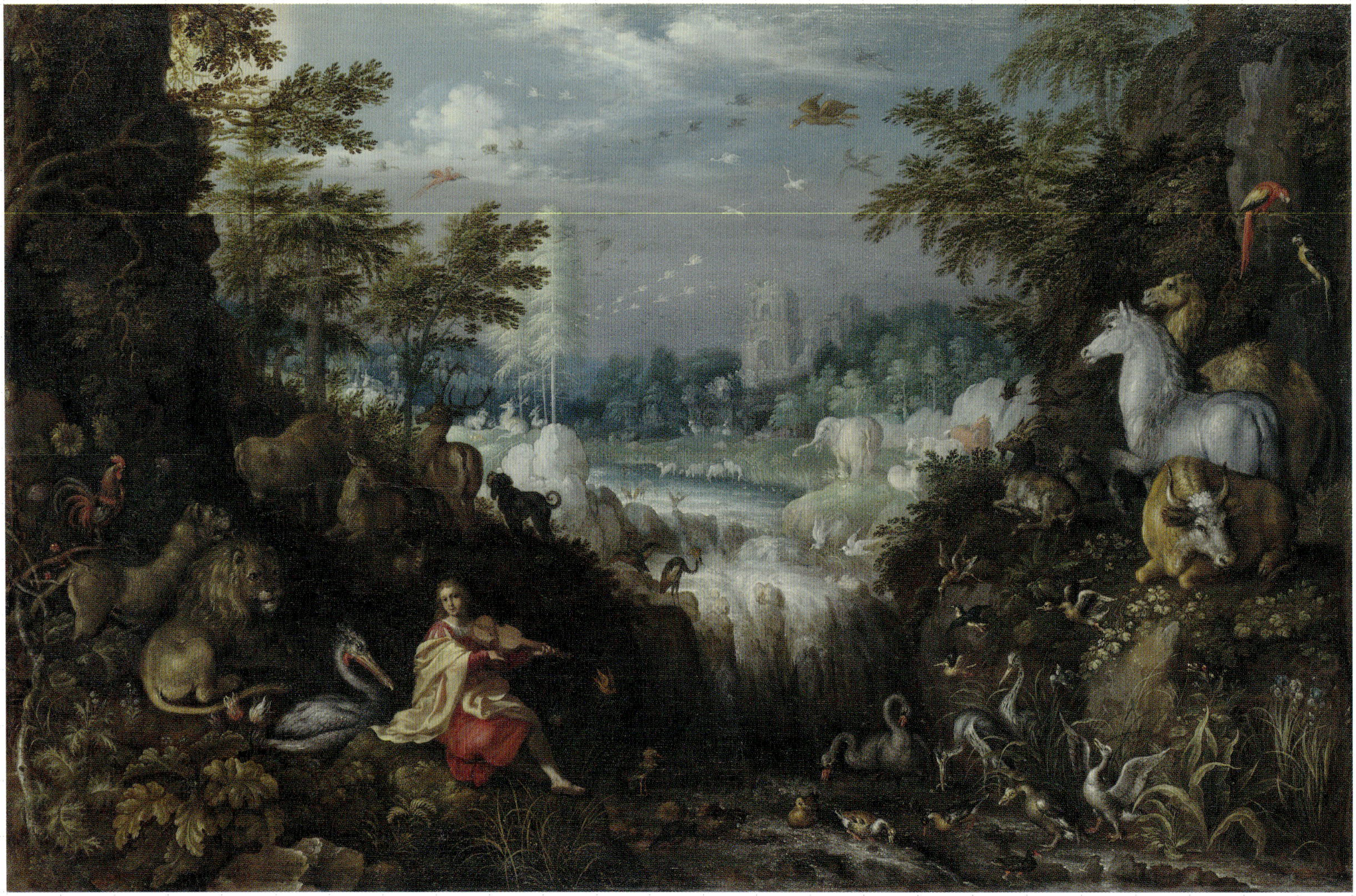

ORPHEUS
Roelandt Savery (1576–1639)
1628
Oil on oak

In this enchanting scene, Orpheus is surrounded by animals captivated by his violin playing. His music had the ability to charm all living creatures, even the trees and rocks. Lions, deer, bovines, horses, a camel, an elephant and an array of wonderful birds are among his audience. See how many birds you can identify.

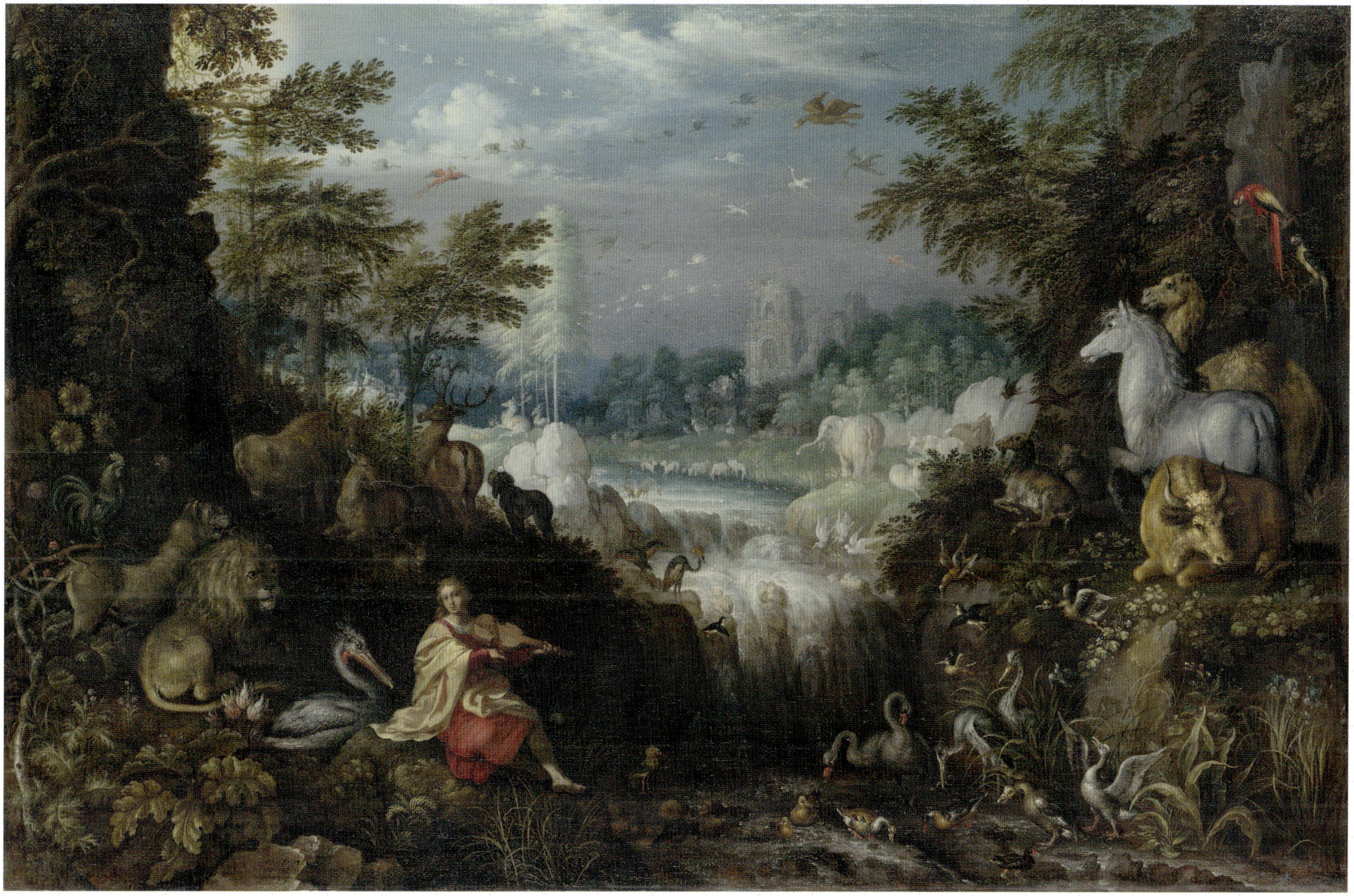

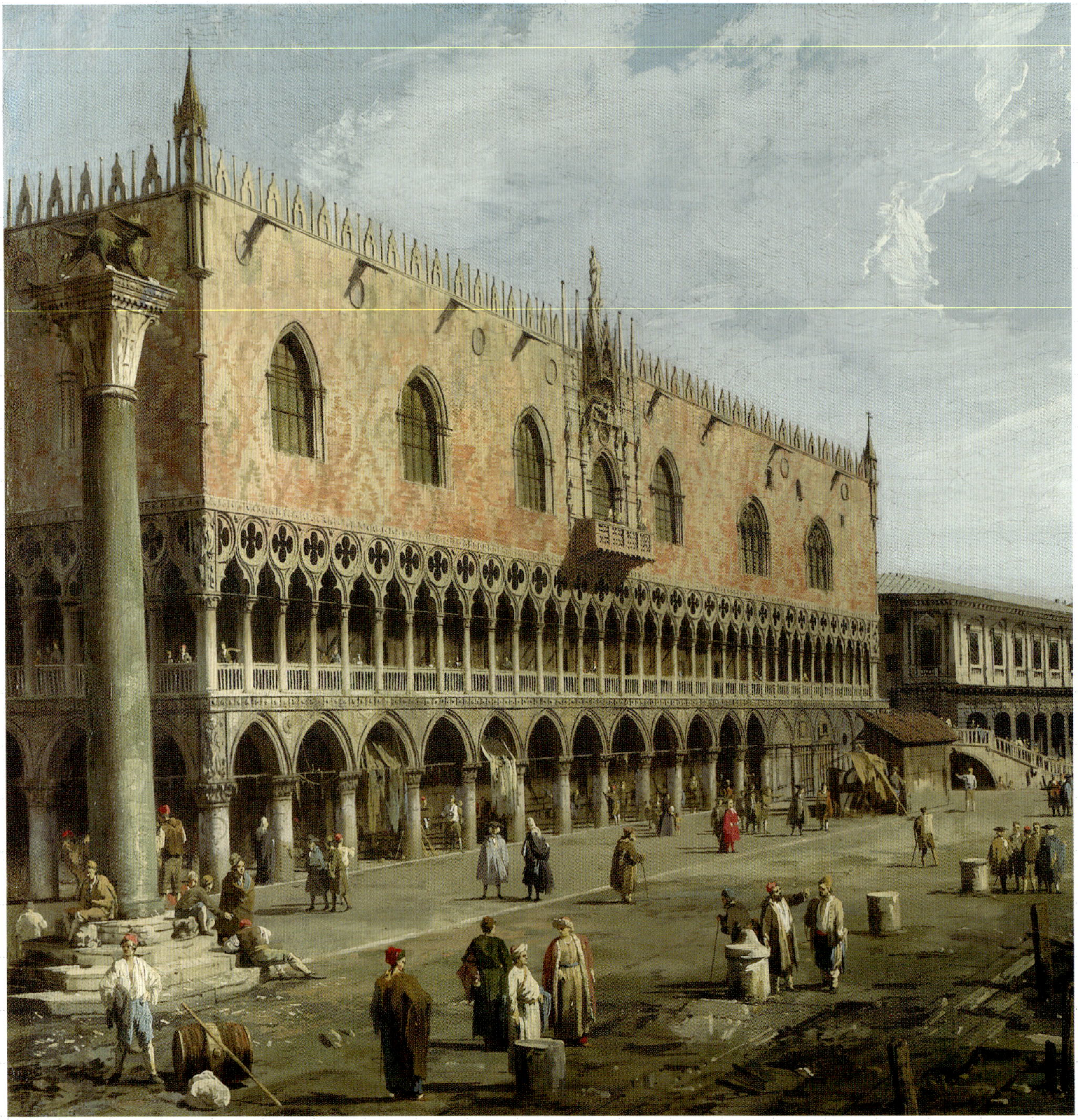

VENICE: THE DOGE'S PALACE AND THE RIVA DEGLI SCHIAVONI (DETAIL)

Canaletto (1697–1768)
Late 1730s
Oil on canvas

Venetians go about their daily life on a bright, sunny day. The architectural detail and use of perspective are striking. From the column of St Mark (symbolised by a lion) on the left, the eye is drawn into the distance by the archways of the Doge's Palace. Sun beams off the brickwork while the corridors are steeped in shadow.

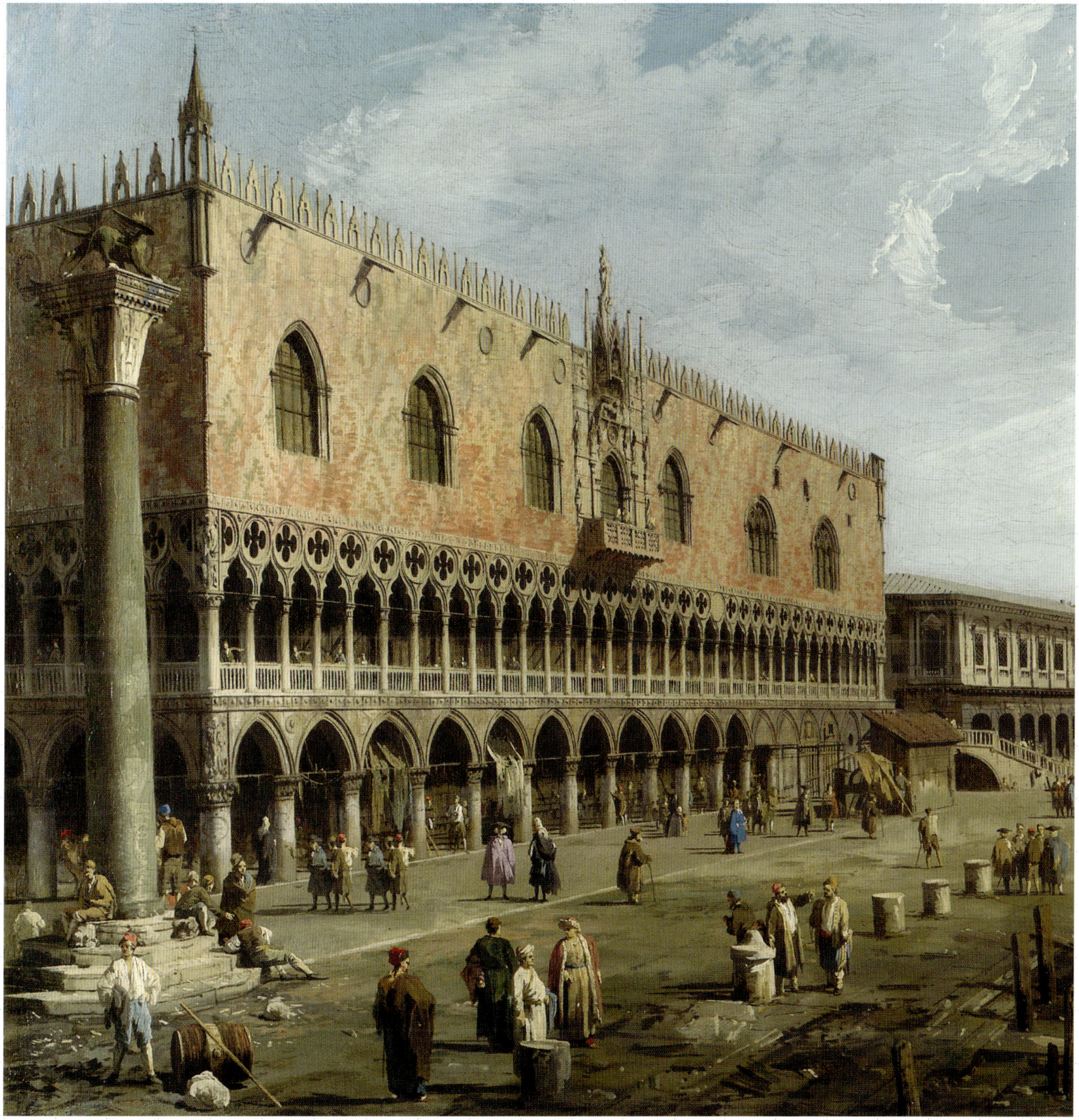

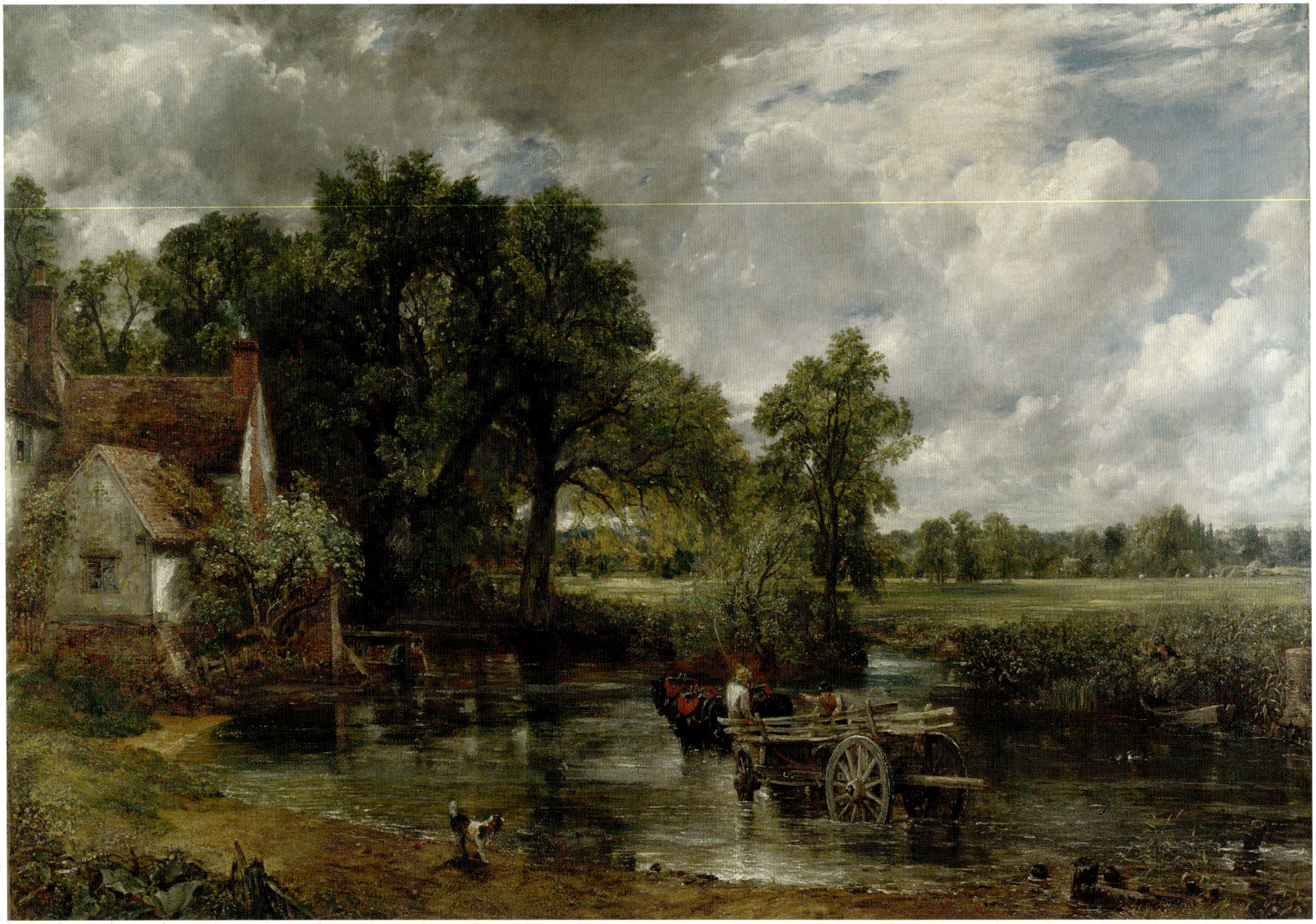

THE HAY WAIN

John Constable (1776–1837)
1821
Oil on canvas

In this picturesque landscape, one of Constable's most famous paintings, three horses pull a hay wain (cart) across the river Stour. A dog watches on from the bank, and in the distance haymakers can just be made out, working in the fields. A figure emerges from the bushes on the right, and two ducks swim alongside a boat.

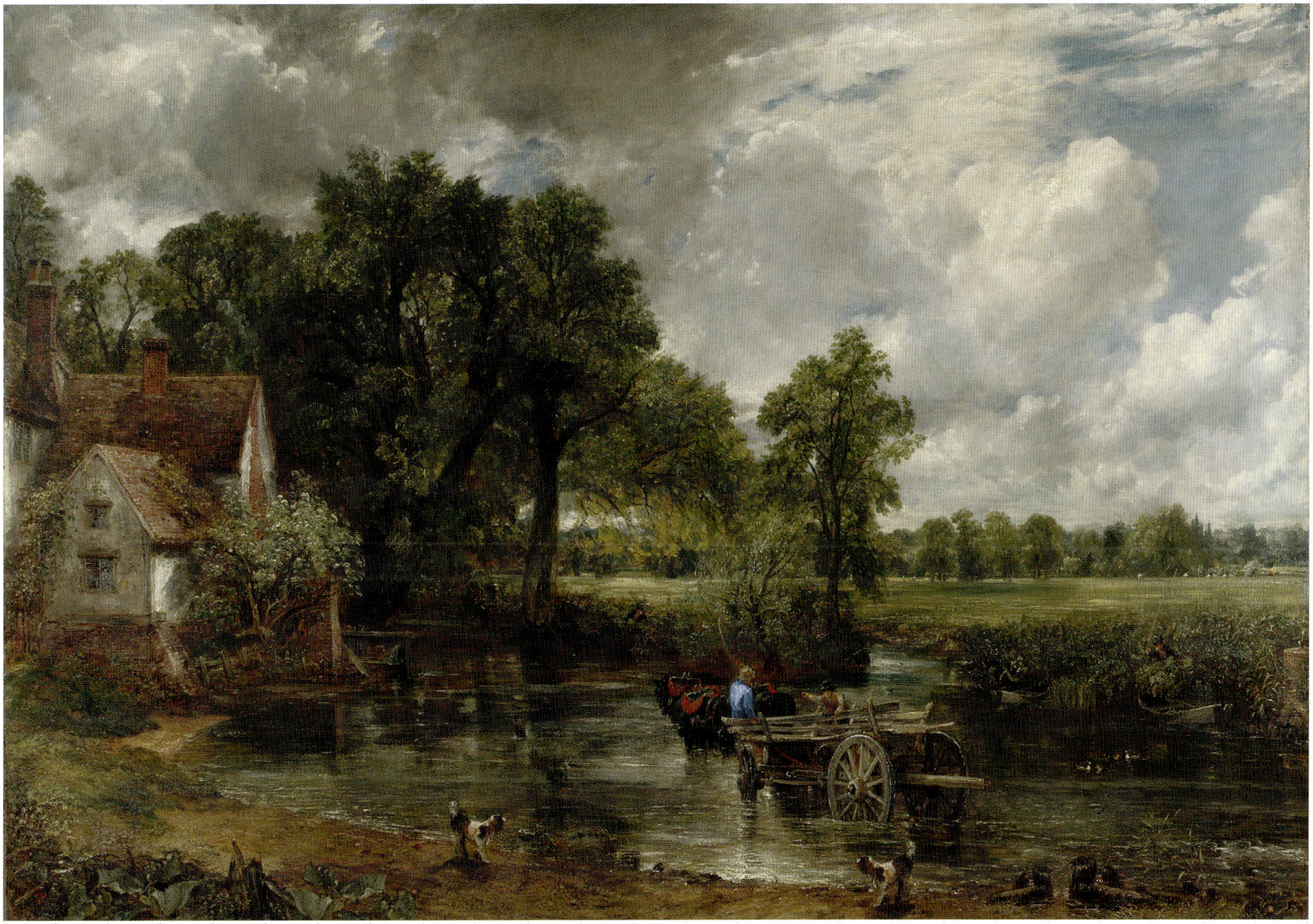

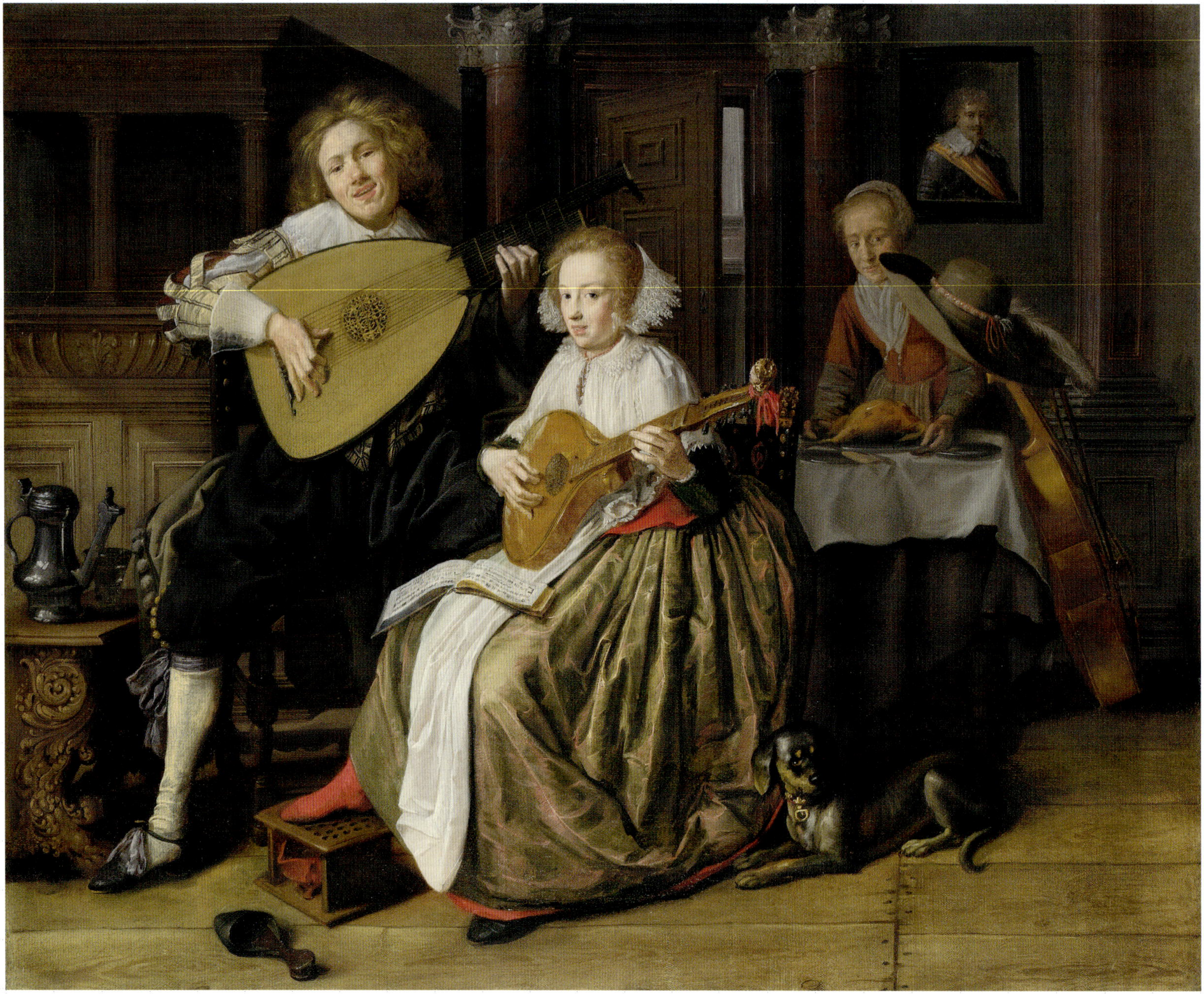

A YOUNG MAN AND WOMAN MAKING MUSIC

Jan Miense Molenaer (about 1610–1668)
about 1630–1632
Oil on canvas

Here a young woman plays a cittern – music book resting on her lap – in duet with the young man on her left. It's thought to refer to the harmony of true love, while the foot-warmer could be a symbol of the effort a man has to make to win a woman's affection. A dogs sits loyally at her feet.

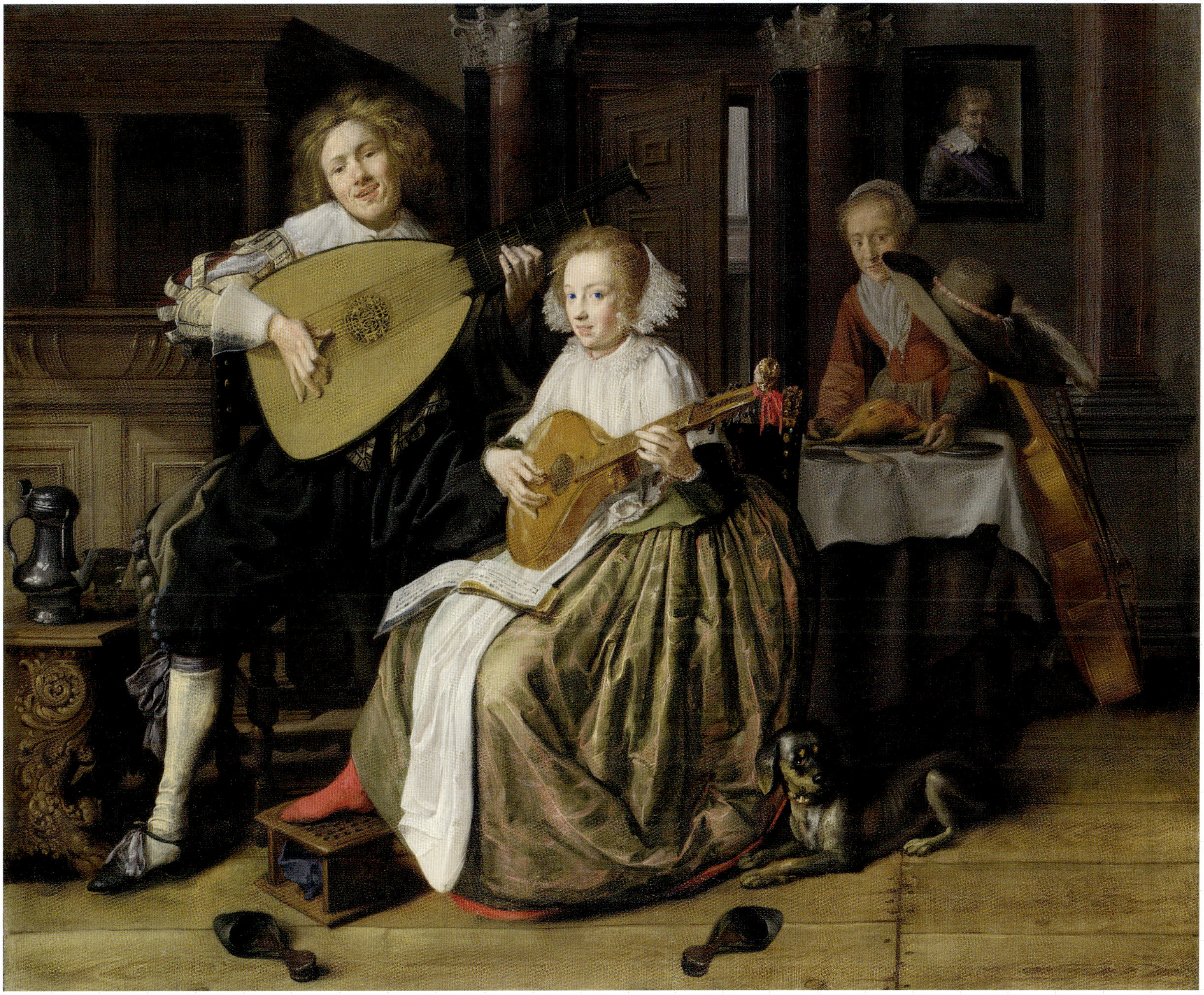

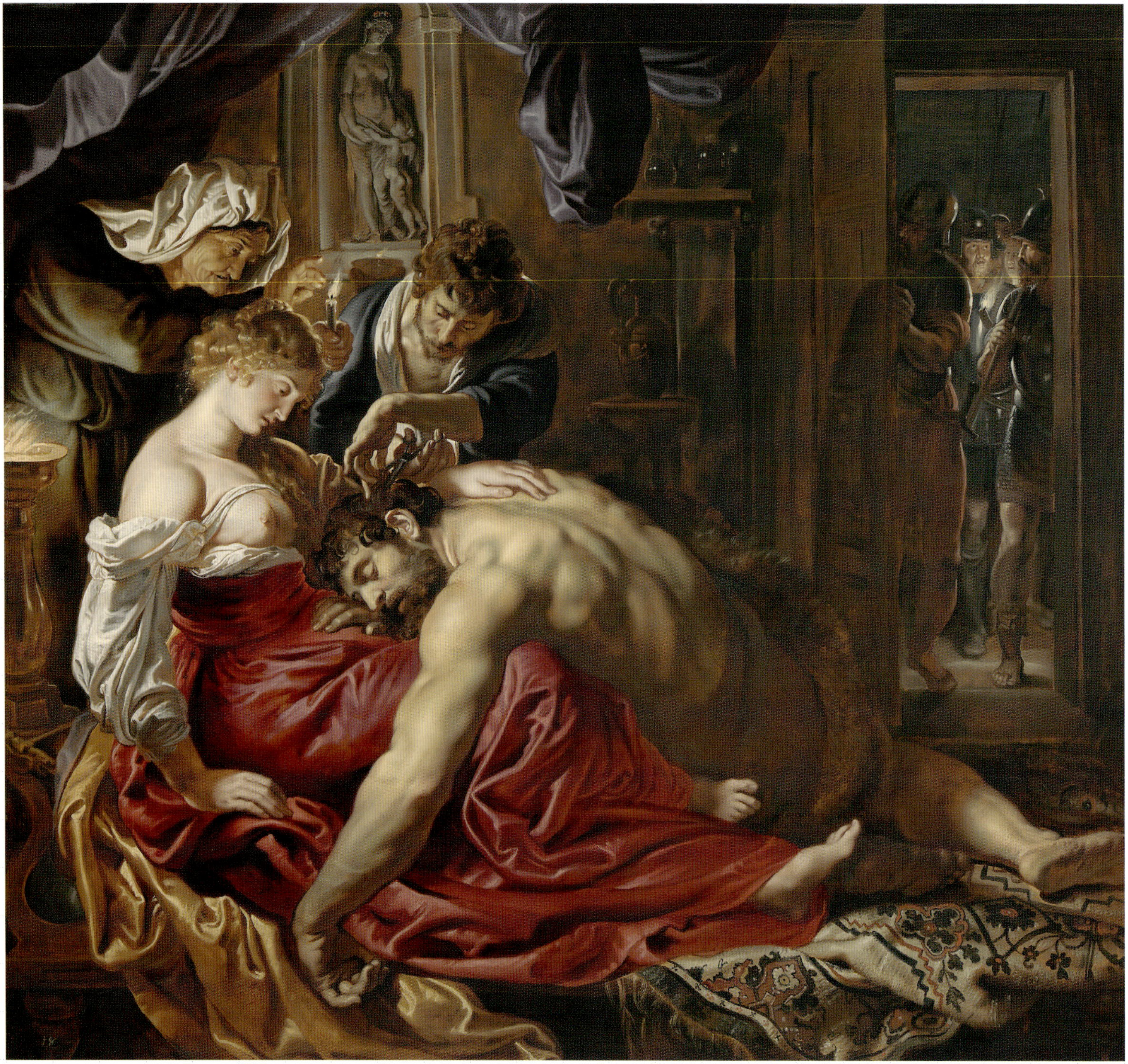

SAMSON AND DELILAH

Peter Paul Rubens (1577–1640)

about 1609–1610

Oil on wood

Bribed by the Philistines, Delilah tricks the Jewish hero Samson into revealing the source of his strength – his uncut hair. While he sleeps a barber takes a pair of scissors to his locks, the Philistines wait at the door. A statue of Venus and Cupid alludes to love being the cause of his downfall.

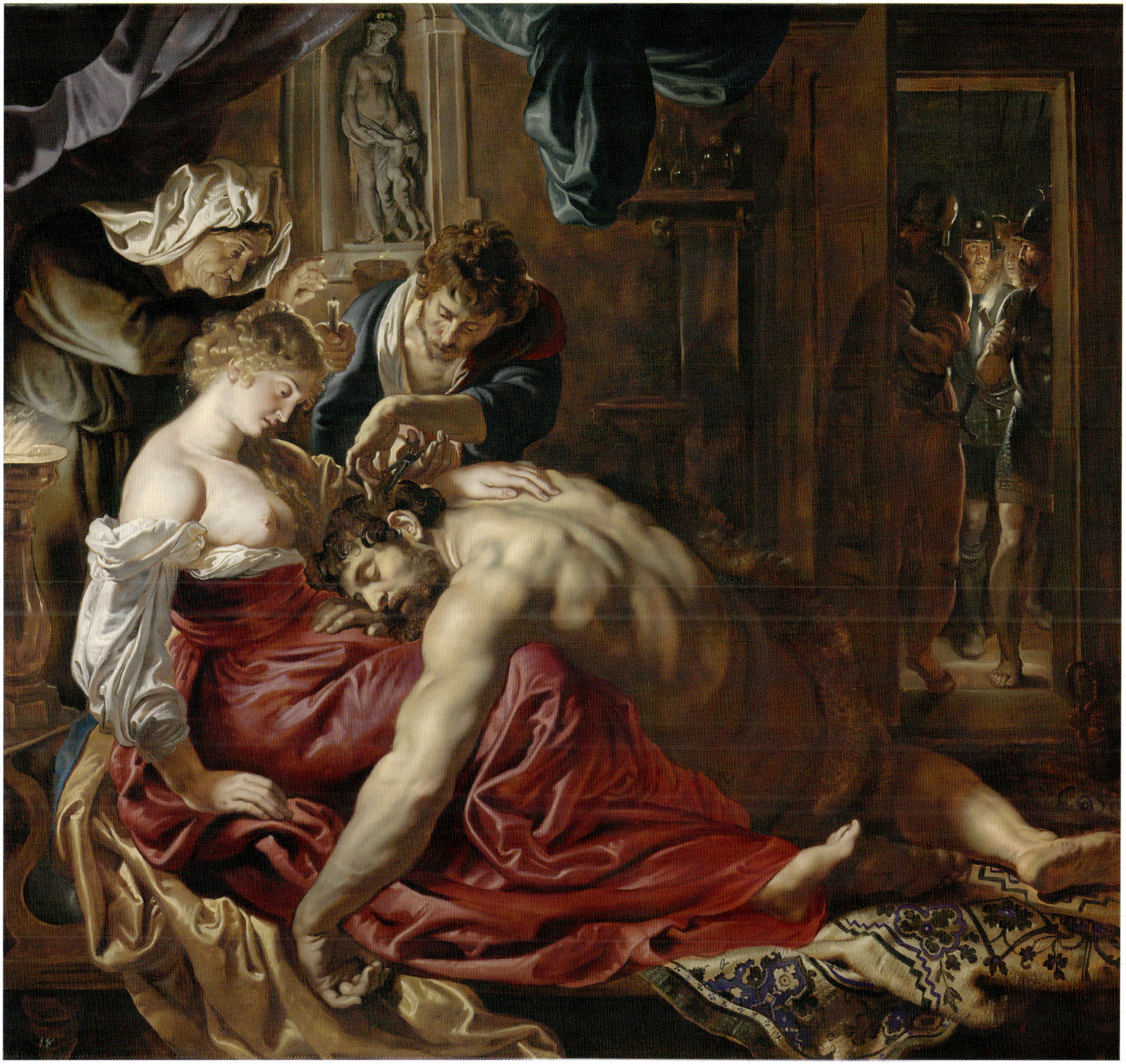
A B C D E F G H I J K L M N O P Q R S T U V W X Y Z
1 2 3 4 5 6 7 8 9 10 11 12 13 14 15 16 17 18 19 20 21 22 23 24 25 26
A B C D E F G H I J K L M N O P Q R S T U V W X Y Z

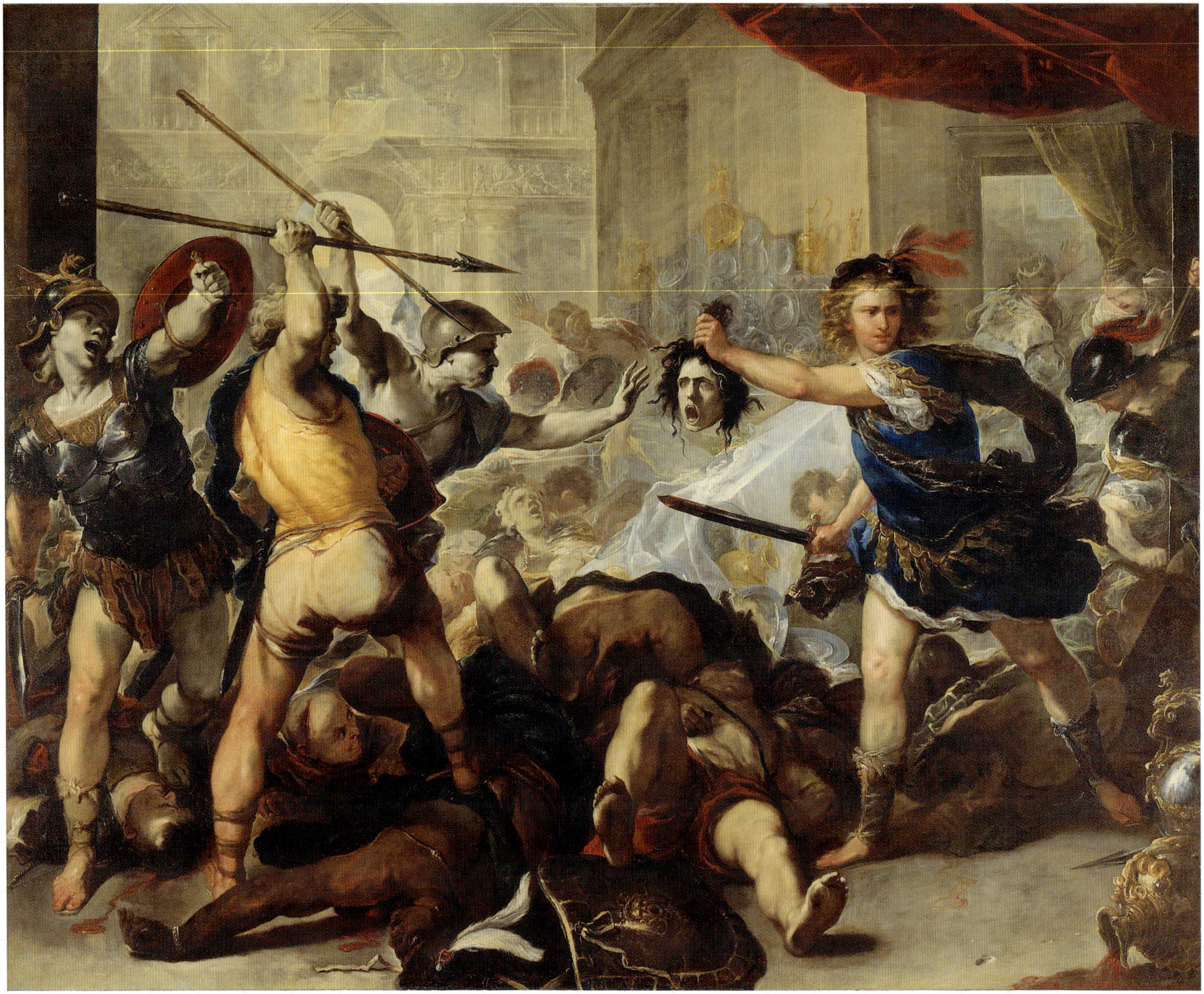

PERSEUS TURNING PHINEAS AND FOLLOWERS TO STONE

Luca Giordano (1634–1705)
Early 1680s
Oil on canvas

Having rescued Andromeda from a sea serpent, Perseus wins her hand in marriage and a wedding banquet is held. Phineas (far left) and his followers attack in an attempt to reclaim the bride. Outnumbered, Perseus holds up the head of Medusa in defence. Frozen in action, the ambushers begin to turn to stone.

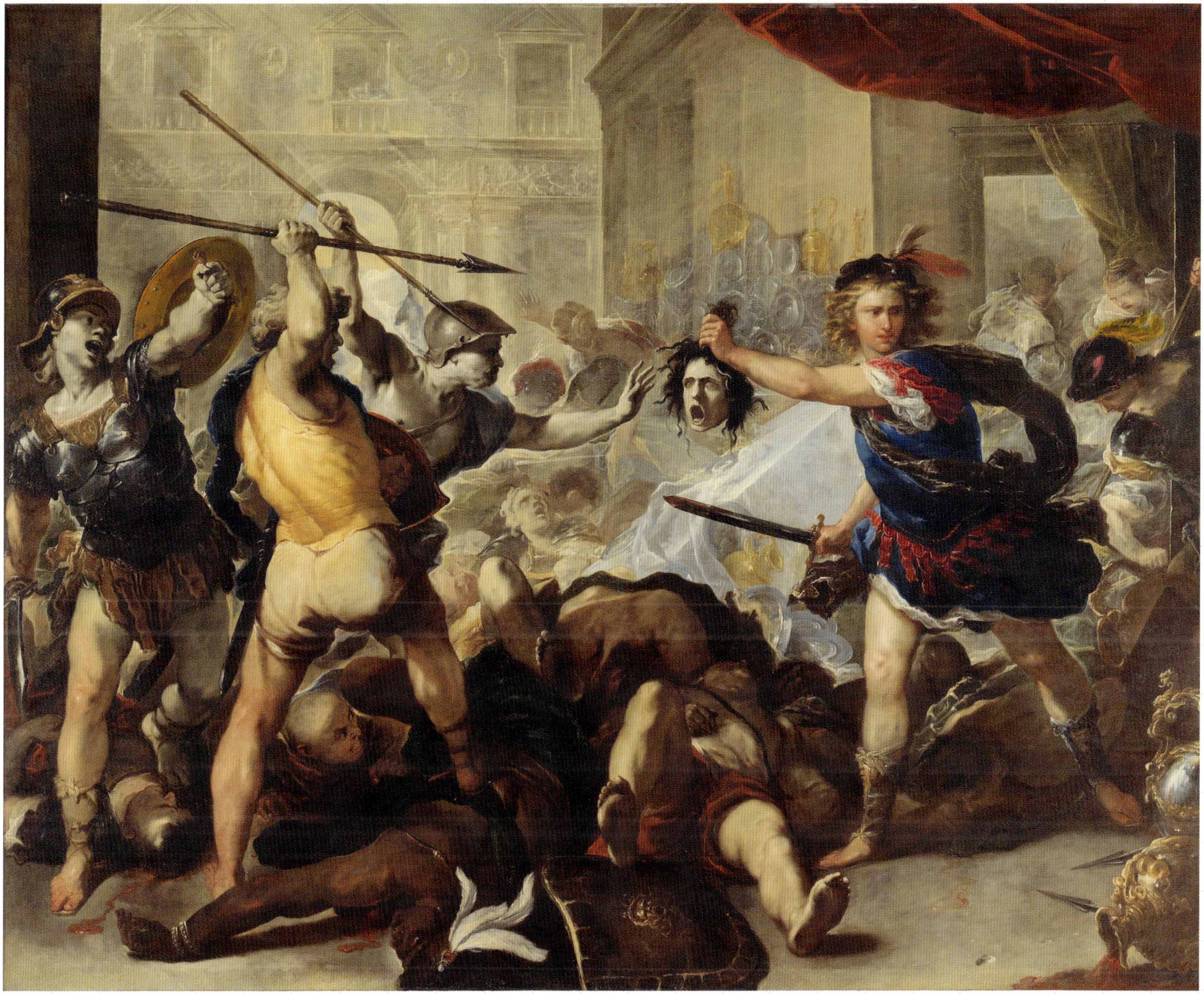

A B C D E F G H I J K L M N O P Q R S T U V W X Y Z

1 2 3 4 5 6 7 8 9 10 11 12 13 14 15 16 17 18 19 20 21 22 23 24 25 26

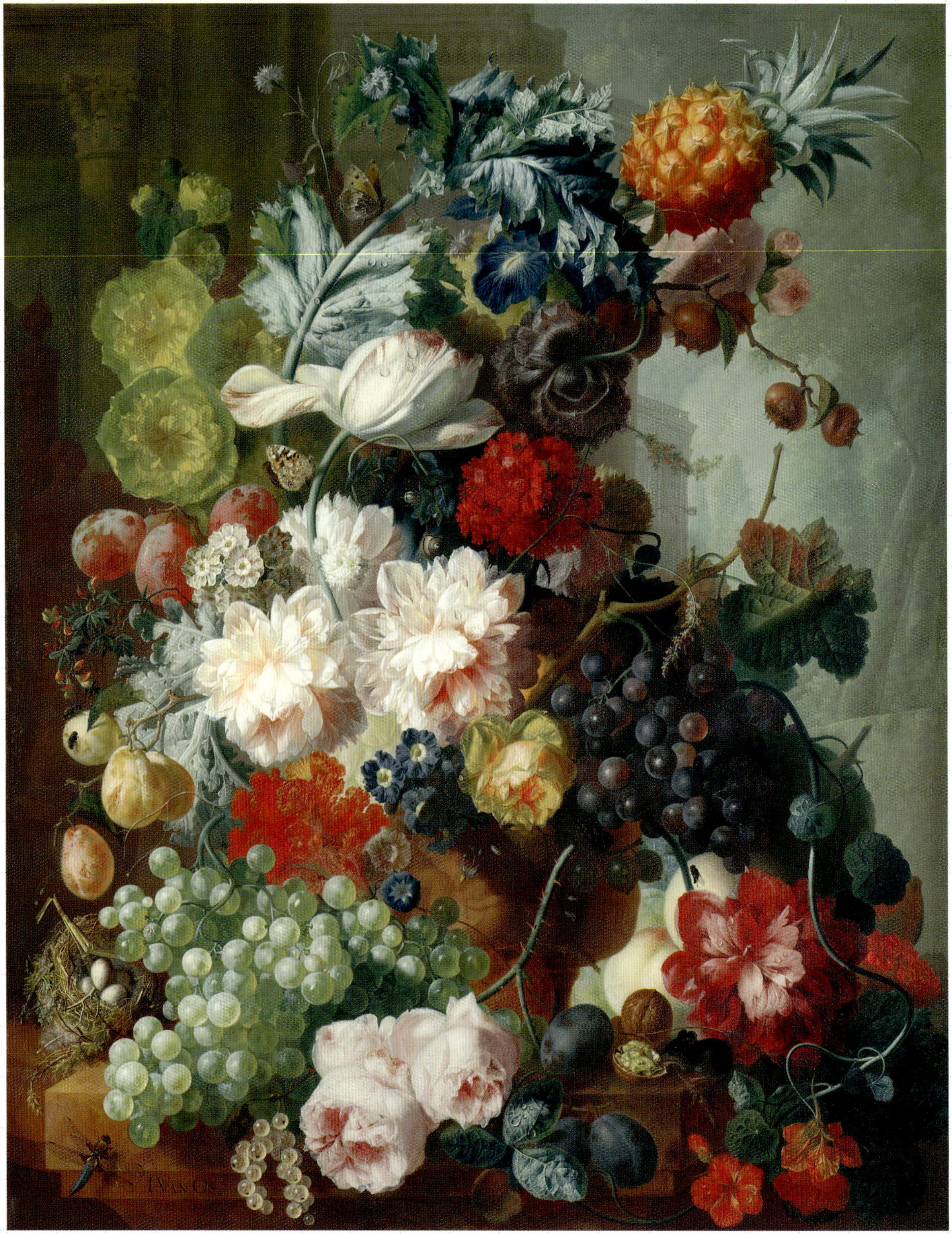

FRUIT AND FLOWERS IN A TERRACOTTA VASE

Jan van Os (1744–1808)
1777–1778
Oil on mahogany

In this vibrant still life, colourful fruits and flowers overflow from a terracotta vase. A bright pineapple perches top right, and in the opposite corner a dragonfly inspects some grapes. Two flies and a wasp can be seen silhouetted against ripe yellow fruits. Can you find the little mouse enjoying an open walnut?

 A B C D E F G H I J K L M N O P Q R S T U V W X Y Z

A B C D E F G H I J K L M N O P Q R S T U V W X Y Z

1 2 3 4 5 6 7 8 9 10 11 12 13 14 15 16 17 18 19 20 21 22 23 24 25 26

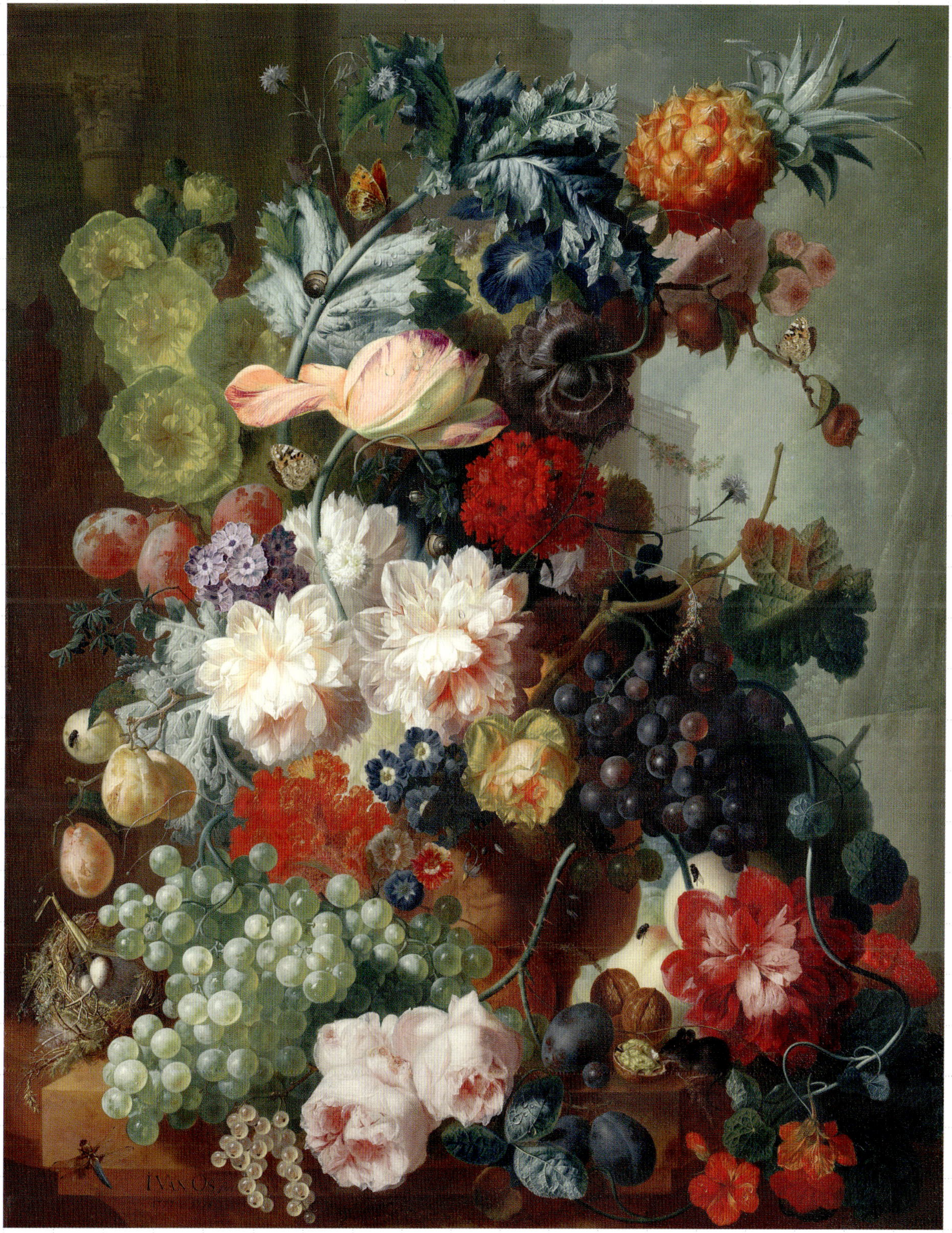

A B C D E F G H I J K L M N O P Q R S T U V W X Y Z

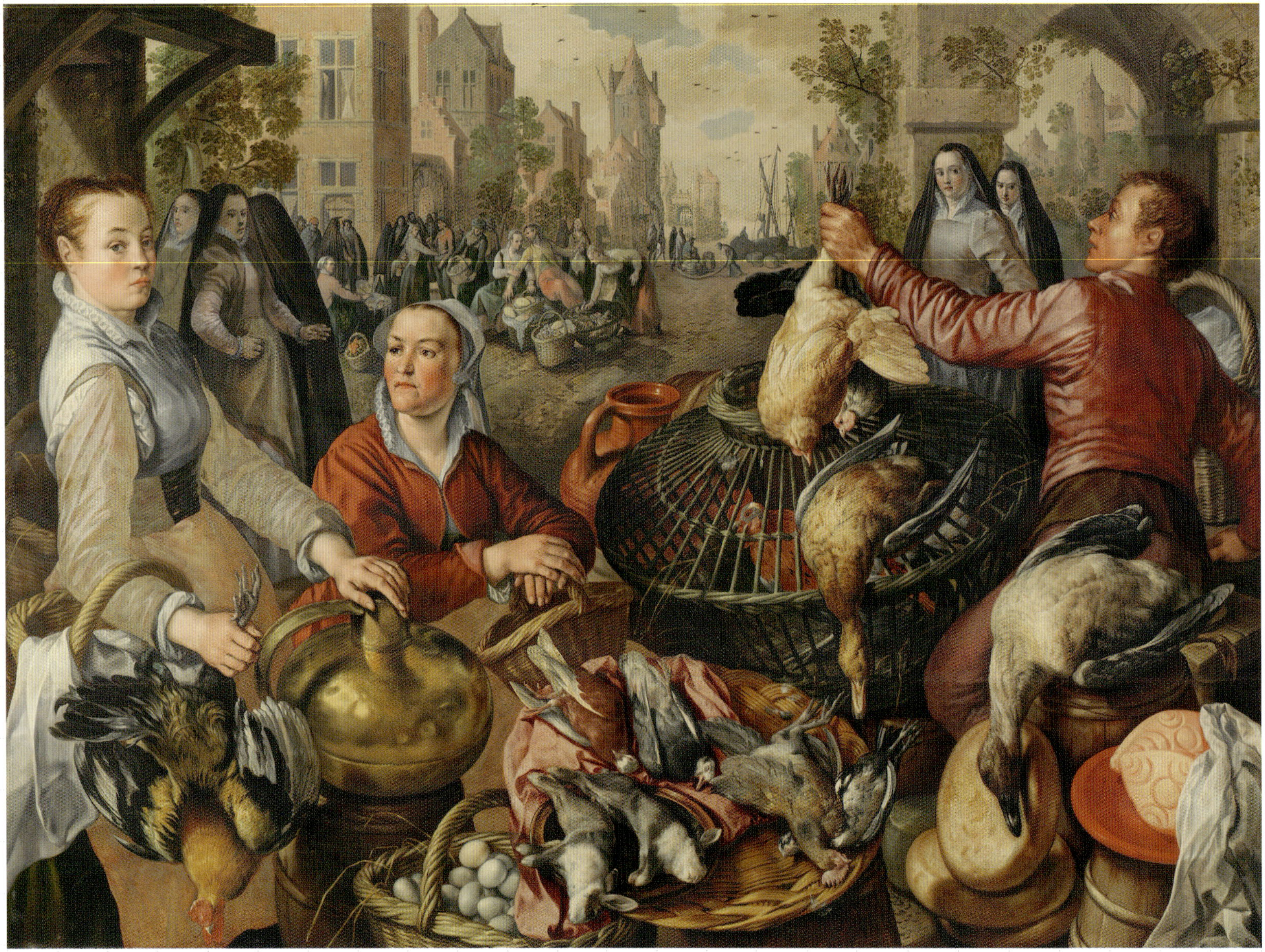

THE FOUR ELEMENTS: AIR

Joachim Beuckelaer (about 1535–died 1575)
1570
Oil on canvas

The third in Beuckelaer's series linking the four elements with Biblical scenes, here a market stall selling poultry represents "air". On offer are chickens, geese and other fowl, along with rabbits, eggs and cheese. Find the Prodigal Son among the market goers. Hint: he is louchely leaning against a woman.

A B C D E F G H I J K L M N O P Q R S T U V W X Y Z

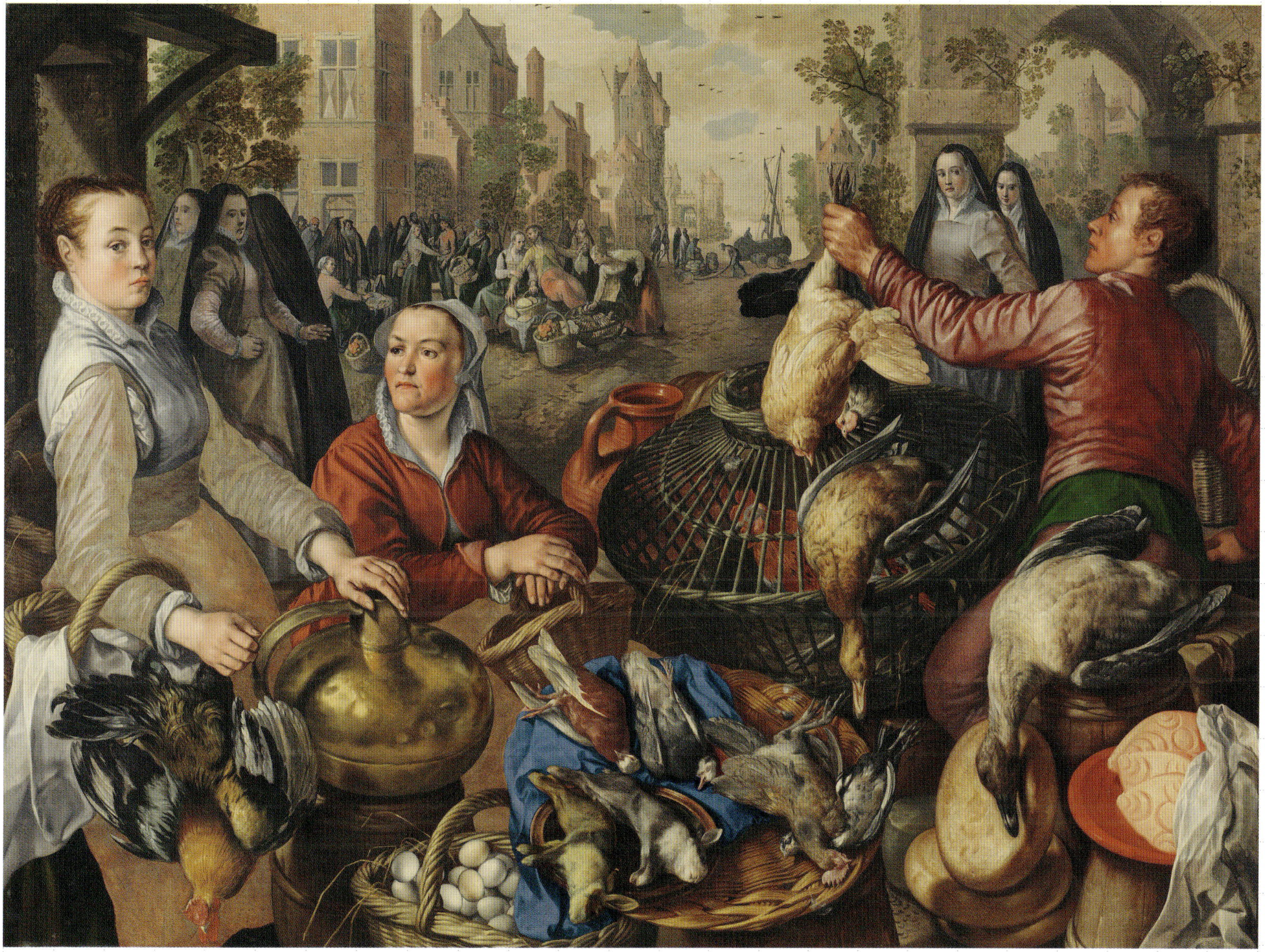

A B C D E F G H I J K L M N O P Q R S T U V W X Y Z

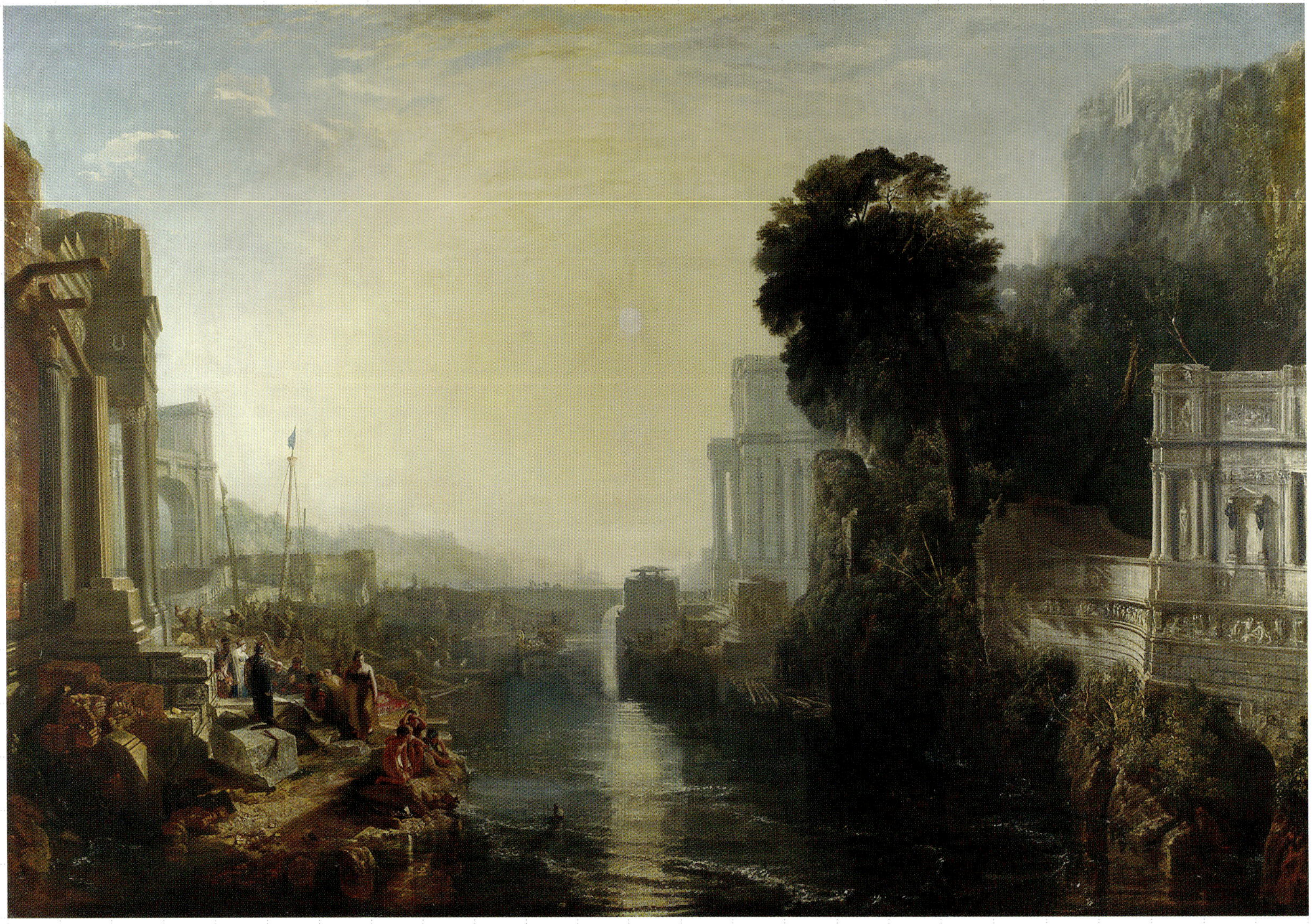

DIDO BUILDING CARTHAGE

Joseph Mallord William Turner (1775–1851)
1815
Oil on canvas

This painting depicts the city of Carthage being built. Dido, the white figure dressed in blue, is standing before a group of builders who have their plans laid out in front of them. The armoured figure next to Dido is her lover Aeneas. Her husband's tomb is on the right. Four boys play by the water's edge with a toy boat.

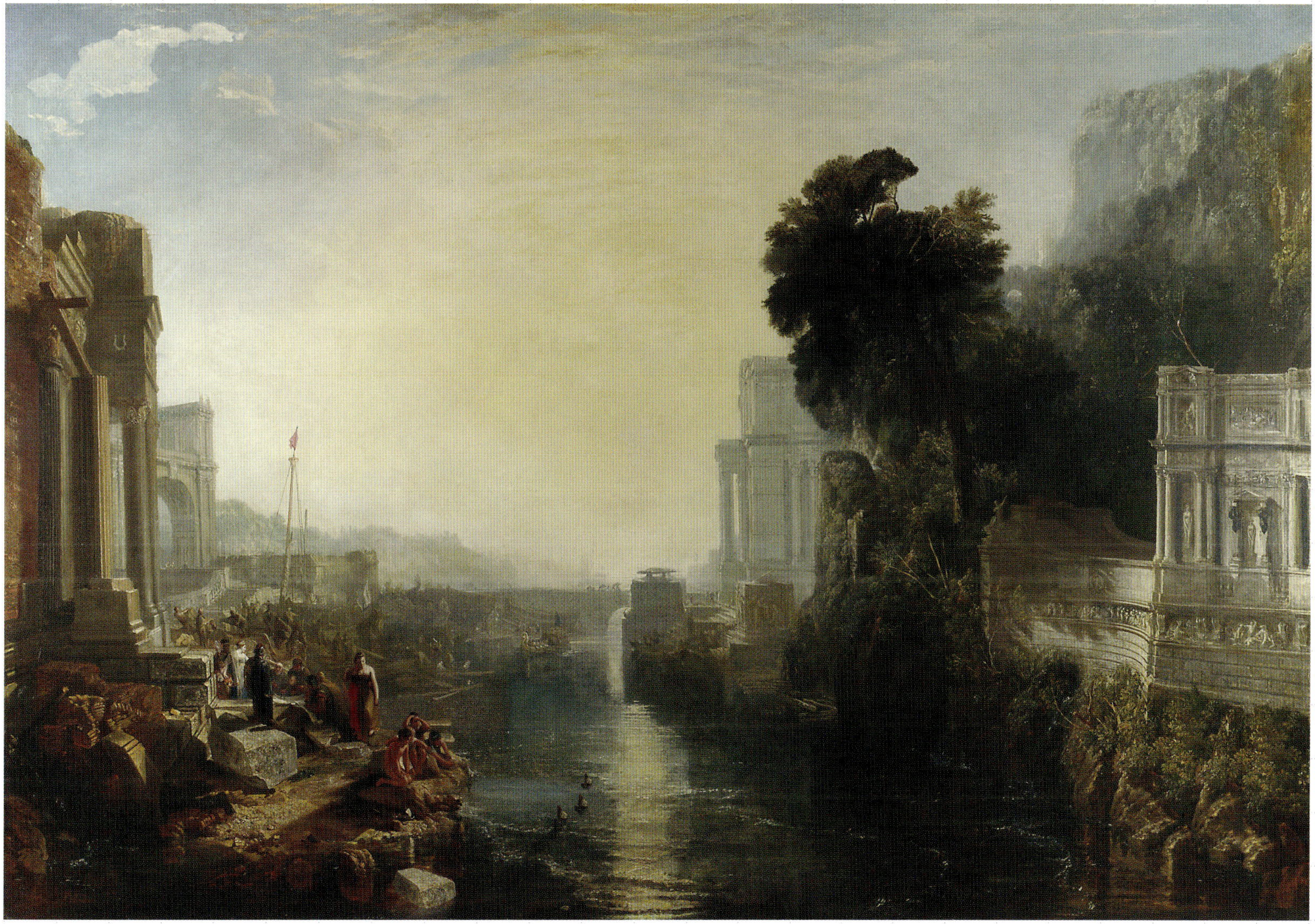

A B C D E F G H I J K L M N O P Q R S T U V W X Y Z

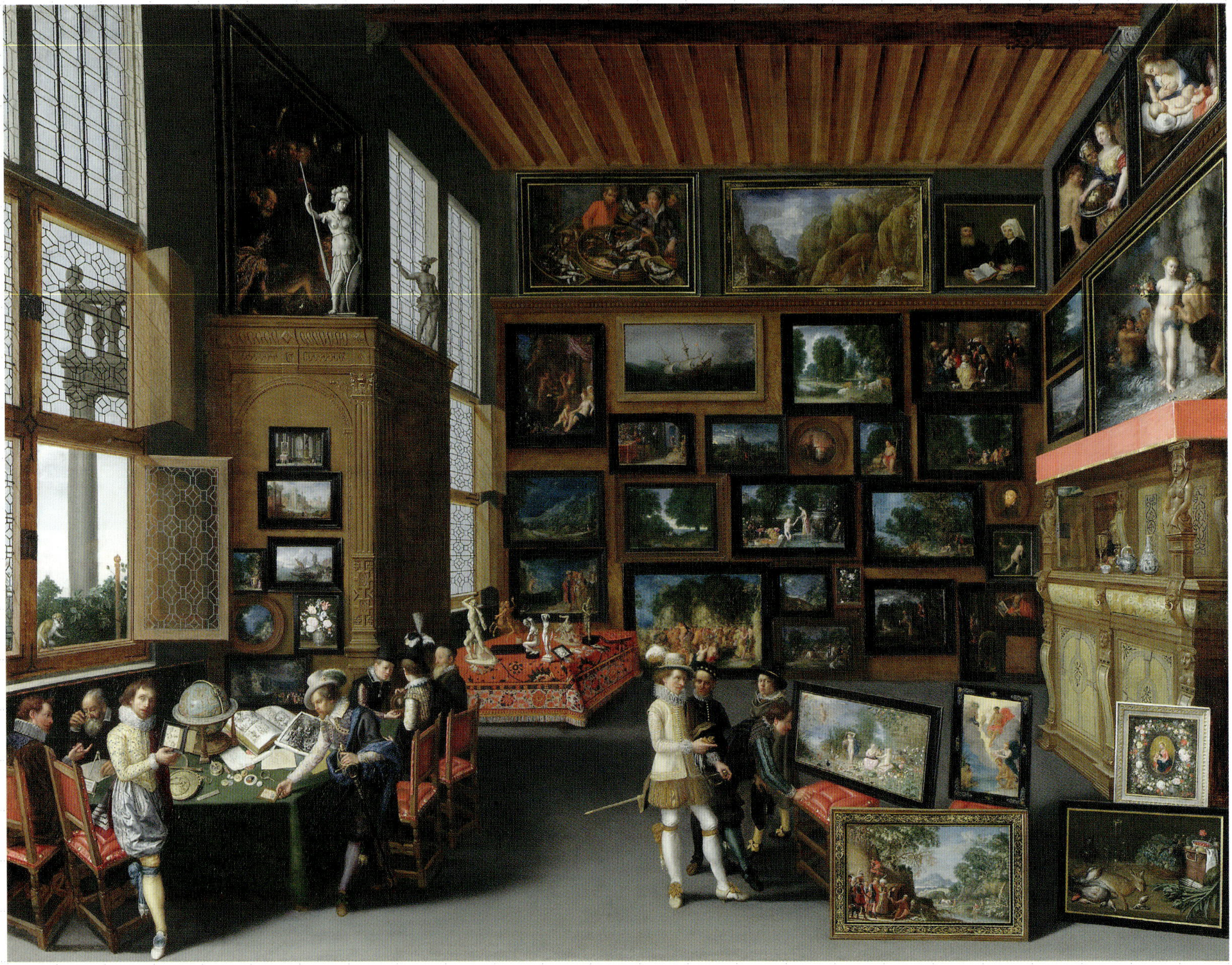

COGNOSCENTI IN A ROOM HUNG WITH PICTURES

Artist unknown
about 1620
Oil on oak

In this scene, cognoscenti – those who are knowledgable on a subject – admire artworks and collectors' items. At the window a curious monkey peers in. Famous paintings by mostly Antwerp artists adorn the walls – do any look familiar? There is one that looks as though it could be part of a series in this book.

A B C D E F G H I J K L M N O P Q R S T U V W X Y Z

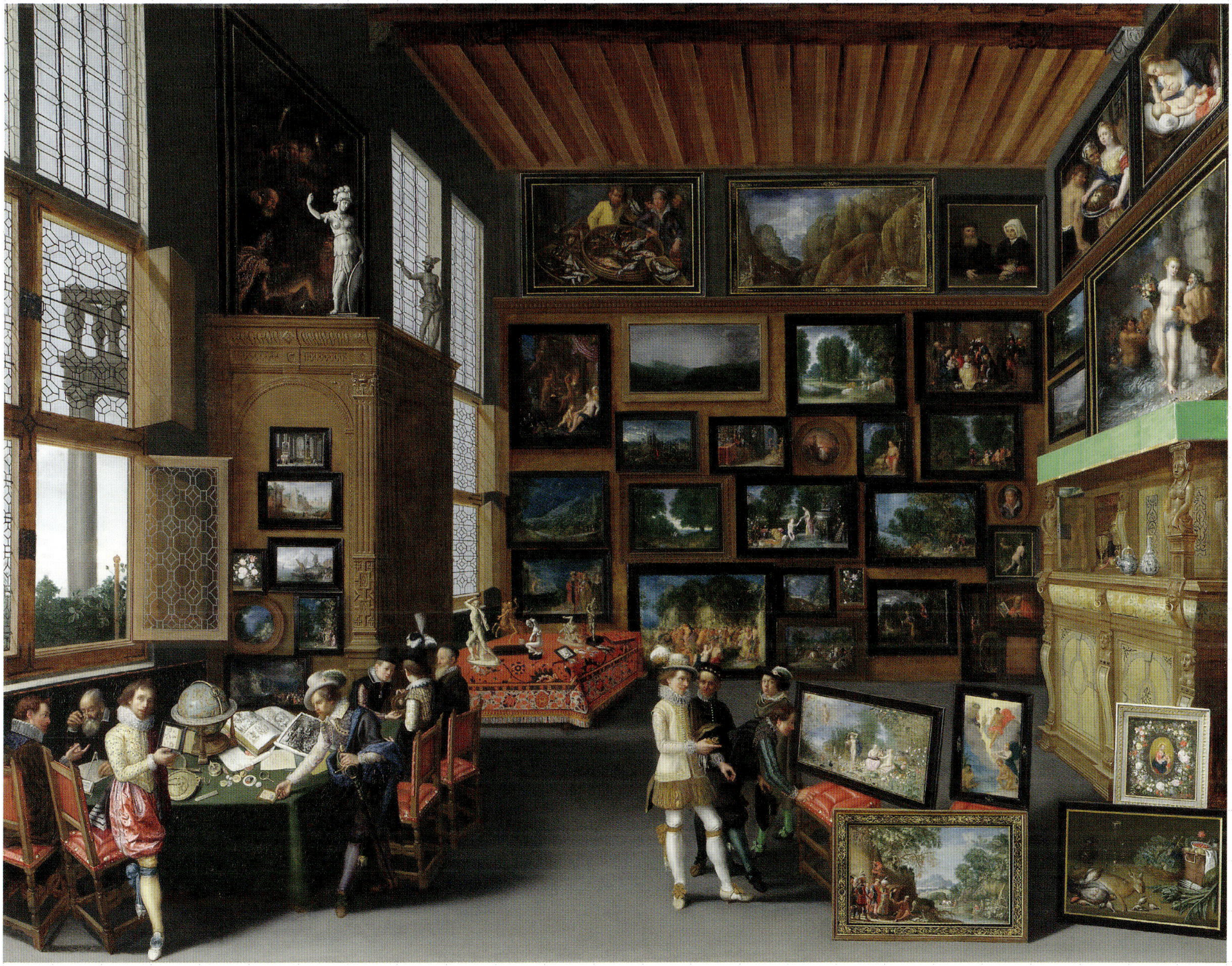

ANSWERS

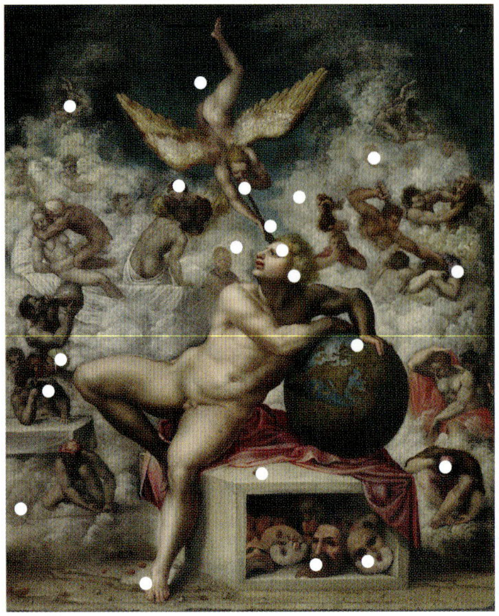

P8
THE DREAM OF HUMAN LIFE
After Michelangelo
22G, 17H, 16H, 6I, 24L, 9M, 5O, 9P, 12P, 21P, 11Q, 12Q, 13R, 10S, 24S, 15U, 24U, 8U, 20X, 12Y

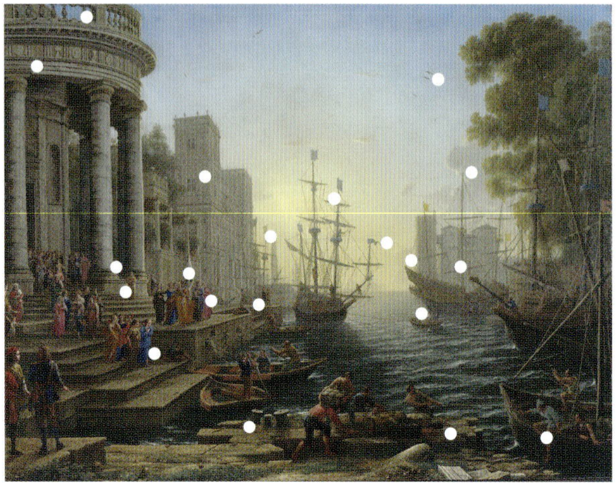

P10
SEAPORT WITH THE EMBARKATION OF SAINT URSULA
Claude Lorrain
4B, 3D, 13E, 14F, 16G, 13H, 9I, 14I, 19K, 14K, 11L, 10N, 11P, 13R, 15R, 5S, 19S, 9T, 13T, 19X

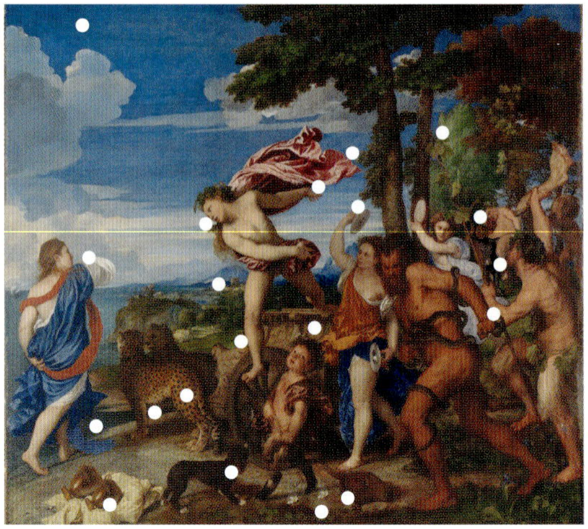

P12
BACCHUS AND ARIADNE
Tiziano Vecellio, known as Titian
2D, 11L, 18D, 22E, 18H, 18I, 10I, 13I, 20J, 15J, 14N, 22N, 9N, 10P, 22O, 7O, 6S, 10T, 14V, 13V

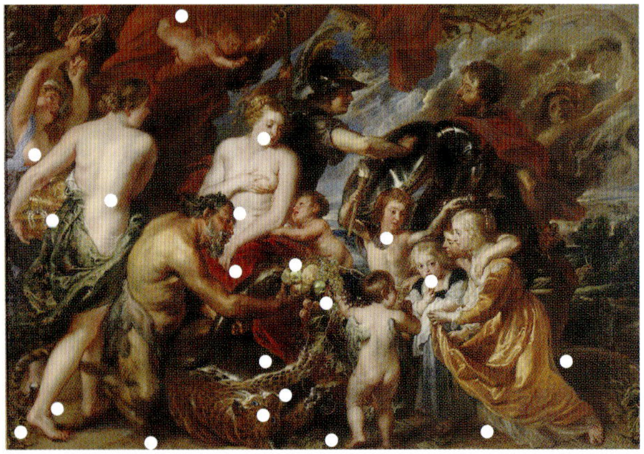

P14
MINERVA PROTECTS PAX FROM MARS ('PEACE AND WAR')
Peter Paul Rubens
9A, 19A, 11B, 18C, 11E, 19F, 4G, 13I, 11J, 8J, 19K, 17K, 18K, 13L, 14M, 19M, 12O, 14Q, 19T, 17W

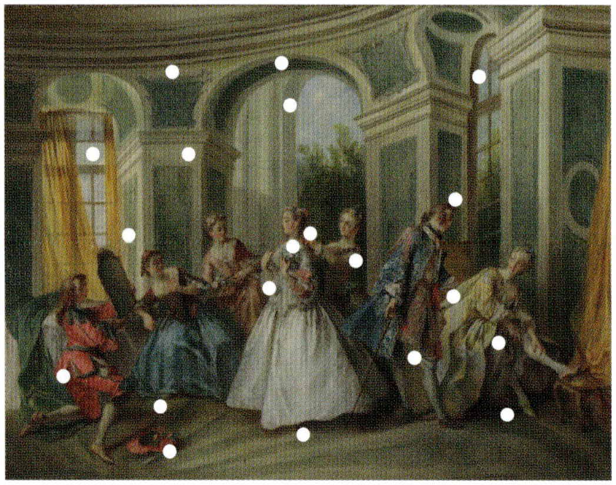

P16
THE FOUR AGES OF MAN: YOUTH
Nicolas Lancret
17C, 8E, 12F, 18G, 20H, 5H, 8H, 13L, 4L, 6M, 11M, 19M, 11N, 12O, 16R, 14S, 9S, 4U, 15U, 18V

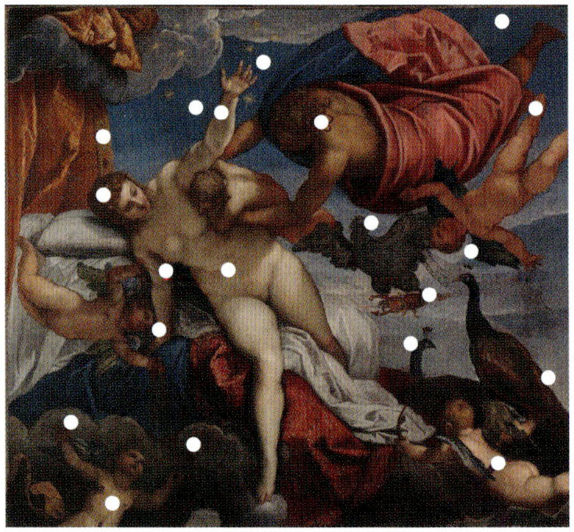

P18
THE ORIGIN OF THE MILKY WAY
Jacopo Tintoretto
19D, 7F, 9F, 21F, 15H, 12I, 20J, 5J, 5K, 12K, 4M, 6O, 10R, 15S, 13T, 11V, 2X, 21W, 5Y, 15Y

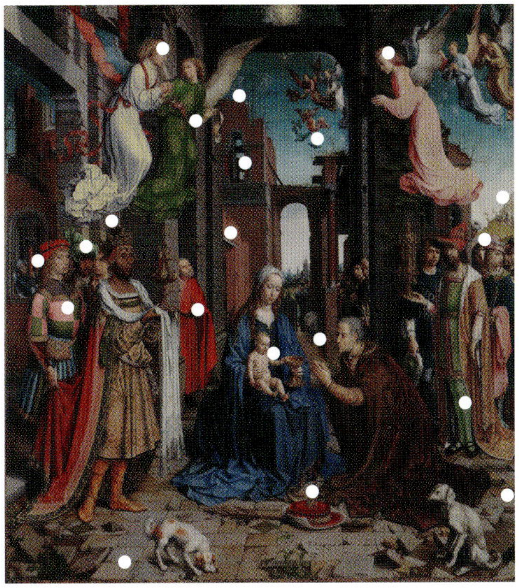

P20
THE ADORATION OF THE KINGS
Jan Gossaert
11D, 13E, 10F, 9G, 22H, 2I, 13K, 5K, 10L, 4L, 7L, 14M, 20O, 14O, 6O, 3R, 16U, 10V, 8W, 20W

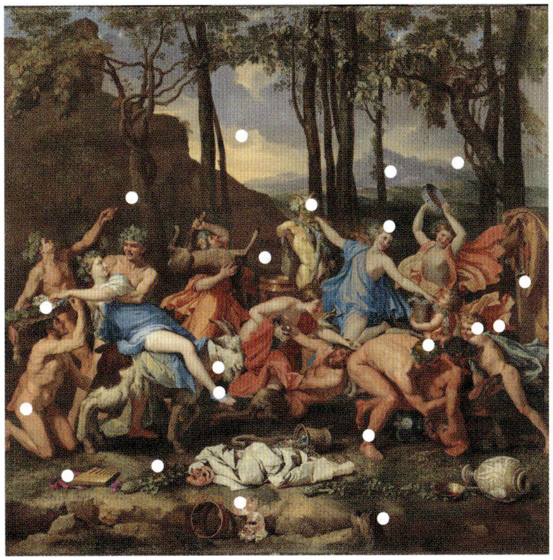

P22
THE TRIUMPH OF PAN
Nicolas Poussin
17C, 13C, 20D, 9G, 20I, 15K, 17K, 21L, 6L, 11M, 9N, 18O, 21R, 10R, 8R, 15S, 8U, 14V, 14W, 12X

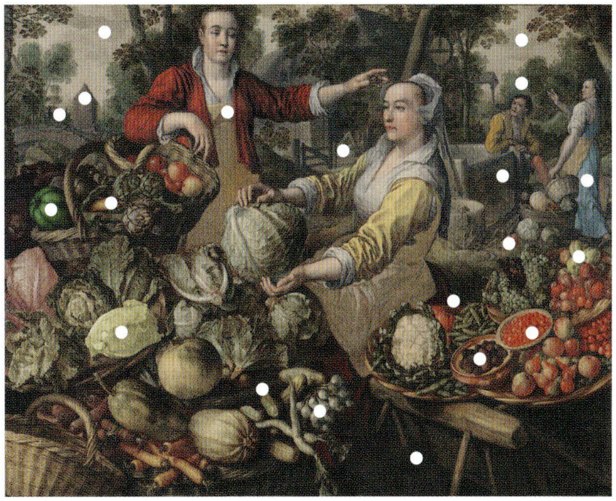

P24
THE FOUR ELEMENTS: EARTH
Joachim Beuckelaer
10C, 6C, 5D, 2E, 9E, 16E, 7J, 17K, 18N, 8O, 20N, 14S, 16U, 8V, 11U, 3V, 5V, 14V, 11Y, 8Y

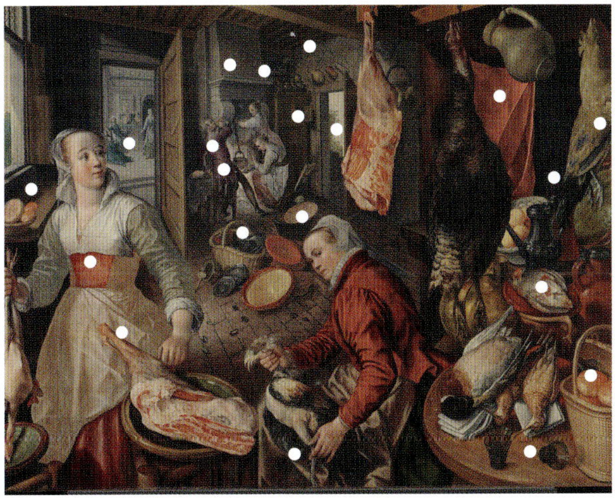

P26
THE FOUR ELEMENTS: FIRE
Joachim Beuckelaer
9B, 12D, 15E, 7F, 7J, 8J, 4J, 11K, 5L, 20L, 6M, 10M, 4N, 7O, 6U, 20W, 13W, 9X, 17Y, 6Y

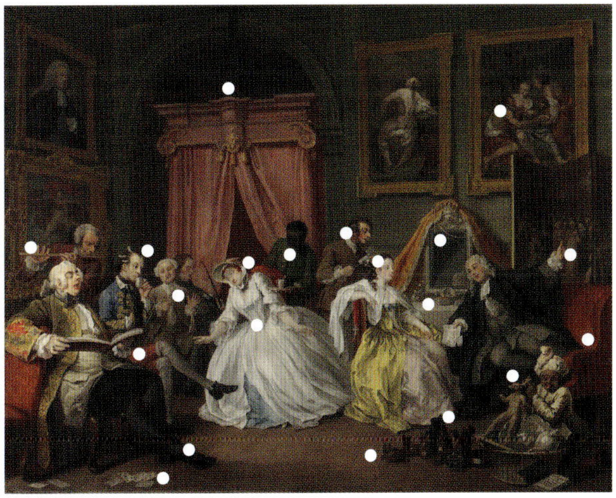

P28
MARRIAGE A-LA-MODE: 4, THE TOILETTE
William Hogarth
11B, 16F, 12F, 21G, 20H, 14H, 5J, 12J, 15K, 11M, 11O, 19P, 12P, 14R, 11S, 18S, 6U, 17V, 12X, 15Y

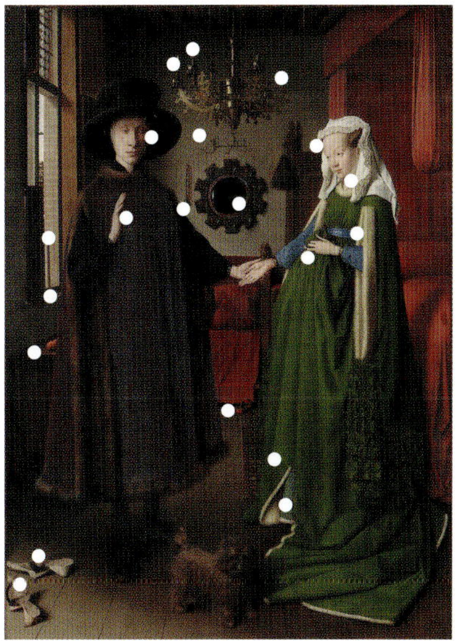

P30
PORTRAIT OF GIOVANNI(?) ARNOLFINI AND HIS WIFE
Jan van Eyck
24F, 23G, 14G, 12H, 10G, 9K, 6L, 3M, 9M, 3N, 6N, 17O, 9O, 19Q, 4Q, 20Q, 11R, 7R, 8T, 10T

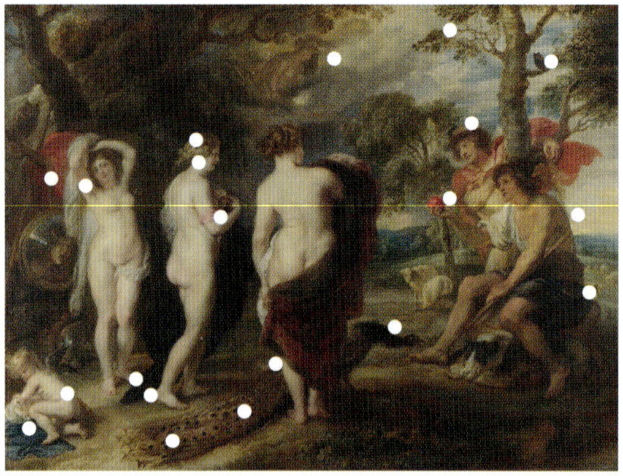

P32
THE JUDGEMENT OF PARIS
Peter Paul Rubens

18B, 9C, 17C, 9D, 16F, 17G, 19M, 7I, 8I, 10I, 18K, 16L, 3O, 15Q, 10S, 3R, 6T, 4W, 9Y, 13Y

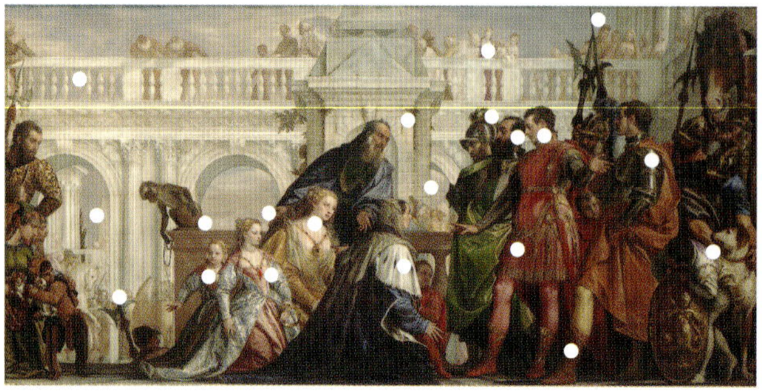

P34
THE FAMILY OF DARIUS BEFORE ALEXANDER
Paolo Veronese

7C, 12D, 14E, 12M, 14M, 11J, 14I, 12L, 13N, 18O, 11O, 6Q, 8Q, 9R, 13R, 9S, 15T, 5U, 10W, 13X

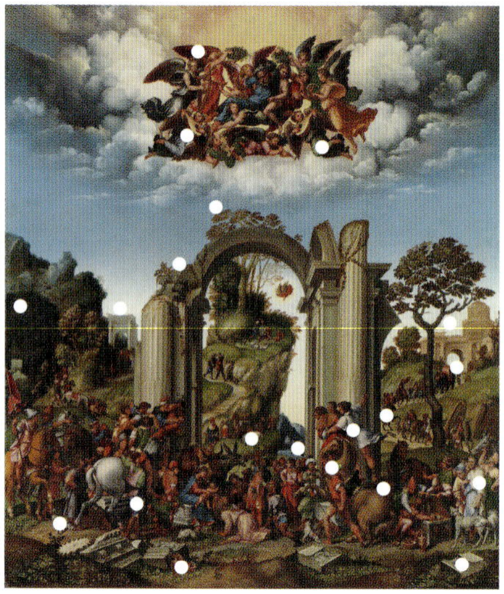

P36
THE ADORATION OF THE KINGS
Girolamo da Treviso

15F, 24M, 15K, 23K, 13M, 25M, 8M, 5N, 11N, 20P, 21R, 9S, 21S, 20T, 22U, 19V, 15X, 17X, 25Y, 22Y

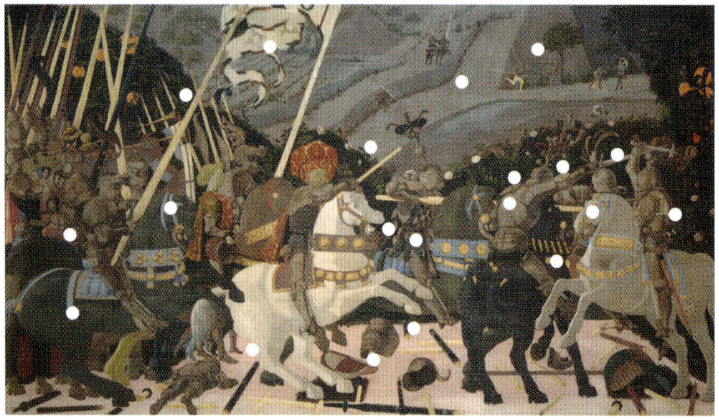

P38
THE BATTLE OF SAN ROMANO
Paolo Uccello

13C, 16C, 12G, 8G, 17I, 7J, 10N, 17N, 13N, 16P, 13O, 8Q, 12S, 11S, 7S, 14U, LLT, 10V, 12V, 12Y

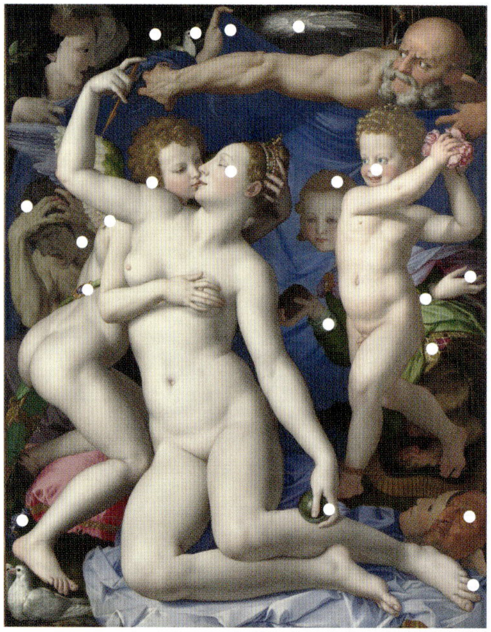

P40
AN ALLEGORY WITH VENUS AND CUPID
Agnolo di Cosimo, known as Bronzino

22F, 9G, 10I, 12I, 10J, 8L, 2L, 3N, 2O, 7O, 2S, 23S, 14S, 8S, 7V, 13W, 15X, 12Y, 22Y, 25Y

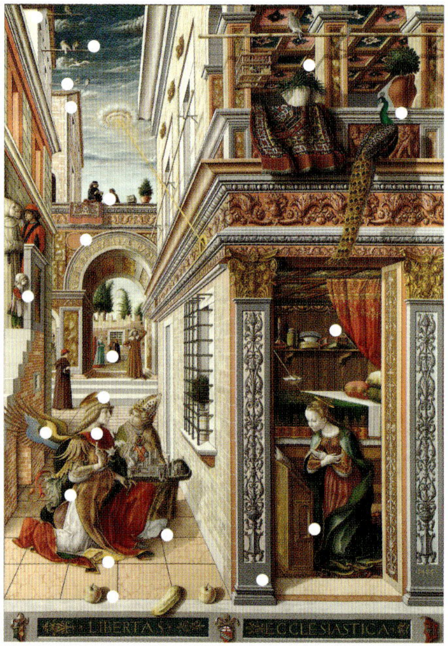

P42
THE ANNUNCIATION, WITH SAINT EMIDIUS
Carlo Crivelli

12H, 1H, 18H, 20I, 4I, 5I, 10J, 3J, 18J, 16K ,23K, 9K, 15K, 25K, 22M, 23Q, 3S, 21S, 14T, 5V

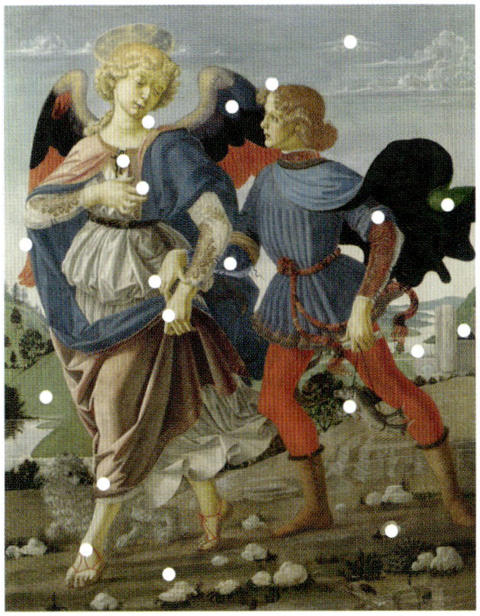

P44
TOBIAS AND THE ANGEL
Workshop of Andrea del Verrocchio
11G, 17H, 23I, 21J, 7K, 8K, 6L, 12L, 14M, 24M, 11O, 5O, 4Q, 3U, 18U, 10V, 23V, 15W, 9Y, 14Y

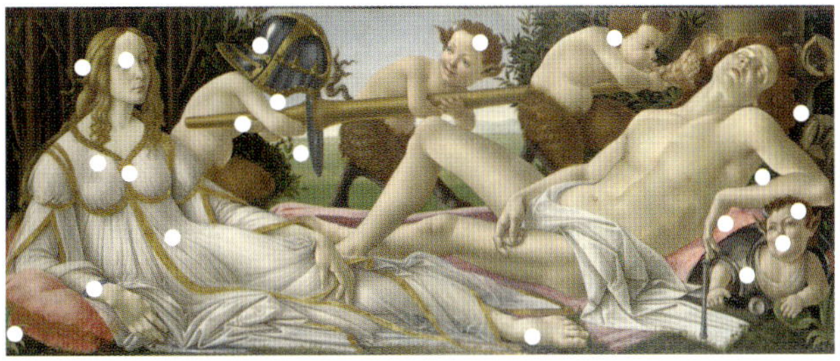

P46
VENUS AND MARS
Sandro Botticelli
15A, 7C, 13D, 9D, 6E, 9E, 12F, 8H, 6I, 8I, 9J, 6O, 15Q, 6S, 11W, 12W, 10X, 12X, 11Y, 8Y

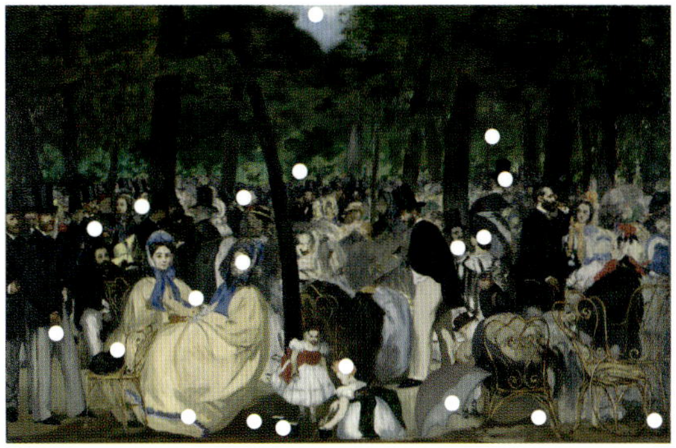

P48
MUSIC IN THE TUILERIES GARDENS
Edouard Manet
16C, 12D, 17E, 11F, 19H, 15H, 13J, 11J, 19J, 19K, 10L, 14L, 17N, 19R, 13R, 12S, 9S, 10T, 19U, 19Z

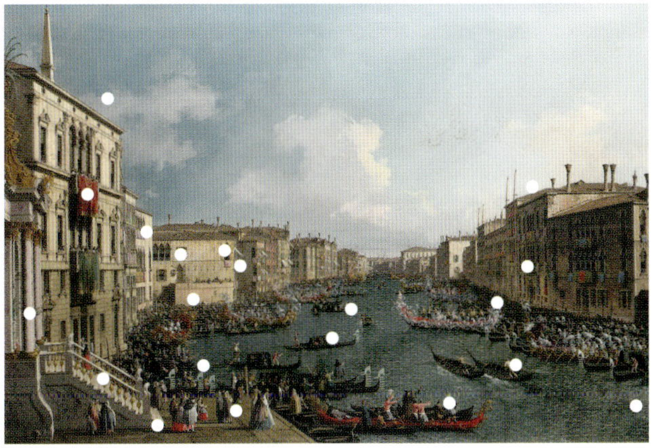

P50
A REGATTA ON THE GRAND CANAL
Canaletto
14B, 9D, 17E, 6E, 11G, 18G, 12M, 14M, 16M, 12J, 18J, 13J, 15M, 14N, 17R, 14T, 16U, 12U, 9V, 18Z

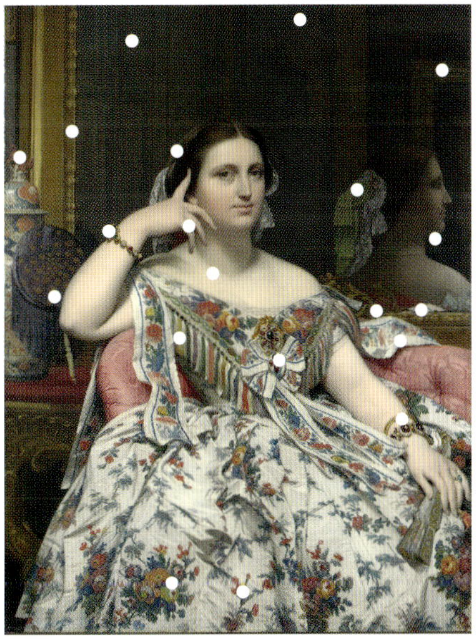

P52
MADAME MOITESSIER
Jean-Auguste-Dominique Ingres
7F, 13H, 6I, 10J, 3K, 24M, 7M, 14M, 10N, 12O, 24P, 15Q, 2R, 8U, 13U, 18V, 15V, 13W, 11X, 4X

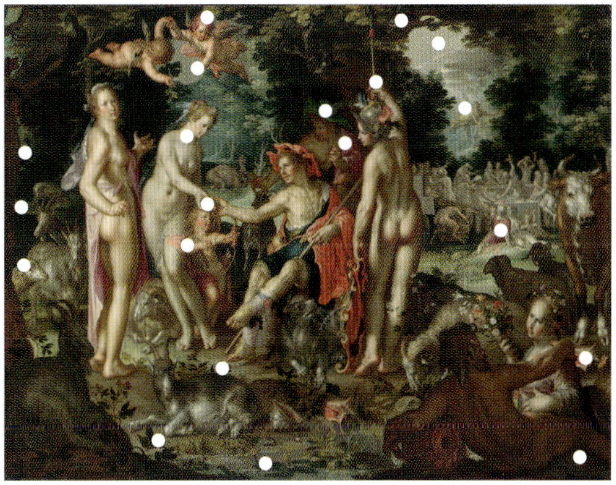

P54
THE JUDGEMENT OF PARIS
Joachim Wtewael
9B, 11B, 7B, 19G, 6I, 11H, 4I, 9I, 2I, 15J, 20L, 5N, 6O, 4P, 2Q, 2S, 5T, 10U, 19Y, 15Y

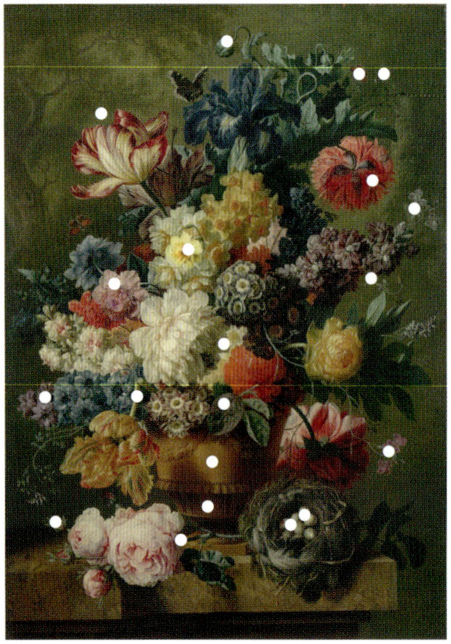

P56
FLOWERS IN A VASE
Paulus Theodorus van Brussel
16G, 22H, K5J, 12J, 16L, 24M, 11M, 21O, 19O, 17O, 14O, 3O, 21Q, 21R, 4T, 8U, 12U, 3U, 19V, 9W

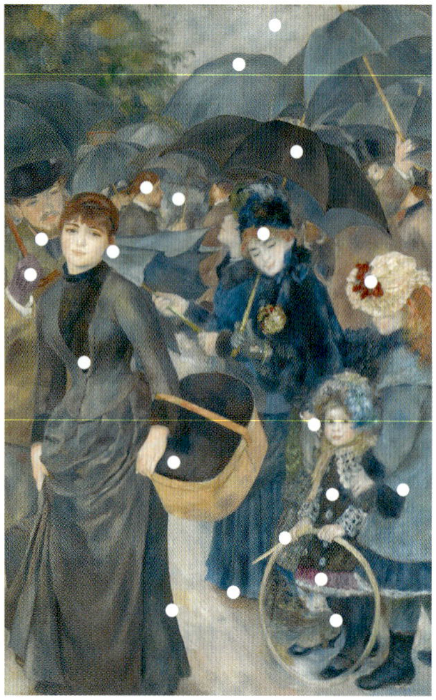

P58
THE UMBRELLAS
Pierre-Auguste Renoir
11G, 9G, 14I, 10J, 7K, 23M, 18L, 8M, 22N, 3O, 9P, 2P, 20Q, 17Q, 22R, 19R, 23R, 11S, 18T, 8Q

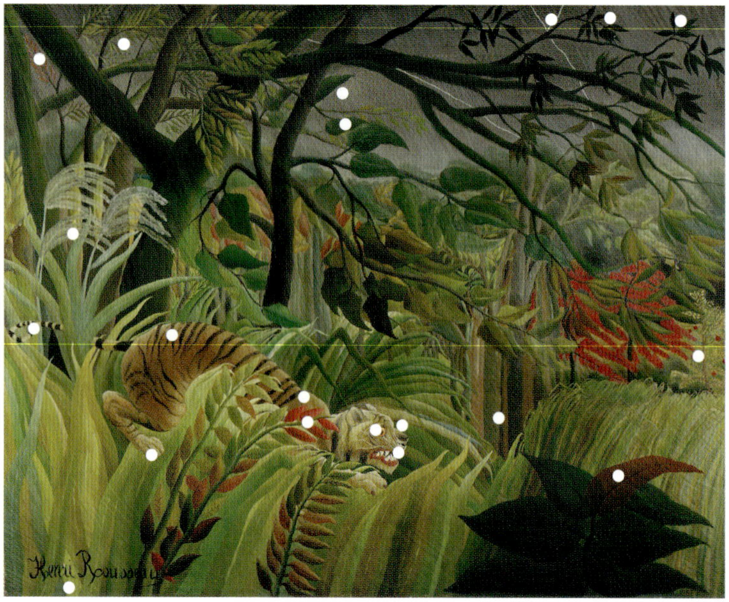

P60
SURPRISED!
Henri Rousseau
3B, 12B, 21C, 9D, 3E, 16F, 12G, 14K, 15L, 4M, 5M, 15N, 16O, 15O, 15R, 2T, 1W, 17V, 2X, 12Y

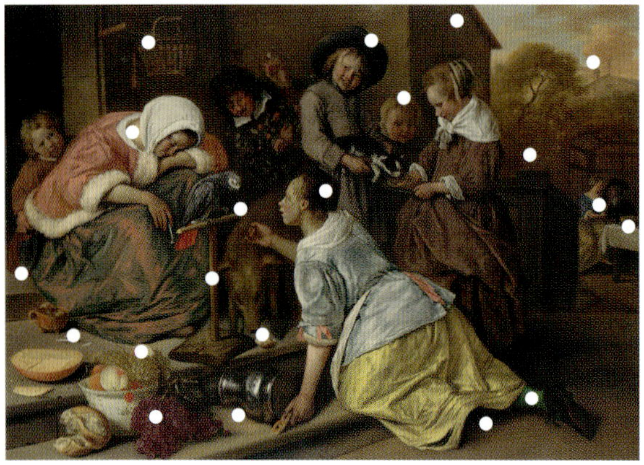

P62
THE EFFECTS OF INTEMPERANCE
Jan Steen
13B, 15C, 8F, 16F, 4F, 19G, 13I, 18J, 11J, 16K, 10N, 4P, 6Q, 3R, 19S, 8V, 18V, 5X, 10X, 11Z

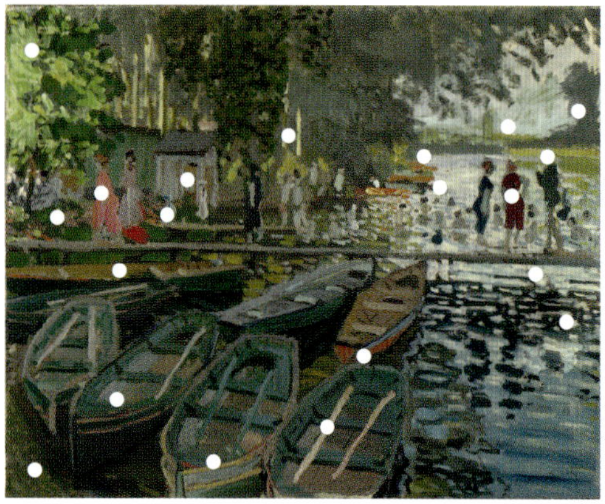

P64
BATHERS AT LA GRENOUILLÈRE
Claude Monet
3B, 20B, 9B, 9E, 17F, 12E, 10H, 8I, 20J, 7M, 18O, 15P, 7S, 9S, 6V, 9V, 12W, 7X, 13Y, 5Y

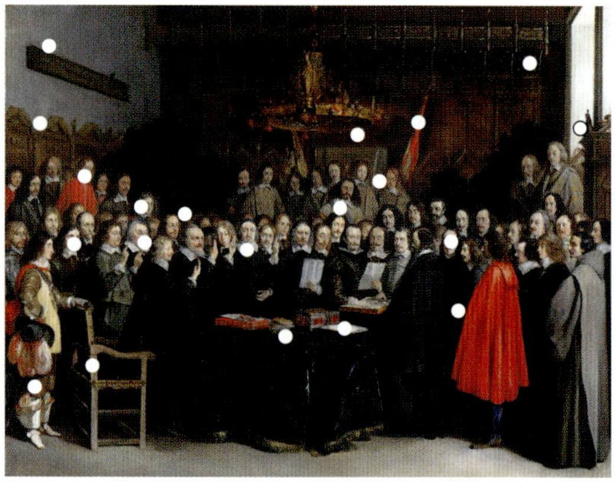

P66
THE RATIFICATION OF THE TREATY OF MÜNSTER
Gerard ter Borch
16B, 6B, 3C, 11D, 8D, 15D, 9G, 11G, 9H, 11K, 14M, 9O, 14O, 6P, 8P, 6R, 10S, 12T, E2, 6Y

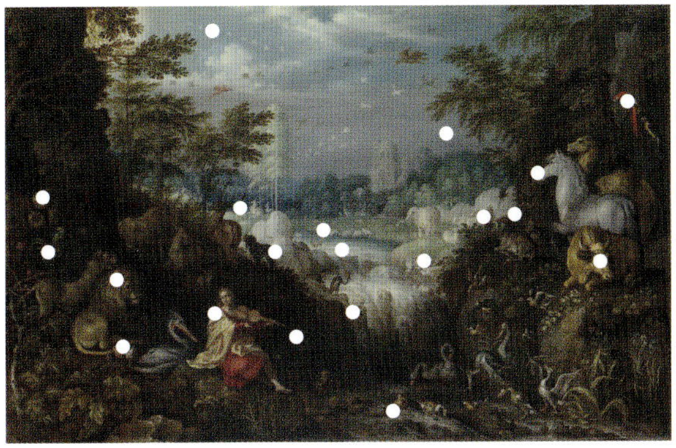

P68
ORPHEUS
Roelandt Savery

10B, 12B, 13F, 16E, 4H, 14I, 10J, 12K, 15L, 11M, 12M, 14N, 18O, 13P, 8R, 11S, 11T, 9U, 12W, 7X

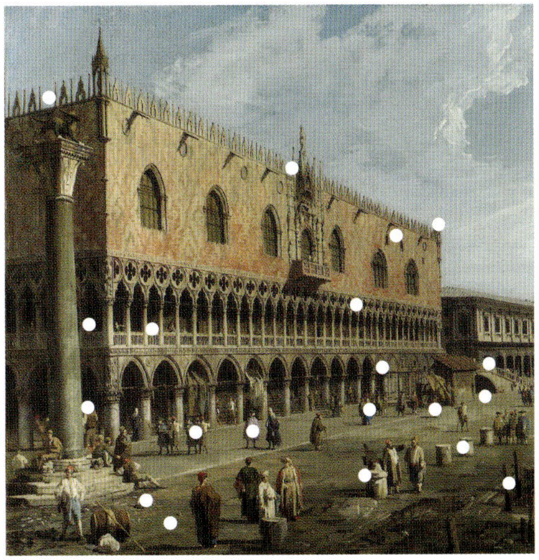

P70
VENICE: THE DOGE'S PALACE AND THE RIVA DEGLI SCHIAVONI (DETAIL)
Canaletto

5E, 16F, 13F, 20H, 13H, 20I, 17J, 18L, 7N, 12Q, 19Q, 17Q, 15R, 10R, 16T, 9T, 18U, 15V, 16V, 19W

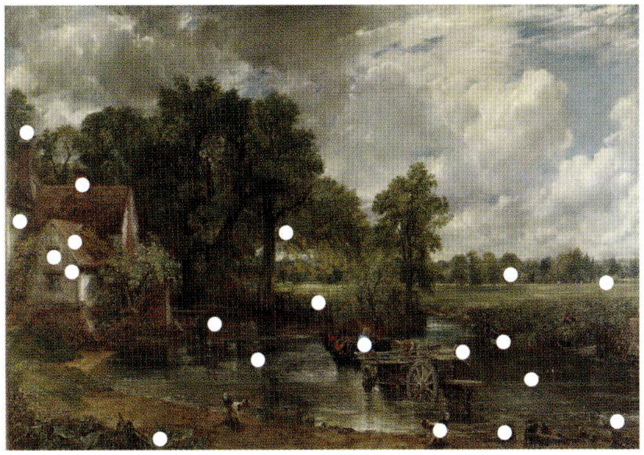

P72
THE HAY WAIN
John Constable

11A, 8B, 12C, 13D, 12D, 10D, 20G, 15I, 16K, 12L, 14M, 16Q, 19R, 16S, 16T, 19U, 13U, 17W, 14X, 19Y

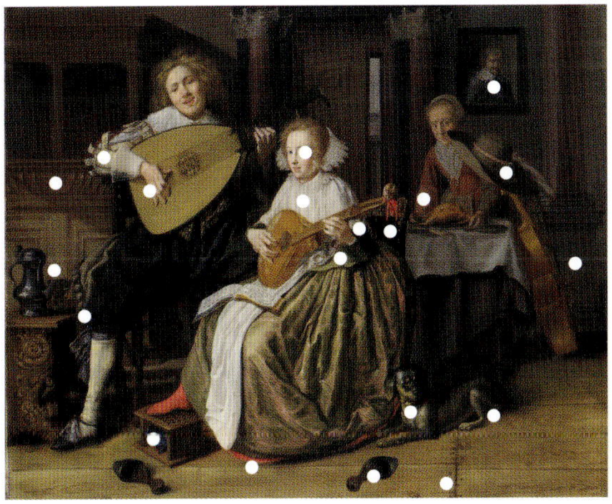

P74
A YOUNG MAN AND WOMAN MAKING MUSIC
Jan Miense Molenaer

12C, 8C, 14D, 7E, 9G, 19G, 20K, 9M, 7M, 11O, 10P, 20Q, 10Q, 18R, 9R, 21T, 18U, 4U, 8V, 12Y

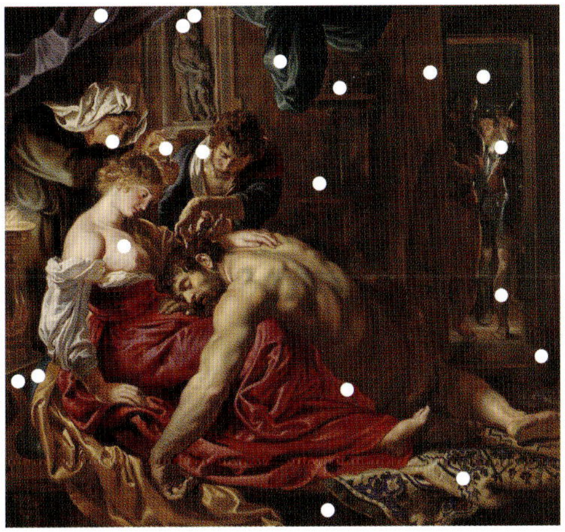

P76
SAMSON AND DELILAH
Peter Paul Rubens

17B, 17C, 2F, 7G, 11G, 7I, 2J, 1J, 8J, 4N, 9O, 23O, 5P, 17Q, 4T, 21U, 4W, 8W, 14W, 16Y

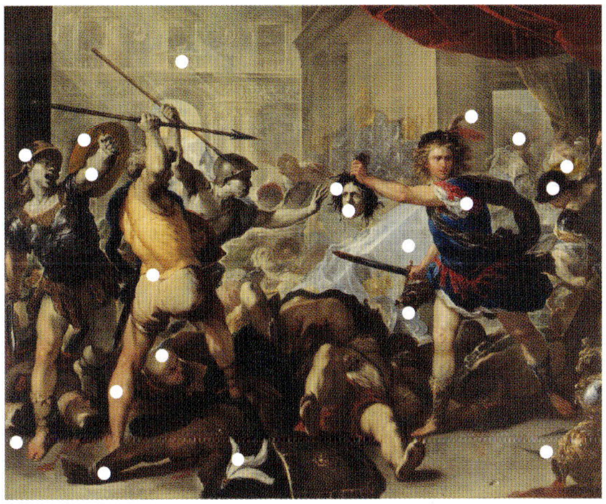

P78
PERSEUS TURNING PHINEAS AND FOLLOWERS TO STONE
Luca Giordano

19A, 7B, 6D, 8D, 20E, 18F, 12G, 16G, 3H, 19J, 8O, 9O, 14R, 11R, 9T, 6T, 7V, 19W, 8X, 8Y

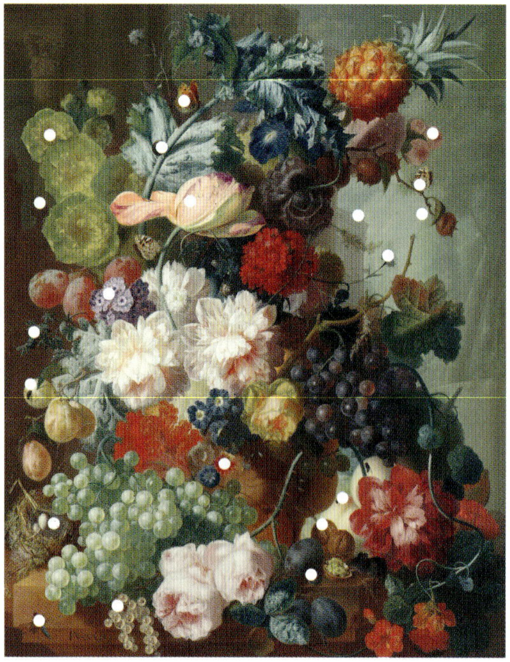

P80
FRUIT AND FLOWERS IN A TERRACOTTA VASE
Jan van Os
16G, 15G, 25G, 10H, 7H, 21H, 13J, 24K, 7L, 6M, 10M, 19O, 23R, 21R, 20S, 10S, 12T, 9V, 10V, 7V

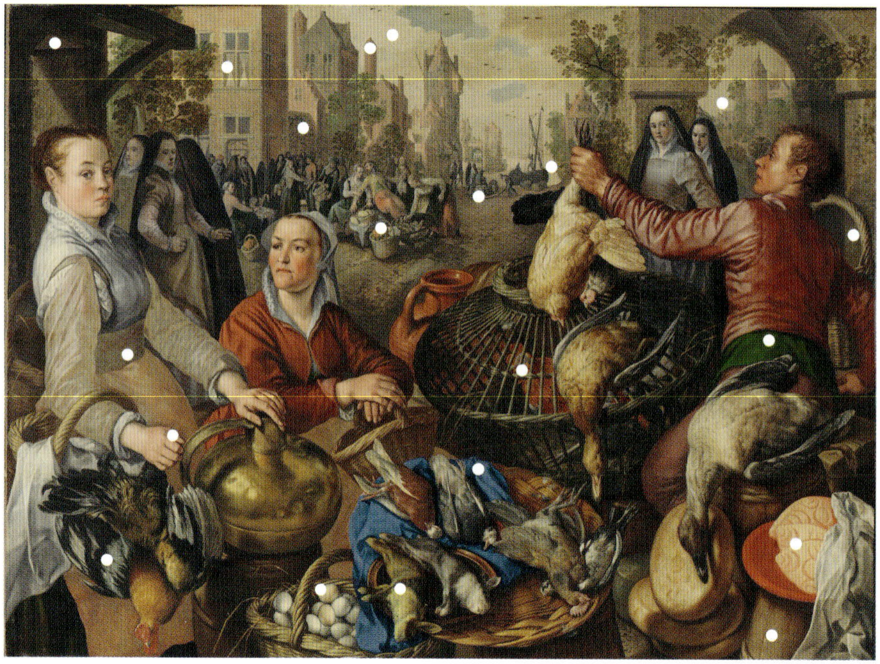

P82
THE FOUR ELEMENTS: AIR
Joachim Beuckelaer
3B, 18D, 11D, 14F, 4G, 5I, 19J, 3K, 8L, 3L, 18M, 7O, 15O, 12P, 7Q, 5V, 11W, 19W, 17X, 8Y

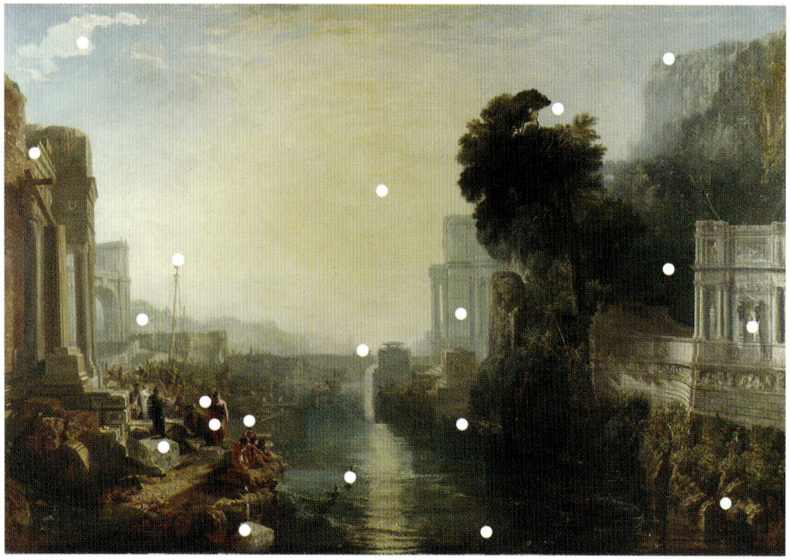

P84
DIDO BUILDING CARTHAGE
Joseph Mallord William Turner
8B, 4D, 13E, 17F, 11F, 15G, 16H, 19I, 16I, 18L, 14L, 9M, 13O, 16P, 19P, 6R, 11V, 5W, 18X, 13Y

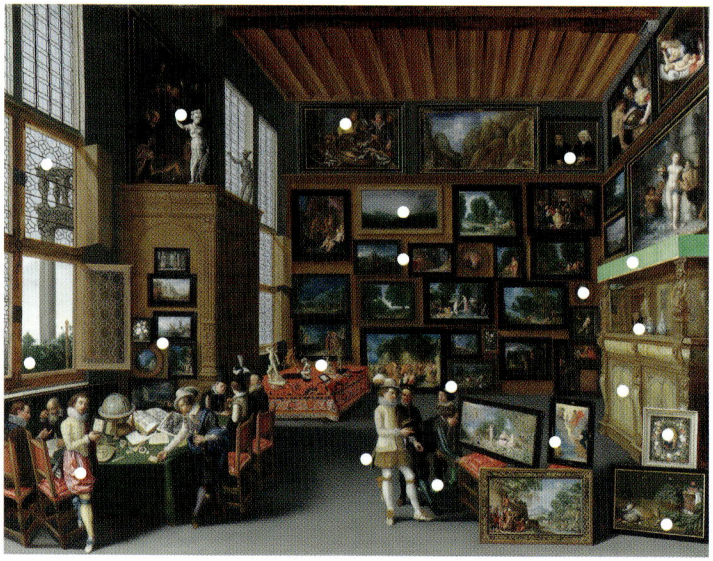

P86
COGNOSCENTI IN A ROOM HUNG WITH PICTURES
Artist unknown
B6, B14, D17, F12, G5, L14, M5, N17, O8, O9, P17, Q14, T17, U6, V13, W14, X9, X12, Y16, Y19

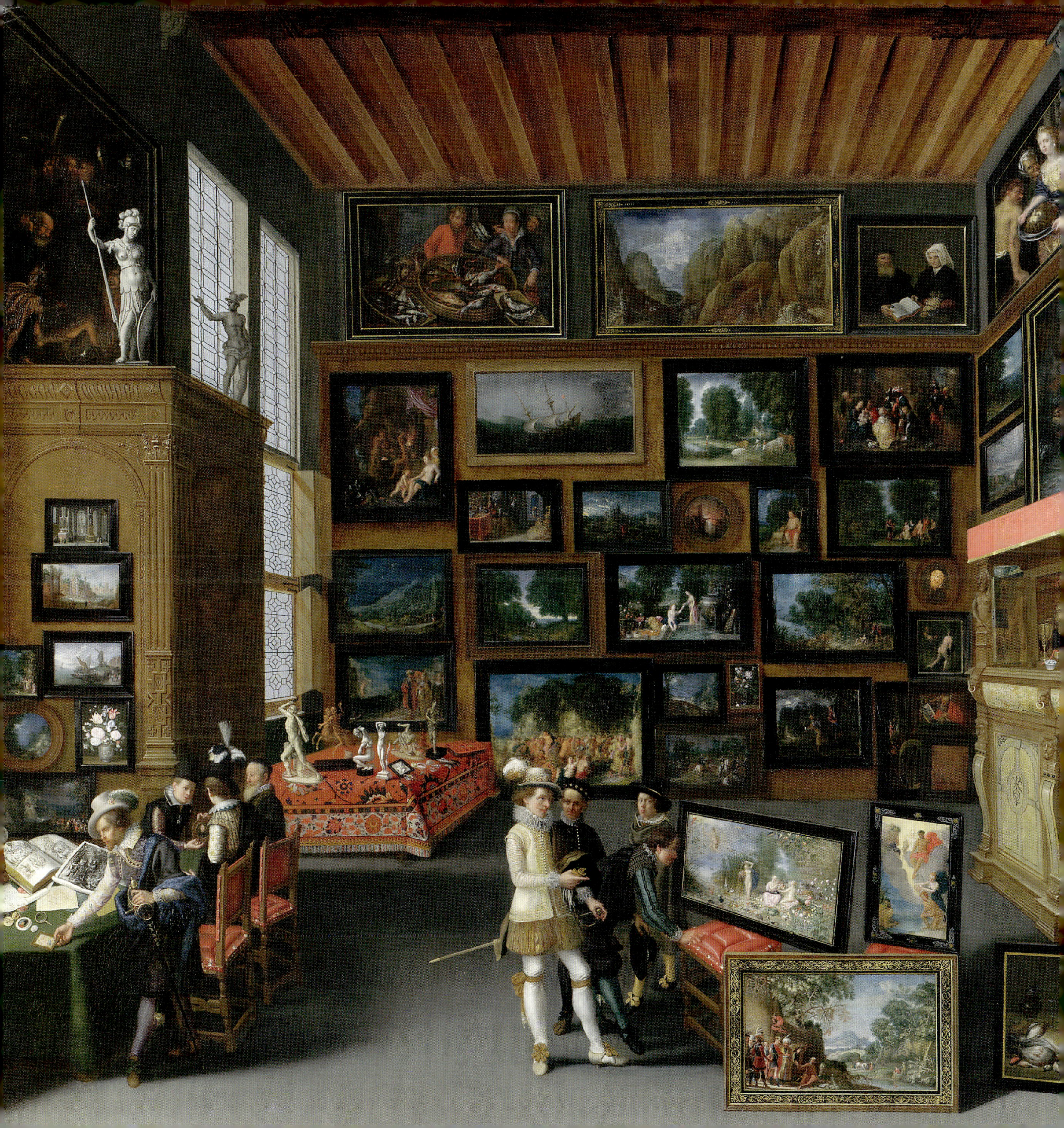

THE NATIONAL GALLERY

GREAT PAINTINGS SPOT-THE-DIFFERENCE

40 FINE-ART PUZZLES